New Frontiers in Regional Science: Asian Perspectives

Volume 12

New Frontiers in Regional Science: Asian Perspectives

This series is a constellation of works by scholars in the field of regional science and in related disciplines specifically focusing on dynamism in Asia.

Asia is the most dynamic part of the world. Japan, Korea, Taiwan, and Singapore experienced rapid and miracle economic growth in the 1970s. Malaysia, Indonesia, and Thailand followed in the 1980s. China, India, and Vietnam are now rising countries in Asia and are even leading the world economy. Due to their rapid economic development and growth, Asian countries continue to face a variety of urgent issues including regional and institutional unbalanced growth, environmental problems, poverty amidst prosperity, an ageing society, the collapse of the bubble economy, and deflation, among others.

Asian countries are diversified as they have their own cultural, historical, and geographical as well as political conditions. Due to this fact, scholars specializing in regional science as an inter- and multi-discipline have taken leading roles in providing mitigating policy proposals based on robust interdisciplinary analysis of multifaceted regional issues and subjects in Asia. This series not only will present unique research results from Asia that are unfamiliar in other parts of the world because of language barriers, but also will publish advanced research results from those regions that have focused on regional and urban issues in Asia from different perspectives.

The series aims to expand the frontiers of regional science through diffusion of intrinsically developed and advanced modern regional science methodologies in Asia and other areas of the world. Readers will be inspired to realize that regional and urban issues in the world are so vast that their established methodologies still have space for development and refinement, and to understand the importance of the interdisciplinary and multidisciplinary approach that is inherent in regional science for analyzing and resolving urgent regional and urban issues in Asia.

Topics under consideration in this series include the theory of social cost and benefit analysis and criteria of public investments, socio-economic vulnerability against disasters, food security and policy, agro-food systems in China, industrial clustering in Asia, comprehensive management of water environment and resources in a river basin, the international trade bloc and food security, migration and labor market in Asia, land policy and local property tax, Information and Communication Technology planning, consumer "shop-around" movements, and regeneration of downtowns, among others.

More information about this series at http://www.springer.com/series/13039

Xiaochun Li
Editor

Labor Transfer in Emerging Economies

A Perspective from China's Reality to Theories

Springer

Editor
Xiaochun Li
Business School
Nanjing University
Nanjing, China

ISSN 2199-5974 ISSN 2199-5982 (electronic)
New Frontiers in Regional Science: Asian Perspectives
ISBN 978-981-10-3568-5 ISBN 978-981-10-3569-2 (eBook)
DOI 10.1007/978-981-10-3569-2

Library of Congress Control Number: 2016963170

Printed on acid-free paper

This Springer imprint is published by Springer Nature
The registered company is Springer Nature Singapore Pte Ltd.
The registered company address is: 152 Beach Road, #21-01/04 Gateway East, Singapore 189721, Singapore

Contents

Chapter 1
Introduction

Xiaochun Li

The term "emerging economies" has no single, exact definition. In the year 2010, the China Boao Forum for Asia defined the concept of 11 emerging countries (E11)[1] for the first time. Among those countries, China, Brazil, India, Russia, and South Africa – also known as the BRIC countries – are relatively affluent, particularly in comparison to the world's developing countries. According to data released by IMF, economic growth in developed economies in 2015 was 2.4%, while in emerging economies it was 4.3%.[2] India, Russia, and Brazil, of whose GDP exceeded one trillion US dollars, have had seats in the top 12 economic entities of the world. Today, China, India, and Russia have contributed more than half to the economic global growth. Moreover, China's economy scale is over $ 10 trillion, ranking second in the world.

It is noteworthy that the current rapid development of emerging economies occurred mainly in the last three or four decades, which is different from developed countries.

During this period, due to new technologies, such as IT and the Internet, coupled with increasing population and land areas of emerging countries, which have never been seen in developed countries, new economic phenomena are springing up en masse. Many problems about which conventional economic studies have shown relatively little concern (hereinafter referred to as "the new economy") have been given a new economic significance in this era. For example, the environmental pollution emerging in China is more severe than any developed country has ever

[1]E11 refers to Argentina, Brazil, China, India, Indonesia, Korea, Mexico, Russia, Saudi Arabia, South Africa, and Turkey in the Group of Twenty.

[2]IMF: In the year 2015, developed economies led global economic growth by 3.5% http://china.huanqiu.com/News/mofcom/2015–04/6200548.html

X. Li (✉)
Business School, Nanjing University, Nanjing, China
e-mail: xiaochun@nju.edu.cn

X. Li (ed.), *Labor Transfer in Emerging Economies*, New Frontiers in Regional Science: Asian Perspectives 12, DOI 10.1007/978-981-10-3569-2_1

experienced. Additionally, China's immigrant remittances scale is equivalent to the size of New Zealand's GDP in 2015.[3] Moreover, the construction of China's modern agriculture and other sorts of things is all producing unprecedented impacts on economic development. The study of economics is inseparable from economic realities. What we need is to concentrate on the market mechanisms and economic policies brought by the new economic phenomenon under the new historical conditions. Amid the emergence of these new economic problems, this book endeavors to ascertain whether the old labor-transfer theory is no longer applicable to the current economic reality of developing countries. We are also curious about how to apply the traditional model to these new economic problems and what kinds of conclusions we may then derive. By conducting theoretical research on new economic problems arising from emerging economies, we can obtain relevant theories and politics, which is precisely the purpose of this book.

1 China's Labor Transference, Background and Factors

Emerging economies share various characteristics such as a large population and vast territory, which China and India, as large, heavily populated countries, certainly typify. China's economic boom started in 1978, and, after nearly 40 years of development, the country has been transformed. In the process, the transference of rural labor to nonagricultural sectors has had a significant influence on economic development.

A large number of farmers have transferred from rural life to urban areas since the 1980s. The data from China's Bureau of Statistics shows that, in the year 2015, approximately 277 million[4] farmers flooded the cities in search of work. These people (also known as "migrant workers") have two characteristics: One is a low level of human capital, as a consequence of which, they can secure only low wages in the city. The other is that they must take care of their rural families, so they have to economize on their living costs as much as possible in order to send money back home. In regard to the first point, with the increasingly rapid economic development, our government has increased investment in education and vocational training. Therefore, China's labor force is accruing more in terms of its human capital. However, as with the long-term dual economic structure, education in rural areas is the other side of the coin with respect to urban education. This is evidenced by a lower average of the number of years of education in rural areas. Many farmers chose work over school simply because they need to escape poverty as soon as

[3]World Bank, "World Development Indicators" http://databank.worldbank.org/data/reports.aspx?source=2&type=metadata&series=NY.GDP.MKTP.CD

National Bureau of Statistics, "2014 Survey and Monitoring Report of Migrant Workers" http://www.stats.gov.cn/tjsj/zxfb/201504/t20150429_797821.html

[4]National Bureau of Statistics, "2015 Survey and Monitoring Report of Migrant Workers" http://www.stats.gov.cn/tjsj/zxfb/201604/

possible. According to statistics, in the year 2015, 74% of migrant workers had not even finished junior high school. This is little different from 30 years earlier, when their parents went to the city in search of employment.[5] Regarding the second point, with China's continued economic development, a more advanced educational institution and infrastructure give migrant workers more opportunities to assimilate into urban life, particularly those born after the 1980s. Their concept of life and livelihood is closer to urban standards; as a matter of fact, they are more willing or more able to live in the city, in which case helping to reduce migrant workers' remittances. However, the income level of the rural population is still low compared to the overall economy. Thus, the amount of remittance from migrant workers continues to rise. According to national statistics and by the authors' estimation, remittances reached nearly 1.06 trillion RMB (around 170 billion US dollar) in 2014.[6] Those remittances play an essential role in rural development. In some regions, the scale of remittances has exceeded the local fiscal revenue,[7] being an economic force whose impact is beyond argument.

Compared to developed countries, however, China's agricultural sector lags behind. Thus, the focus on developing modern agriculture has become an important orientation of national development policies in China, as is the case in other emerging countries. Modern agriculture is based on the higher levels of human capital as well as the higher input of technology and investment. Therefore, it is not only more efficient than traditional agriculture but also more environmentally responsible, despite its higher output. China began to develop its modern agriculture in the mid-1990s, and it has made various achievements. It has also satisfied the conditions for accelerated development.[8] However, due to a weak foundation, it is difficult for China to fully popularize modern agriculture, i.e., to make agriculture a business and livelihood equal to any endeavor of similar input in terms of human capital.

Finally, it must be emphasized that environmental problems, including those incurred by labor transference, are prominent in emerging economies such as China and India. This is because emerging countries often focus on the economic benefits while neglecting the cause of environmental protection as an essential part of economic development. In fact, labor transference in emerging economies is often accompanied by environmental pollution. The relationship between them is presented below:

---

[5]National Bureau of Statistics, "2015 Survey and Monitoring Report of Migrant Workers" http://www.stats.gov.cn/tjsj/zxfb/201604/

[6]Source: http://www.stats.gov.cn/tjsj/zxfb/201504/t20150429_797821.html

[7]Liu Feng. Hometown Remittance and Integration into Urban Life of Rural Migrant Workers: An empirical study based on survey in three Jiangsu's cities. Mathematics in Practice and Theory. June 2016.

[8]Tian Cuijie. Thoughts on the Construction of Modern Agricultural Public Service System. Agricultural Economy. No. 11, 2011.

Labor transference → Upgrading the level of industrialization
→ Environmental pollution

Labor transference is the foundation of industrialization in developing countries. American economists Grossman and Krueger (1991, 1995) conducted an empirical study on the relationship between economic activity and the environment. They noted that economic activity can affect the quality of the environment, mainly in three aspects:

1. Economic scale: The larger the economy in general, the more adverse its environmental impact will be.
2. Technical level: The higher the technical level is, the more beneficial it will be to environmental improvement and preservation.
3. The factors, such as economic structure, are interconnected.

Their point of view has been accepted by many economists. Generally, early in the process of economic development, most developing countries choose an extensive mode of high input, high consumption, and high pollution in order to achieve a target rate of growth, and this tendency has caused widespread environmental damage. Now, many emerging countries have crossed or are about to cross this stage, whereupon they will emerge in a new "green" era of sustainability. In China's case, environmental pollution remains a serious problem: Environmental protection legislation is imperfect, and the standard of sewerage charge is too low, as is the cost of violating the law. In fact, some companies would rather accept the punishment than purchase the machinery needed to deal with pollution. Meanwhile, financial investment in environmental protection is insufficient.[9]

2 Mathematical Analysis of Economics

The term "mathematical analysis of economics" is interchangeable with theoretical analysis. First, as it pertains to the later chapters in this book, I will share some opinions on the method of mathematical economic analysis. Secondly, I will offer a brief introduction to the Lewis (Lewis 1954) and Harris-Todaro models (Todaro 1969; Harris and Todaro 1970), as they are mentioned often in this book.

[9]Li Li. The Choice of Fiscal Policy to Promote Environmental Protection. Special Zone Economy. 2007, No. 3.

2.1 *Mathematical Analysis of Economics*

2.1.1 Scientific Methodology

Economics is a discipline that observes and studies society on the basis of input and output or cost and benefit. Along with political science, sociology, psychology, and other disciplines, it belongs to the general category of social sciences. Viewed in the larger context, science is divided into social sciences and natural sciences such as mathematics, physics, chemistry, biology, etc. Thus, the difference between social and natural sciences is found in their subject matter and objectives. Whereas the social sciences focus on humanities and social conditions, the natural sciences study such things as physical geography. The so-called scientific methodology considers how to use scientific methods to conduct research on social issues or natural problems. In the field of theoretical economics, mathematics – as one of the scientific methodologies in economic study – is the primary mode of research. Regardless of the area to be studied in the realm of economics, the research process employing mathematical tools consists of a "trilogy": First, we should make a mathematical treatment to the hypothesis, translating economic problems into mathematical expressions, usually through means of mathematical equations or formulas. This is the so-called mathematical modeling. We then use mathematical methods to derive the quantitative results and deduce our qualitative judgments. Finally, we restore the mathematical results into the economic expression. Generally, the conclusions we draw through the use of mathematical tools must be verified as to their "correctness" with respect to the real economy. When the conclusion is consistent with the reality, the hypothesis can be seen as correct, whereupon it is known as a "theorem." Otherwise, the hypothesis is incorrect, being known as a "paradox."

Generally, empirical analysis is used to judge whether the conclusion is consistent with the reality. Such a trilogy involves the process of mathematical analysis, but such a process is also scientific methodology, which can be summarized as shown below:

$$\text{Setting hypothesis and mathematicization} \rightarrow \text{mathematical deduction}$$
$$\rightarrow \text{restoration into economic issues}$$

Of course, in the above process, it is better to set fewer conditions and deduce more conclusions.

2.1.2 Modeling the Economic Phenomenon

A hypothesis is called a theorem once it is proved to be right. So, the theorem should be as general as possible.

Highly abstract concepts are presented as models so that they may be expressed in relatively concrete forms. Usually, scholars make abstractions and generalizations by presenting one or several mathematical equations, sometimes doing so in the form of geometric patterns. The Lewis model and the Harris-Todaro model are examples, being frequently mentioned in the study of labor economics.

Mathematical analysis in economics cannot be accomplished without the principles and concepts of economics. Often it requires that the researcher have a solid basis of knowledge in microeconomics and macroeconomics. Shown below are some concepts that are essential when building a model in economic empirical study. Normally, these concepts are requisite conditions.

First is the definition of "economic subjects."

Society is made up of humans. Human interaction is considered to be social activity. Because economics closely correlates society to economic activity, we consider the economy of society to consist of the "economic man" and the "economic activity." Here, the term "economic man" is also known as "rational economic entity." In addition to a natural person in the biological sense, an entity such as an enterprise or an organization can also have status as a legal person. Thus, the term "rational economic entity" refers to any natural person or legal person who counts one's own interests in the economic activities. Such a natural person or legal person is hereinafter referred to as an "economic entity."

The economy of society, in turn, consists of the following two elements:

- An economic entity conducting consumption and production activities
- A market

The elementary economic theory assumes, in regard to market conditions, that the prices of goods and services form naturally, while an economic entity only needs to decide whether or how to trade according to its prices. This is the so-called perfect competition assumption. Here, the economic entity is the price-taker. Of course, the circumstances may be such that other complex economic theories can also be considered.

Let us consider the economic entity's code of conduct in the market.

Given the above, economic men are economic entities who take action after calculating their self-interest, which is in turn calculated on the basis of internal and external price information. When tracking changes in market prices, the economic entity considers its own internal situation in order to estimate the loss of consumption, production, and trade. Generally, the economic entity is divided into consumers and producers. Among them, the consumers act on the basis of maximized utility, which is the degree of satisfaction they can obtain from goods and services. It is significant that there are too many kinds of goods and services in the world, so the degree of utility often cannot be measured by a unified unit. In a market economy, the producers take action on the basis of maximized benefits.

The difficulty of the theoretical economy is that, in the real world, it is impractical to precisely divide consumption activities from production activities. For example, for a family business or the self-employed household, it is difficult to distinguish productive activity from consumption activity. If a company is considered an economic body, then consumption activity is also productive activity. If an enterprise is seen as an economic entity, its business must include consumption as well as production. In the following pages, we will break down these circumstances and examine their relationship to the whole.

2.1.3 Testing the Conclusions of Theoretical Analysis

Any conclusion derived from a mathematical model should be tested in the real world. In the study of economics, such tests are often conducted by means of an econometric method called the "empirical analysis" in economic methodology. If the conclusion derived from the model isn't fully supported by evidence, it can only be seen as a hypothesis. However, this doesn't mean that all of the theoretical analysis must be supported by real evidence in order to merit inclusion in an empirical report. As the theoretical analysis often appears before the corresponding policies do, there isn't enough statistical data to facilitate empirical analysis. Therefore, many theoretical papers lack a section on empirical analysis. Some chapters in this book also finish without an empirical part, so their ultimate improvement depends on the results of future research.

Not all the conclusions derived by using mathematical tools can be validated in the real economy. Another reason is that the conditions set forth in the first step in our trilogy are relatively abstract, being difficult to establish or verify in the real economic environment. Some readers will say, "In this case, those unpractical conditions should not have been set in the first place!" I have heard similar opinions in symposiums attended by scholars and experts. However, in order to solve a problem or launch a new policy, it is often necessary to go through multiple arguments. People's cognition gradually deepens, going from the theoretical to the practical. Without a relatively abstract stage, we may find that we can't reach the ideal. I don't propose that we should set the hypothesis without considering the real economic conditions. On the contrary, I urge that the world of the real economy be considered, so that we can transfer from a "hypothesis" to a "theorem" as soon as possible, on the basis of scientific methodology.

Let's return to the problem of the environment. Ultimately, we must decide which kind of policy is required and how it should be implemented. We need to consider the comprehensive social and economic situation before choosing which disciplines of social sciences should be referenced. Not all the conclusions derived from our model should be adopted by authorities, as we consider only the factors in economic areas. Therefore, our conclusions can only provide advice from an economic perspective. In fact, in the process of making environmental policy around the world, there is constant argument between critics and economists. Although this book presents a series of policy-making recommendations, I do not think the conclusions derived merely from the standpoint of economics will suffice as the basis of policy. However, I don't think policies can be made without taking economics into consideration. Hopefully, this research can help improve our

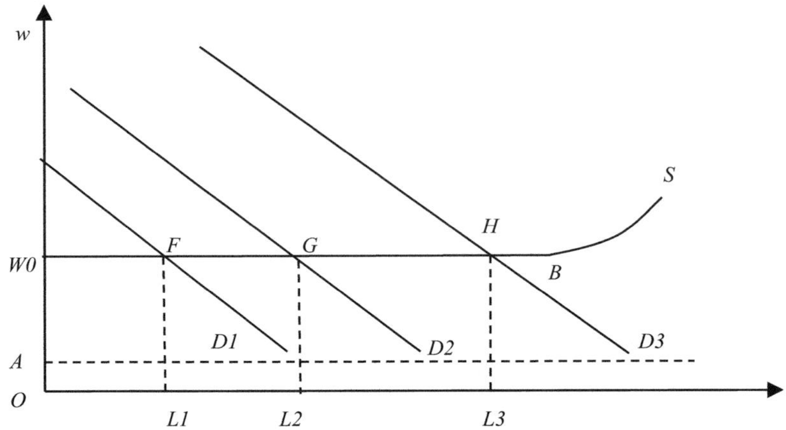

Fig. 1.1 The Lewis model

country's environment while also benefiting the development of China's economic discipline.

2.2 *The Lewis and Harris-Todaro Models*

2.2.1 The Lewis Model

The respected British economist and 1979 Nobel laureate William Arthur Lewis (Sir Arthur Lewis) proposed "dual economies" in his 1954 paper titled "Economic development with unlimited supplies of labor." He explained that, in many developing countries, there are two different economic sectors: One is the urban modern industrial sector, with a large concentration of capital and high labor productivity, and the other is traditional agricultural sector, which lacks capital and has low labor productivity. Thus, farmers can only maintain a minimum standard of living. Nevertheless, there is a vast surplus of labor, but the marginal productivity of rural surplus labor is zero. Therefore, as long as the industrial sector requires, it can tap an unlimited supply of labor from the agricultural sector. According to Fig. 1.1, under the dual structure in developing countries, we use *OA* to represent the average income of agricultural labor to maintain a family's minimum standard of living, i.e., survival income; *Ow* is the real wage offered by the urban industrial sector, for which the supply of labor from the traditional agricultural sector is unlimited. The urban industrial sector continues to take profits and reinvest them as a means to expand the scale of capital, with the real wage being constant, whereby the marginal production curve of labor continues to move right from *D1*, to *D2*, to *D3*. This in turn creates more labor opportunities, attracting more agricultural labor from *L1*, to *L2*, to *L3*. Thus, the cycle is repeated. Meanwhile, in the urban industrial sector, the scale of capital expands, absorbing the surplus of labor from the traditional agricultural sector. As long as there is surplus labor in the agricultural sector, the urban industrial sector will be able to expand the scale of investment, doing so on the basis of such labor. This situation continues until the labor-supply curve *S* reaches its turning point *B* (the Lewis turning point). At that point, surplus labor in the agricultural sector is fully absorbed by the industrial sector, and the marginal productivity of labor in the agricultural sector is no longer zero, that is, agricultural output reduced because of the loss of agricultural labor. In this case, the labor-supply curve *S* became right-up sloped, and the industrial sector will not be supplied of agricultural labor until wages are raised. Then the structure of these two basic production sectors, namely, the agricultural and industrial sectors, is transformed, achieving a balanced state of development. The net result is that the difference between the urban sector and the rural sector is reduced and the dual economic structure is implemented as a unitary economic structure, moving toward simultaneous industrialization and urbanization. The dual economic structure put forward by Lewis was widely used in economic research in developing countries. However, the Lewis theory did not discuss unemployment, which cannot be avoided in a market economy. So, the application of the Lewis theory is limited to research of economic problems at the industrial takeoff stage.

2.2.2 The Harris-Todaro Model

The Harris-Todaro model is a succession, critique, and development of the Lewis model. As with the latter, the former has a dual economy as its general environment, and consequently, criticism and development in the two models are reflected in urban unemployment. This is because the downward rigidity of wages in the urban sector causes urban unemployment, inhibiting the flow of rural labor toward the urban zones. In 1969, the American economist Michael Todaro was the first to conduct systematic research into the phenomenon that although urban unemployment exists, rural labor still transfers into urban areas. He then cooperated with the American economist John R. Harris and published, in *American Economic Review,* a creative paper titled "Migration, unemployment and development: a two-sector analysis." Todaro was just 31, which was the beginning of the two men's rise to fame. Their research drew wide attention and enjoyed a high reputation in global economic circles. Moreover, the mechanism of labor transfer, as described in the paper, became known as the Harris-Todaro model.

Precondition

We consider a small open economy with two products being composed of two departments, namely, urban and rural sectors. The research hypotheses are as follows:

- The urban sector produces importable industrial products; the rural sector produces exportable agricultural products.
- The factors of production in both sectors are labor and capital.

The original Harris-Todaro model also takes into account the effect of another factor in agricultural sector land on agricultural production. For convenience of explanation, we leave the land factor consideration aside. As for capital, according to the requirement of research, in general, there are two settings: One is free flow capital between sectors, and another is immovable capital. Here, we take the latter, setting capital which is sector-specific, i.e., capital cannot move between sectors. Sector-specific capital is also called "special capital." At this point, the capital employed by each sector can be seen as a constant.

Production Function

Under these above preconditions, the production of urban sector and rural sector is X_m and X_a, respectively. Production function can be expressed as:

$$X_m = F^m(L_m)$$

$$X_a = F^a(L_a)$$

where L_i ($i = a, m$) is labor employment in urban sector and rural sector, respectively. F^m and F^a are strictly quasi-concave and first-order homogeneous functions.

Labor Allocation Mechanism

Supposing urban wage is higher than rural wage, rural laborers are attracted by the high urban wage and move into urban areas. But because of the downward rigidity of wage, unemployment exists in the urban sector. Thus, rural laborers who transfer into urban areas may not find a job and become unemployed even if they have reached urban areas. Therefore, the rural labor in determining whether transfer will compare the rural wage rate with the urban wage rate may be obtained in:

$$w_m L_m / (L_m + L_u)$$

where w_m is urban wage rate, L_u is urban unemployment rate, $L_m/(L_m + L_u)$ is the employment rate in the urban sector, while $w_m L_m/(L_m + L_u)$ is the expectation wage in the urban sector, also called "the expected wage." If the expected wage is higher than the rural wage, rural labor will flow into urban areas looking for a job, and the transfer process will continue until the expected wage equals the rural wage. This is the famous Harris-Todaro labor-transfer balance. In other words, the labor resources are allocated in urban and rural sectors as:

$$w_a = w_m L_m / (L_m + L_u)$$

where w_a is the real wage rate in the rural sector. Note that there is downward rigidity in urban wage, and is an exogenous variable, while there is flexibility in rural wage, and is an endogenous variable. Let $\lambda = L_u/L_m$, then the above equation can be expressed as:

$$w_a = w_m / (1 + \lambda) \tag{1.1}$$

Here, λ is the ratio of unemployment to employment in the urban sector and is defined as "unemployment rate" in some economic textbooks (note the difference between the definition in this text and the "unemployment rate" in macroeconomics). This is convenient for later analysis. Equation (1.1) is the core relation of labor allocation in the Harris-Todaro model.

Equilibrium in Labor Market

If the amount of labor endowment in the whole economy is L, then

$$L = L_m + L_u + L_a$$

Substituting $\lambda = L_u/L_m$ into the above equation can be obtained:

$$L = (1 + \lambda) L_m + L_a \tag{1.2}$$

On the other hand, profit of the urban sector can be described as the following equation:

$$\pi = pX_m - w_m L_m$$

where π is the urban profit and p is the price of industrial product in terms of agricultural product, that is, supposing the price of agricultural product is 1 and then the price of industrial product is p. According to the profit maximization of the urban sector, we calculate the first-order condition of the above equation and obtain:

$$pF_L^m = w_m \tag{1.3}$$

Similarly, from the profit maximization of the agricultural sector, we obtain:

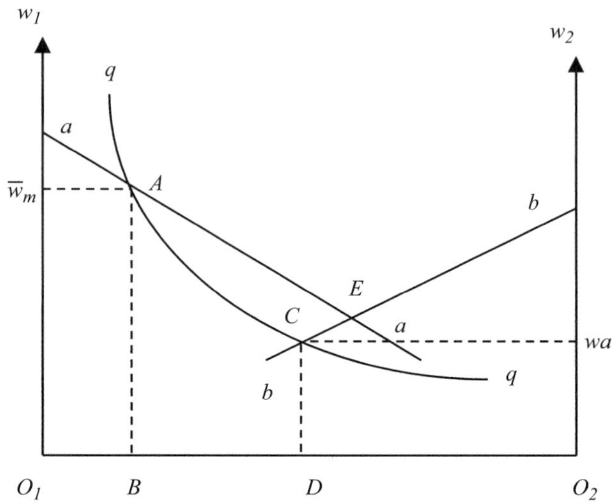

Fig. 1.2 The labor distribution mechanism of Harris-Todaro model

$$F_L^a = w_a \tag{1.4}$$

here, $F_L^m = \partial F^m / \partial L_m, F_L^a = \partial F^a / \partial L_a$. The economic meaning of (1.3) and (1.4) is that under perfect competitive condition, wage equals the marginal production of the labor factor.

We focus on the labor market and its general equilibrium which is composed of four equations, (1.1), (1.2), (1.3), and (1.4); we call it "the basic Harris-Todaro model." There are three exogenous variables, w_m, p, and L, and four endogenous variables, w_a, λ, L_a, and L_m. Given the exogenous variables, the system can determine the endogenous variable. The Harris-Todaro basic model is mainly used to study economic issues related to the labor factor in dual economy. For example, when study on the economic effect of the government policy is aimed at subsidize farmers' income under rural labor-transfer condition, the income ratio of subsidized policy can be implanted into sequence 4, calculating the equations in the Harris-Todaro basic model to obtain the results we are interested in (refer to relevant sections of this book for specific calculation methods and approaches). When we are interested in the labor-transfer-induced environmental issues, we need to expand the scope of the market under consideration, adding equations related to the association between environment and production. Refer to the second chapter of the book and succeeding chapters for specific approaches.

3 Ustrate Harris-Todaro Model in Figure

The role of labor distribution is illustrated in Fig. 1.2, where the vertical axes on the left and right sides refer to the wages of the urban and rural sectors, respectively. The horizontal axis is the total endowment of labor in the economy; *aa* and *bb* are the demand curves and also the marginal production curves of the urban and rural sectors, respectively.

In the traditional labor-transfer model, the equilibrium point can be reached in point *E*. The urban and rural sectors have the same wage rate and have no unemployment. But in the Harris-Todaro model, the wage of the urban sector $(\bar{w}_m)$ is exogenously fixed; we draw a line parallel to the horizontal axis and passing through $\bar{w}_m$; it crosses *aa* at *A*; then, we draw another line passing *A* perpendicular to the horizontal axis; it meets the horizontal axis at *B*; O_1B is the employment of the urban sector L_m, and *qq* is a rectangular hyperbola through point *A*. We draw a line parallel to the horizontal axis, passing through the intersection *C* of *qq* and *bb*; it crosses the right side of the vertical axes at w_a; w_a is the rural wage rate. We draw a line parallel to the vertical axes, passing through *C*; it crosses O_1O_2 at *D*; DO_2 is the employment of the rural sector L_a. Meanwhile, *BD* is the unemployment in the urban sector L_u. According to the nature of the hyperbolic, the rectangular shadow area of $\bar{w}_mABO_1$ equals the rectangular shadow area of w_aCDO_2, so we have $\bar{w}_mL_m = w_a(L_m + L_u)$, which is expressed by Eq. (1.1).

The general consensus, during the initial stage of the pair's research, was that the problem would be the cumulative effect of various government policies like wage-subsidy policy or the promotion (or the restriction) of labor-transfer policy on the economy or social welfare. Later, scholars expanded the scope of study by inserting human capital, industrial upgrading, industrial clustering, and the environment into the Harris-Todaro model as problems to be examined and rectified. In recent years, research has concentrated on environmental protection, and scholarly research has made many achievements. It also reflects another aspect: that the importance of environmental protection in less developed countries extends beyond national/political boundaries to become a significant issue for the world.

4 The Structure of This Book

It was in September 2003 that, after studying in Japan for many years, I returned to China and entered the Business School of Nanjing University. I have been so fortunate to participate in the process of China's economic development in this great era and to witness the rapid development of China as a representative emerging economy. This great privilege continues to be the basis for my research. Each chapter in this book is independent but also connected to the others. The work pursues research from four aspects: the level of human capital, migrant workers' remittances to their hometowns, environmental protection, and the development of modern agriculture. We cannot say that the four aspects encompass the economic panorama of emerging nations, but they do grasp the main context of emerging nations such as China. The following is a brief introduction to the structure of this book.

This book has four parts and 12 chapters, in which there is an introduction and 11 chapters. This research is the result of my thinking in regard to various economic phenomena incurred by labor transfer in emerging nations.

The initial chapter includes the reason for the publication of this book, the related background of Chinese labor transfer, the basic knowledge in that subject, and an introduction to the book.

The portion on human capital discusses economic influences of human capital level in dual economy countries in three perspectives: urban-rural human capital gap, training rural-urban migrants, and the minimum wage on employment in the labor buyer's market.

The portion concerning migrant remittances is made up of two chapters. In the existing literatures, theoretical research on migrant remittances has produced little. This portion in the book investigates the economy effect of migrant remittance from unskilled labor working in the urban sector and the influence of migrant remittance on the urban economy.

The portion on environmental protection analyzes the impact on economic development and environmental protection from three perspectives of migration remittances, inter-sector labor transfer, and trans-boundary pollution.

The part on modern agriculture analyzes the economic effect of policies to promote advanced agricultural development.

Readers of this book should be made aware that the problems discussed in the above chapters are derived from emerging economies, particularly from the observation of China's economic phenomena. Dualistic (or multiple) economic structure models abstracted from these phenomena are effective for economies of a dualistic (or multiple) economic structure.

This book has benefited from the consistent support of Professor Makoto Tawada (Department of Economics, Aichi Gakuin University) at the Japan Section of the Regional Science Association International, without whose encouragement and advice it would not have been published. I am sincerely grateful to him. I am also thankful to the Business School of Nanjing University for providing such a great environment for work and research, so that I could devote myself to the project. In the process of compiling this book, we also received financial support from the Key Project of 2014 for Key Research Bases for Humanities and Social Sciences of the Ministry of Education No. 14JJD790016. The name of this research project is "Comparison of the Modern Economic Development Modes of Jiangsu, Zhejiang and Shanghai." Jiangsu Province, Zhejiang Province, and Shanghai, in the regional division known as the Yangtze River Delta, constitute China's manufacturing heartland. They also contain the bulk of rural transfer in China, so many of the observations of China's new economic problems stem from that region.

It took approximately 5 years to finish this book. Because I started my research in the absence of experience and serious research, the early accumulation is also relatively weak, so I have to work harder than others. The spirit of perseverance shown by my students will always be foremost in my memory. The following individuals participated in the compilation of this work: Dianshuang Wang, Ph.D.; Jing Zhou, Ph.D.; Yunyun Wu; Xiaoying Qian; Qin Shen; Yuanting Xu; Ping He; Chunlei Gu, Ph.D.; Zheyu Dong, Ph.D.; Guoqing Zhang, Ph.D.; and Yu Zhou, Ph.D, participated in the manuscript's proofreading and translation work. These individuals are my students at Nanjing University, and this book is the crystallization of our accumulated knowledge. Our efforts have been rewarded, over the course of nearly 5 years, with the publication of approximately 20 papers in domestic and international journals, and the research results have received attention in China and abroad. Thus, we call for Nanjing University to be accorded entry to the highest echelon in the study of labor transfer. I selected a portion of the results to form this book, but I sincerely hope that this research won't be limited to a single volume. In fact, I hope this book will allow more people to sharpen their perceptions of the "new economy" generated by labor transfer. Thus, we will have the opportunity to deal with labor-transfer problems in the academic and practical work of emerging economies and ultimately become the model for other societies to emulate.

References

Grossman, G. M., & Krueger, B. A. (1991). *Environmental impacts of a North American free trade agreement, NBER working paper no. 3914*. Cambridge, MA: National Bureau of Economic Research.

Grossman, G. M., & Krueger, B. A. (1995). Economic growth and the environment. *Quarterly Journal of Economics, 110*(2), 353–377.

Harris, J. R., & Todaro, M. P. (1970). Migration, unemployment and development: A two-sector analysis. *American Economic Review, 60*, 126–142.

Lewis, W. A. (1954). Economic development with unlimited supplies of labor. *Manchester School, 22*(2), 139–191.

Todaro, M. P. (1969). A model of labor migration and urban unemployment in less developed countries. *The American Economic Review, 59*, 138–148.

Part I
Human Capital

This portion comprises three chapters. Chapter 2 examines the real economic influences of the urban-rural human capital gap in China, which should not be ignored by other emerging nations. The general equilibrium model developed in this chapter is a basic one, but many problems can be extrapolated on the basis of such a model. Additionally, this chapter illustrates the Harris-Todaro model, which comprises three sectors. Chapter 3 analyzes the economic and environmental effects of training rural-urban migrants. Such training affects the environment by facilitating the improvement of work efficiency and content once the human capital is developed. Chapter 4 investigates the effect of minimum wage on employment in the labor buyer's market. Labor buyer's market means hire market, in which hired people have little bargaining power; this mostly happens when the human capital level is very low. The conclusion of this chapter is contrary to common sense that "setting minimum wage will decrease employment"; we prove that setting minimum wage will increase employment in the labor buyer's market, and we use the actual data of the Yangtze River Delta region of China to verify this conclusion.

Chapter 2
Economic Analysis on the Urban–Rural Disparity in Human Capital in China

Xiaochun Li and Xiaoying Qian

Abstract With China's economic development and capital accumulation in the industrial sectors, the human capital level of the labors moving from the rural areas could no longer meet the demand of the industrial sectors. Therefore, "structural shortage of technical labor" emerged in the labor market as a result of excess of demand for high-skilled workers. Previous literature mostly focused on the relationship between rural human capital level and labor movement, income change, and economic growth, but in this article, the authors focus on the study of the relative disparity of urban and rural human capital and labor movement, as well as the effect of the change of urban–rural human capital gap on industrial output, profit, and social welfare. This article shows that bridging the urban–rural gap in respect of human capital level could not only improve the situation of the "structural shortage of technical labor" but also have a positive effect on the general social welfare.

Keywords Transfer of labor • Harris–Todaro model • Disparity of urban and rural human capital • Structural shortage of technical labor • Informal sector • Formal sector

1 Introduction

The human capital level of labor refers to the education level, working skills, and health level of a labor. Human capital level is an important factor in the process of production. If there is a huge gap between high level of material capital and low level of human capital, it would cause controversy between high-tech production measures and products and low-skilled labor, which would further lead to loss of economic efficiency, increase of production cost, and lower competitiveness of the firms.

Since the mid-1980s, a huge number of rural labors have been flooding to the coastal cities from the interior regions for higher wages guided by the market

X. Li (✉)
Business School, Nanjing University, Nanjing, China
e-mail: xiaochun@nju.edu.cn

X. Qian
School of Economics, Nanjing University, 22 Hankou Road, Nanjing, Jiangsu 210093, China

X. Li (ed.), *Labor Transfer in Emerging Economies*, New Frontiers in Regional Science: Asian Perspectives 12, DOI 10.1007/978-981-10-3569-2_2

mechanism, which forms a large-scaled "wax-and-wane" moving of labor across regions, namely, "the tide of migrant workers." In the initial stage of the transfer, China was in its preliminary stage of economic growth; thus, its level of industrialization was low, and the low-skilled human capital from the rural area was able to meet the demand of the nonagricultural sector. With the development of China's economy, material capital in the urban sector is accumulating, while accumulation of human capital in rural China has not fundamentally changed.

According to a sample study of national population based on their education level, which was published in the Chinese Demographic Statistics Yearbook, the weighted average length of education in the rural area increased from 6.46 years in 1997 to 7.70 years in 2007 and that in the urban area increased from 11.42 years to 13.44 years during the same time period.[1] The improvement in the rural area is less than that in the urban area. The average education level of people in the rural area is junior high school, and it is still much lower than that in the urban area, which is high school. Hence, the human capital level of the transferred labor from the rural area is lagging behind the progress of modernization. Since late 2004, a shortage of labor occurred in part of the Pearl River Delta region, southeast of Fujian Province, and the Yangtze River Delta region since there was an excess of demand for high-skilled labor, which was called a "structural shortage of labor." Later, the "technical labor shortage" also happened in some labor-exporting interior provinces, such as Jiangxi, Hunan, and Anhui. Since the second half of the year 2009, as China is recovering from the global financial crisis and moving steadily back to growth, the "shortage of labor" is heard again in some regions, which is largely deemed as a structural shortage. This phenomenon is mainly due to the low level of education, lack of vocational training, low-working skills, and, in general, low level of human capital of the migrant labors from the rural area. In fact, before the "shortage of labor" problem hurts China's economy, many scholars have conducted comprehensive studies on the impact of human capital level on China's economy.

In the study of the impact of human capital of rural labors on movement of labor and individual income in China, Zhao (1997) discussed the impact of the human capital difference among rural labor on their job-hunting behavior. According to his observation, education level of rural labor is positively correlated with the rate of working in the cities, and the higher the education level they have, the higher incomes they get for working in the cities. Taking the cost of moving into consideration, labor with relatively high human capital tends to seek employment in industrial sectors in the rural area first and then employment in the cities. On the other hand, for those with lowest human capital, their first choice is to stay on their land.

[1]Data source: Chinese Demographic Statistics Yearbook from 1997 to 2007. The detailed approach sees: Delong, H. (2005). Empirical analysis of the contribution of human capital to economic growth in Jiangxi. In J. Shaoseng and H. Delong (eds), Development in the Interior Regions of China and Regional Corporation. Beijing: People's Press of Beijing, 168–169.

Du (1999) conducted a study of the transfer of rural labor in the poor region to nonagricultural sectors, focusing on the factors that influence education level. He thinks that basic education is the premise for rural labors to find a job in the cities. Jamison and Gaag (1987), economists of the World Bank, evaluated valid data of 481 rural households in Hui County of Gansu Province and calculated the yield of rural education around the year 1985. Zhou and Zhu (2003) calculated the contribution of different education levels to incomes among rural residents. Assuming complete illiteracy contributes to income by 1, primary school level of education would contribute 1.070, junior high school 1.254, high school 1.308, and college education 1.634, respectively. Hou (2004) made a quantitative analysis on the human capital level of migrant workers from the rural areas and their benefits and pointed out that a government-funded training system for rural labor, which is integrated with the urban area vocational training, is crucial to increasing urban-working opportunities and incomes for rural labors.

In respect of the impact of rural labor's human capital on economic growth, Cai and Wang (1999) discussed the change of labor-use models, the growth of the labor market, and its stimulating effect on economic growth and structural change and estimated the contribution of relocation of human capital and labor resources on China's economic growth. They thought that improvement of efficiency of labor-resource location contributed a significant ratio of 20.23 % to economic growth. Pan and Cheng (2002) established a model for per capita agricultural gross product of rural labor to study the contribution of rural educational investment on rural economic growth and concluded that the social return for educational investment is 32.88 %.

As can be seen, the above domestic and international literature mostly focused on the relationship between rural human capital level and labor movement, income change, and economic growth but rarely combined the study of the relative disparity of urban and rural human capital and labor movement or focused on the effect of the change of gap of urban–rural human capital level on industrial output, profit, and social welfare. This article will focus on the issues that were neglected by past studies. On the other hand, the investors of human capital mainly comprise of individuals, firms, and governments. Yet, currently, the urban–rural human capital disparity is still significant. This is partly due to the inactiveness of the investing entities, which is largely caused by their lack of awareness of the significance of reducing urban–rural human capital disparity on the economy.

In order to clarify the author's points, this article will establish a theoretical model to analyze the significance of the change of urban–rural human capital disparity on solving "structural shortage of technical labor" and its influences on wages, outputs, profits, social welfare, etc. Finally, the authors will provide policy proposals for reference.

2 Theoretical Model

Harris and Todaro (1970), in a thesis of creativity and originality, established a labor transfer model based on the urban–rural dual economic structure. This model puts the focus of labor transfer on the unemployment of the urban sector. Since the wages in the urban sector have inelasticity at the lower end, unemployment exists in the urban sector. However, for rural labors, even though they are transferred to the cities, they would not necessarily be able to get into the urban sector. Therefore, when rural labors are willing to transfer to the urban sector for higher wages, they would not compare their rural income with the wage in the urban sectors. Rather, they compare it to the expected wage of urban sectors. Expected wage is the volume of urban wage multiplied by the probability of finding a job in the cities.

The labor transfer mechanism of Harris–Todaro model is that when the rural wage is below the expected wage of the urban sector, the rural labors move to the urban sector. With the growing number of transferred labors, the unemployment in the urban sector increases, and then the expected wage of urban area would decrease. When the rural wage equals the expected wage of the urban sector, the transfer of rural labor to the urban sector will halt. This article expands the two-sector model of Harris–Todaro and makes an economic analysis with consideration of factors of disparity in the urban–rural human capital levels.

2.1 *Description of the Initial Status*

In this article, the economy is divided into three sectors: the urban formal sector, the urban informal sector, and the rural sector. It was Grinols (1991) who raised the notion of urban informal sector. He thinks that as the rural labors move to the cities but could not find a job, they would take on jobs such as selling newspapers, working as babysitters, vendors, etc. All those jobs share the commonality of lacking organization and small investment; thus, they are called urban informal sector in general. In this way, he divided the urban sectors to two: the formal and the informal. The urban former sector refers to the ordinary industrial sectors. Such division basically matches the current situation in China. Thus, this article adopts the same theoretical model of the division and makes the following premises about the model.

It is assumed that the three sectors all rely on capital and labor as factors for production; capital does not move among sectors; the formal sector produces importable goods, while the rural sector produces exportable goods. Wages of the urban formal sector are inelastic at the lower end, but wages of the urban informal or rural sectors are elastic. The transfer of labor has two phases, the initial phase and the transferring phase. In the initial phase, all rural labors are employed in the rural sector, while all urban labors are employed in the urban sectors, some of which are in the formal sector, and the others are in the informal sector. In the authors' model, transfer cost is not counted.

The labor endowment in the economy is L. L_U and L_R refer to urban and rural labor endowment, respectively, with $L = L_U + L_R$.

The production functions for each sector are

$$M_{11} = F^1\left(L_{11}, \overline{K_{11}}\right)$$
$$M_{21} = F^2\left(L_{21}, \overline{K_2}\right)$$

and

$$M_{31} = F^3\left(L_R, \overline{K_3}\right)$$

Of the two-digit footnotes, the first represents the sectors, with 1, 2, and 3 representing the urban formal sector, the urban informal sector, and the rural sector, respectively. The second digit represents the phase, with 1 and 2 representing the initial phase and the transferring phase, respectively. Single digit refers to the sector, irrelevant to the phase. $F^{\xi}(i = 1, 2, 3)$ means the production function of the formal sector, the informal sector, and the rural sector, all are strictly quasi-concave, linearly homogeneous function. M_{11}, M_{21}, and A_{31} mean the production of the formal sector, the informal sector, and the urban sector, respectively. L_{11}, L_{21}, $L_R, \overline{K_{11}}, \overline{K_2}$, and $\overline{K_3}$ refer to the labor and capital invested in production of the formal sector, the informal sector, and the rural sector, respectively. $\overline{w_1}$ is the wage level of the formal sector, which is taken as the fixed baseline, while w_{21} and w_{31} refer to the wage levels of the informal and rural sectors. With the condition of maximized profit of each sector, we have the formulas as follows:

$$p_1 F_L^1\left(L_{11}, \overline{K_{11}}\right) = \overline{w_1} \tag{2.1}$$
$$p_2 F_L^2 = w_{21} \tag{2.2}$$
$$F_L^3 = w_{31} \tag{2.3}$$

F_L^i means the first derivative of the production function ($i = 1, 2, 3$) on the labor; p_1 and p_2 are the relative prices of the products of the formal and informal sectors, respectively, while price of the rural sector is assumed as 1. Considering the features of the economy, we assume that p_1 and p_2 are given. Thus, the urban labor L_U satisfies the following formula

$$L_U = L_{11} + L_{21} \tag{2.4}$$

From Eqs. (2.1), (2.2), (2.3), and (2.4), there are four formulas to determineL_{11}, L_{21}, w_{21}, and w_{31}, while other variables in the model are exogenous variables. In the initial stage, the distribution of labor could be shown as in the following graph (Fig. 2.1).

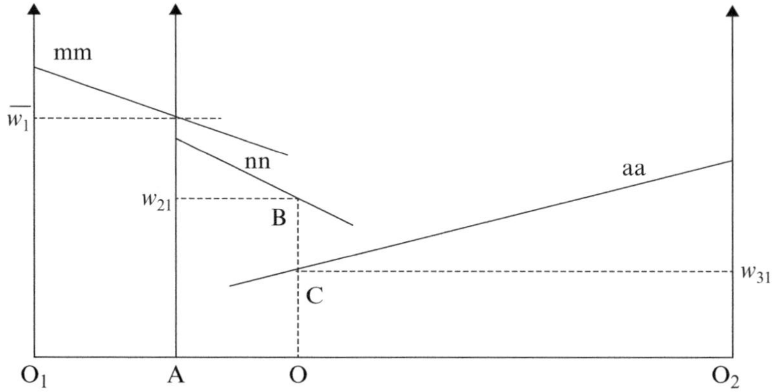

Fig. 2.1 The labor distribution of the three sectors in the initial phase

In the graph, the horizontal axis is the amount of labor of the whole economy, with O_1Oindicating the urban labor and O_2O indicating the rural labor. mm and aa refer to the marginal production curves of the formal sector and the rural sector, respectively. Since the wage of the formal sector $\overline{w_1}$ is fixed, the size of L_{11} is O_1A, and the size of L_{12} is AO. Drawing a perpendicular line against the horizontal axis from point O, it intersects with the marginal production curve of the informal sector nn at B and with the marginal production curve of the rural sector aa at C. Then, drawing a line crossing B and C that parallels with the horizontal axis, we get w_{21} and w_{31}, and this shows the distribution of labor of the three sectors in the initial phase.

2.2 *The General Equilibrium Model of Labor Transfer*

With the increase of capital in the formal sector due to economic development, the intensity of technology increases, and, thus, the demand for high-skilled labor increases $\left(p_1F_L^1\left(L_{11},\overline{K_{11}}\right) > \bar{w}_1\right)$. On the supply side of labor, because of the disparity in economic and educational levels between urban and rural areas, the human capital level of urban labors is relatively high, and that of the rural labors is relatively low; thus, whether the human capital level of the transferred labor from the rural areas could meet the demand of firms largely depends on whether they are well trained. Therefore, in the process of hiring in the formal sector, we assume that the urban labors could be employed in the formal sector directly, while whether the rural labor could enter into the formal sector relies on whether they have received vocational training.

In addition, the formal sector usually tends to attract more young labor (Zhang Zheng 2005). Taking Dongguan of Guangzhou, for example, people between the age of 18 and 28 compose 80% of the labor force, while people between the age of

17 and 25 take 87% of the shortage of labor. This means that most of the labors transferring from the rural areas to the cities are youngsters, which means that young labors are the main source of labor increase. The labors in the urban informal sector, on the other hand, are mostly senior and weak people, who could not be employed in the formal sector. We assume that those people could not work and find opportunities in the formal sector.

We also assume that the transfer of labor from the rural to urban areas would not squeeze out labor in the formal sector. In addition, for the labor transferring from the rural areas, even though they could not enter into the formal sector, geographically moving to the cities would help them acquire more accurate and prompt working information. As a consequence, they enter into the urban informal sector. In this view, rural labors could be employed in the formal, informal, or rural sector, and there is no unemployment in the entire economy.

In the following, we would establish and study the model in details. In the transferring phase, the production functions for each sector are

$$M_{12} = F^1\left(L_{12}, \overline{K_{12}}\right)$$
$$M_{22} = F^2\left(L_{22}, \overline{K_2}\right)$$

and

$$A_{32} = F^3\left(L_{32}, \overline{K_3}\right)$$

Among them, $\overline{K_{12}}\left(\overline{K_{12}} > \overline{K_{11}}\right)$ is the capital stock for the formal sector after the increase, while the capital in the other two sectors stays the same. The formal sector would invest in human capital investment. Assuming that the formal sector makes human capital investment based on a proportion of production, and while the labor quality meets the demand of the employers, it would stop investing in this regard, then $T = \lambda p_1 M_{12}$. Here, T is the investment on human capital by the formal sector; λ is the proportion of production used on human capital investment in the formal sector. Moreover, h is assumed to be the cost of training a rural labor to meet the demand of human capital by the formal sector, which is a measure of the human capital disparity between rural and urban labors. L_{12} is the amount of labor for production in the formal sector. While the employment of urban labors in the formal sector is constant, the amount of labor that could be transferred from the rural area to the formal sector is $L_{12} - L_{11}$, which is

$$L_{12} - L_{11} = \frac{T}{h} = \frac{\lambda p_1 M_{12}}{h} = \frac{\lambda p_1 F^1\left(L_{12}, \overline{K_{12}}\right)}{h} \tag{2.5}$$

Since only trained rural labor would enter into the formal sector, the rest of the labor force $L_{22} - L_{21}$ would enter into the informal sector.

In the transferring phase, the rural labors in each sector would be

$$L_R = (L_{12} - L_{11}) + (L_{22} - L_{21}) + L_{32} \tag{2.6}$$

and the profit functions for each sector would be

$$\pi_1 = p_1F^1 - \overline{w_1}L_{12} - r_1\overline{K_{12}} - \lambda p_1F^1$$
$$\pi_2 = p_2F^2 - w_{22}L_{22} - r_2\overline{K_2}$$

and

$$\pi_3 = F^3 - w_{32}L_{32} - r_3\overline{K_3}$$

Among them, r_1, r_2, and r_3 refer to the capital interest of the three sectors in a perfectly competitive market. With w_{22} and w_{32} indicating the wages of the informal and rural sectors, the following three formulas could be derived from maximization of profit in each sector:

$$(1-\lambda)p_1F_L^1(L_{12}, \overline{K_{12}}) = \overline{w_1} \tag{2.7}$$

$$p_2F_L^2 = w_{22} \tag{2.8}$$

$$F_L^3 = w_{32} \tag{2.9}$$

In the equilibrium of transfer of labor force, the wage in the rural sector equals the sum of expected wages in the formal and the informal sectors, i.e.,

$$w_{32} = \frac{L_{12} - L_{11}}{L_{12} - L_{11} + L_{22} - L_{21}}\overline{w_1} + \frac{L_{22} - L_{21}}{L_{12} - L_{11} + L_{22} - L_{21}}w_{22} \tag{2.10}$$

The above formula could also be written as

$$(L_{12} - L_{11})(\overline{w_1} - w_{22}) = (L_{22} - L_{21})(w_{32} - w_{22}) \tag{2.11}$$

The wage level of the formal sector $\overline{w_1}$ is the highest among all sectors, $L_{12} > L_{11}$ and $L_{22} > L_{21}$. Therefore, $\bar{w}_1 > w_{32} > w_{22}$. With the economic development and transfer of rural labor force, the wage of rural sector gradually increases, while that of the informal sector decreases so that the wage in the informal sector is lower than that of the rural sector. Nonetheless, based on the assumptions of this part, some rural labors are still willing to move to the urban informal sector.

Figure 2.2 shows the labor distribution mechanism of the three sectors expressed by Eq. (2.10). The horizontal axis is the total labor endowment in the economy; O_1O is the labor endowment of the urban households; O_2O is the labor endowment of the rural households; mm and aa are the marginal production curves of the formal sector and the rural sector, respectively. The wage of the formal sector $\bar{w}_1$ is fixed. The size of L_{11} is O_1A. From Eqs. (2.5), (2.6), and (2.7), it could be derived that L_{12}

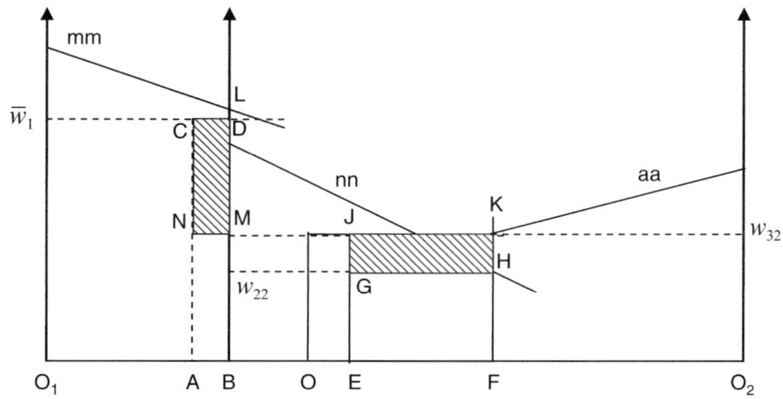

Fig. 2.2 The equilibrium in the labor distribution mechanism of the three sectors

is O_1B. A line that crosses $\bar{w}_1$ and parallels with the horizontal axis intersects with a line that crosses A and B and is perpendicular to the horizontal axis at C and D. Using B as the original point to make a vertical axis, we get the marginal production curve of the informal sector nn and could know that $\lambda = DL/BL$. Let $OE = AB = L_{12} - L_{11}$, then $BE = AO = L_{21}$. By Eqs. (2.6), (2.8), (2.9), and (2.10), we derive that L_{22} equalsBF, and $EF = L_{22} - L_{21}$. Thus, $OF = OE + EF = L_{12} - L_{11} + L_{22} - L_{21}$ is the amount of labor transferring from the rural areas, and $FO_2 = L_{32}$. We then make a line that is parallel to the vertical axis and crosses F; it intersects nn and aa at H and K. Drawing a line that parallels the horizontal axis and crosses H and K, we get w_{22}, w_{32}, and points G, J, M, and N. According to Eq. (2.11), the area of $GHKJ$equals that of $CDMN$(shown as shades in the graph).

In view of the above, from Eqs. (2.5), (2.6), (2.7), (2.8), (2.9), and (2.10), there are altogether six formulas to solve the six endogenous variables L_{12}, L_{22}, L_{32}, λ, w_{22}, and w_{32}. Other variables in this model are exogenous variables. Therefore, the model establishment is complete.

3 Analysis

Based on the established model, we could make a theoretical analysis of change of the urban–rural disparity of human capital on the economy. Total differentiation of the equations of (2.5) and (2.7) are

$$\left(\lambda p_1 F_L^1 - h\right) dL_{12} + p_1 F^1 d\lambda = (L_{12} - L_{11}) dh$$

Fig. 2.3 Comparison of the marginal product and average product in the formal sector

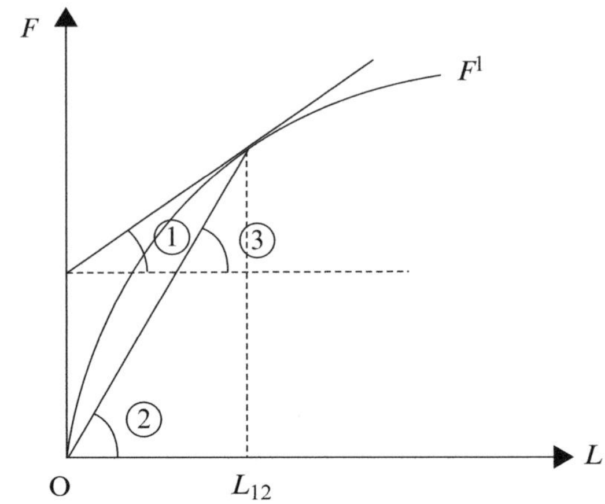

and

$$(1-\lambda)F^1_{LL}dL_{12}F^1_L d\lambda = 0$$

and it could be expressed by the following determinant:

$$\begin{pmatrix} (1-\lambda)F^1_{LL} & -F^1_L \\ \lambda p_1 F^1_L - h & p_1 F^1 \end{pmatrix}\begin{pmatrix} dL_{12} \\ d\lambda \end{pmatrix} = \begin{pmatrix} 0 \\ L_{12} - L_{11} \end{pmatrix} dh \tag{2.12}$$

In the above determinant, F^i_{LL} is the second derivative of the production function F^ξ on labor ($i = 1, 2, 3$). Assuming the determinant of the coefficient matrix of Eq. (2.12) is Δ_1, we have

$$\Delta_1 = (1-\lambda)p_1 F^1 F^1_{LL} + F^1_L\left(\lambda p_1 F^1_L - h\right).$$

Since $F^1_{LL} < 0$, the sign of the above formula is dependent on $\lambda p_1 F^1_L - h$. As F^1 is a strict quasi-concave function, F^1_L is descending on $[0, L_{12}]$. Therefore, we have $F^1_L(L_{12}) < \frac{F^1(L_{12})}{L_{12}}$, which can be shown as the graph below (Fig. 2.3).

Thus, tan ∠ ① < tan ∠ ③ tan ∠ ②, which means, $\lambda p_1 F^1_L(L_{12}) < \frac{\lambda p_1 F^1(L_{12})}{L_{12}} < \frac{\lambda p_1 F^1(L_{12})}{L_{12} - L_{11}} = h$; thus, it could be derived that $\Delta_1 < 0$.

Total differentiation of Eqs. (2.6), (2.8), (2.9), and (2.10) are

$$p_2 F^2_{LL} dL_{22} - dw_{22} = 0,$$
$$F^3_{LL} dL_{32} - dw_{32} = 0,$$
$$dL_{22} + dL_{32} = -dL_{12}$$

and

$$(w_{32} - w_{22})dL_{22} - (L_{22} - L_{21})dw_{22} + (L_{12} - L_{11} + L_{22} - L_{21})dw_{32} \\ = (\overline{w_1} - w_{32})dL_{12}$$

The above could be organized as the following matrix:

$$\begin{pmatrix} w_{32} - w_{22} & 0 & -(L_{22} - L_{21}) & (L_{12} - L_{11} + L_{22} - L_{21}) \\ p_2 F_{LL}^2 & 0 & -1 & 0 \\ 0 & F_{LL}^3 & 0 & -1 \\ 1 & 1 & 0 & 0 \end{pmatrix} \begin{pmatrix} dL_{22} \\ dL_{32} \\ dw_{22} \\ dw_{32} \end{pmatrix} \\ = \begin{pmatrix} \overline{w_1} - w_{32} \\ 0 \\ 0 \\ -1 \end{pmatrix} dL_{12} \tag{2.13}$$

Assuming the determinant of the coefficient matrix of Eq. (2.12) is Δ_2, then the determinant of the above matrix is

$$\Delta_2 = w_{32} - w_{22} - p_2 F_{LL}^2 (L_{22} - L_{21}) - F_{LL}^3 (L_{12} - L_{11} + L_{22} - L_{21}) > 0$$

In order to analyze the change of economic welfare level, we assume that C_1, C_2, and C_3 are the consumption of the formal sector, the informal sector, and the rural sector, respectively. We further assume that $U(\cdot)$ is the social utility function defined on (C_1, C_2, C_3), which is a strict concave function. If $e(p_1, p_2, U)$ is the minimum expenditure under the utility U, then the cost-and-benefit equilibrium condition would be $e(p_1, p_2, U) = p_1 M_{12} + p_2 M_{22} + A_{32}$.

Total differentiation of the above equation could be written as

$$e_U dU = p_1 F_L^1 dL_{12} + p_2 F_L^2 dL_{22} + F_L^3 dL_{32} \tag{2.14}$$

The urban–rural human capital disparity h has an impact on the investment cost on human capital in the formal sector and further on the investment ratio, labor transferred, sector output, and profit. Using the Cramer's rule, Eq. (2.12) could be written as

$$\frac{dL_{12}}{dh} = \frac{(L_{12} - L_{11}) F_L^1}{\Delta_1} < 0$$

and

$$\frac{d\lambda}{dh} = \frac{(1 - \lambda)(L_{12} - L_{11}) F_{LL}^1}{\Delta_1} > 0$$

From the two formulas, we get

$$\frac{dF^1}{dh} = F_L^1 \frac{dL_{12}}{dh} < 0 \tag{2.15}$$

$$\frac{d(\lambda p_1 F^1)}{dh} = \frac{p_1(L_{12} - L_{11})}{\Delta_1}\left[(1-\lambda)F^1 F_{LL}^1 + \lambda\left(F_L^1\right)^2\right](<,=,>)0$$

$$\frac{d\pi_1}{dh} = -p_1 F^1 \frac{d\lambda}{dh} < 0 \tag{2.16}$$

Using the Cremer's rule for Eq. (2.13), we have

$$\frac{dL_{22}}{dh} = \frac{dL_{22}}{dL_{12}} \cdot \frac{dL_{12}}{dh} = \frac{(L_{12} - L_{11})F_L^1\left[(\overline{w_1} - w_{32}) + F_{LL}^3(L_R - L_{32})\right]}{\Delta_1 \Delta_2}(<,=,>)0 \tag{2.17}$$

$$\frac{dw_{22}}{dh} = \frac{dw_{22}}{dL_{12}} \cdot \frac{dL_{12}}{dh} = \frac{(L_{12} - L_{11})p_2 F_L^1 F_{LL}^2\left[(\overline{w_1} - w_{32}) + F_{LL}^3(L_R - L_{32})\right]}{\Delta_1 \Delta_2}(<,=,>)0$$

$$\frac{dL_{32}}{dh} = \frac{dL_{32}}{dL_{12}} \cdot \frac{dL_{12}}{dh} = \frac{-(L_{12} - L_{11})F_L^1\left[(\overline{w_1} - w_{32}) - p_2 F_{LL}^2(L_{22} - L_{21})\right]}{\Delta_1 \Delta_2} > 0 \tag{2.18}$$

$$\frac{dw_{32}}{dh} = \frac{dw_{32}}{dL_{12}} \cdot \frac{dL_{12}}{dh} = \frac{-(L_{12} - L_{11})F_L^1 F_{LL}^3\left[(\overline{w_1} - w_{32}) - p_2 F_{LL}^2(L_{22} - L_{21})\right]}{\Delta_1 \Delta_2} < 0 \tag{2.19}$$

From the above four formulas, we further have

$$\frac{dF^2}{dh} = F_L^2 \frac{dL_{22}}{dh}(<,=,>)0 \tag{2.20}$$

$$\frac{d\pi_2}{dh} = -L_{22}\frac{dw_{22}}{dh}(<,=,>)0$$

$$\frac{dF^3}{dh} = F_L^3 \frac{dL_{32}}{dh} > 0$$

$$\frac{d\pi_3}{dh} = -L_{32}\frac{dw_{32}}{dh} > 0 \tag{2.21}$$

Putting the relevant equations above into Eq. (2.14), which expresses welfare level, we will have

$$\begin{aligned}\frac{e_U dU}{dh} &= p_1 F_L^1 \frac{dL_{12}}{dh} + p_2 F_L^2 \frac{dL_{22}}{dh} + F_L^3 \frac{dL_{32}}{dh} \\ &= \frac{(L_{12} - L_{11}) F_L^1}{\Delta_1 \Delta_2} \left[\frac{\lambda \overline{w_1}}{1-\lambda} (w_{32} - w_{22}) - p_2 F_{LL}^2 (L_{22} - L_{21}) \left(\frac{\overline{w_1}}{1-\lambda} - w_{32} \right) \right. \\ &\quad \left. - F_{LL}^3 (L_R - L_{32}) \left(\frac{\overline{w_1}}{1-\lambda} - w_{22} \right) \right] < 0\end{aligned}$$

In this view, we get Proposition 2.1.

Proposition 2.1 In the model, reducing the human capital disparity between rural and urban labors has the following economic effects:

- It could increase the employment level of the formal sector and the employment of labor transferred from the rural area, reduce the proportion of product used for human capital investment in the formal sector, and increase the output and profit of the formal sector.
- It could have an effect of increasing the amount of labor transferred from the rural areas, decreasing the employment level in the rural sector, raising wage level in the rural sector, but reducing the output and profit of the rural sector. It could increase the social economic welfare level overall.

From Eqs. (2.15) and (2.16), it can be seen that for the relationship of the moving direction of human capital investment in the formal sector lp1F1 and that of h, l and h are moving in the same direction, while F1 and h are moving in the opposite direction. Thus, we could not determine their signs directly, but we could derive that the sufficient and necessary conditions to determine their signs are:

- When $(1-\lambda)F^1F_{LL}^1 + \lambda(F_L^1)^2 > 0$, $\lambda p_1 F_L^1$ and h are moving in the opposite direction, which means that the increase of h goes with a decrease of $\lambda p_1 F_L^1$.
- When $(1-\lambda)F^1F_{LL}^1 + \lambda(F_L^1)^2 < 0$, $\lambda p_1 F_L^1$ and h are moving in the same direction, which means that the increase of h accompanies an increase of $\lambda p_1 F_L^1$.

From Eqs. (2.17), (2.18), (2.19), (2.20), and (2.21), it can be seen that the relationship between the change of direction of several economic variables of the informal sector and that of h could not be determined directly, but it could be done through accurate calculation. When h changes, the amount of labor in the informal sector L_{22}, the wage w_{22}, and the profit π_2 are moved in the same direction, which is opposite to the output F_2. Similar to the previous paragraph, the sufficient and necessary conditions for determining the signs are:

- When $\overline{w_1} - w_{32} + F_{LL}^3(L_R - L_{32}) > 0$, h and L_{22}, F_2, and π_2 move in the opposite directions, but h moves in the same direction withw_{22}, which means that increase of h will lead to decrease of L_{22}, F_2, and π_2 but increase of w_{22}.

- When $\overline{w_1} - w_{32} + F^3_{LL}(L_R - L_{32}) = 0$, the change of h is irrelevant to L_{22},w_{22}, F_2, and π_2.
- When $\overline{w_1} - w_{32} + F^3_{LL}(L_R - L_{32}) < 0$, h and L_{22}, F_2, and π_2 move in the same direction, which is the opposite direction of moving of w_{22}. This means that decrease of h will lead to decrease of L_{22}, π_2, and F_2 but increase of w_{22}.

Thus, we get Proposition 2.2.

Proposition 2.2 In the model, when the human capital level disparity h between rural labors and urban labors is reduced:

- When $(1-\lambda)F^1F^1_{LL} + \lambda\left(F^1_L\right)^2 > 0(< 0)$, the formal sector will increase (decrease) human capital investment.
- When $\overline{w_1} - w_{32} + F^3_{LL}(L_R - L_{32}) > 0(< 0)$, it will have an effect of increasing (decreasing) the level of employment, profit, and output in the informal sector but reducing (enlarging) wages in the informal sector.
- When $\overline{w_1} - w_{32} + F^3_{LL}(L_R - L_{32}) = 0$, the change of h is irrelevant to L_{22},w_{22}, F_2, and π_2.

We may come to the conclusion from Proposition 2.1 that reducing the disparity of human capital between urban–rural sectors can contribute to the increase of the employment rate in formal urban sector. It leads to the alleviation of the shortage of labor. Obviously, the disparity of human capital between urban–rural sectors directly serves as the reason for the shortage of labor. Also, reducing the disparity of human capital helps increase the number of labor force moving from rural to urban sector and reduces the burden of human capital accumulation in formal sector. It also attributes to the increase of the rural sector wage, as well as the improvement of social welfare. All the above effects will exert positive influences on ameliorating the urban–rural dual economic structure and promoting the course of urbanization. Nevertheless, Proposition 2.1 also shows a dilemma. Despite the fact that reducing the disparity of human capital between rural and urban sectors may bring to the increase of the output and profit in urban sector, it decreases the output and profit in rural sector at the same time. Moreover, its impact on the output and in informal profit sector remains uncertain. Yet the two following points should be most emphasized:

1. With the improvement of social welfare, we can infer that reducing the disparity of human capital between urban–rural sectors has more positive effects than negative ones. So it is reasonable to dedicate to it.
2. From Proposition 2.1, special attention should be paid to the rural sector the same time we reduce the disparity of human capital between urban–rural sectors. We should be fully aware of its negative effects on rural sector and be prepared to take protective measures to minimize social welfare losses.

Proposition 2.2 is a supplementary to the economic effects that are not addressed by the Proposition 2.1. It reflects the economic effect produced by narrowing the urban–rural human capital level under certain circumstances.

On the contrary, if the human capital gap between rural and urban labors is becoming larger, it would not only affect the transfer of rural labor but also further decreases the wage level of the rural sector. Thus, it pushes the formal sector to increase its human capital accumulation ratio and raises the burden of human capital accumulation. Thus, it would have a negative effect on the output and profit of the formal sector, as well as on the social economic welfare.

In the following, we would analyze the change of the economic variables based on the graph of the labor distribution mechanism of the three sectors. Assuming $h\downarrow$, according to the previous calculation, $L_{12}\uparrow$, $(L_{12}-L_{11})\uparrow$, the line BL moves rightward, $DL\downarrow$, $\lambda = DL/DB\downarrow$; $L_{32}\downarrow$, the line FKmoves rightward, $w_{32}\uparrow$, $(\overline{w_1}-w_{32})\downarrow$; and the change of L_{12} and w_{22} are uncertain. As for the equal area shade parts, $(L_{12}-L_{11})(\overline{w_1}-w_{32}) = (L_{22}-L_{21})(w_{32}-w_{22})$, which means that under the condition of equilibrium, the difference between the total wage seared by the transferred labor from the rural areas in the formal sector and in the rural sector is the same as that the difference of their total wages between the rural sector and the informal sector. Then, when $h\downarrow$, the area of the shades changes as follows:

$$
\begin{aligned}
\frac{d[(\overline{w_1}-w_{32})(L_{12}-L_{11})]}{dh} &= \frac{(L_{12}-L_{11})F_L^1}{\Delta_1\Delta_2}\{(\overline{w_1}-w_{32})(w_{32}-w_{22}) \\
&\quad + F_{LL}^3(L_{12}-L_{11})[(w_{32}-w_{22})] - p_2F_{LL}^2(L_{22}-L_{21}) \\
&\quad - (\overline{w_1}-w_{32})\ \ (L_{22}-L_{21})(p_2F_{LL}^2+F_{LL}^3)\} \\
&= \frac{(L_{12}-L_{11})F_L^1}{\Delta_1\Delta_2}\{\left[\overline{w_1}-w_{32}+F_{LL}^3(L_{12}-L_{11})\right] \\
&\quad \left[w_{32}-w_{22}-p_2F_{LL}^2(L_{22}-L_{21})\right] \\
&\quad - F_{LL}^3(L_{22}-L_{21})(\overline{w_1}-w_{32})\}
\end{aligned}
$$

It shows that when $\overline{w_1}-w_{32}+F_{LL}^3(L_{12}-L_{11})>0$, $\frac{d[(\overline{w_1}-w_{32})(L_{12}-L_{11})]}{dh}<0$. At the same time, the area of the shade increases; the gap between total wages earned by the rural labor transferred to the cities and their total wage if they were staying in the rural areas decreases. Thus, we derive Proposition 2.3.

Proposition 2.3 When $\overline{w_1}-w_{32}+F_{LL}^3(L_{12}-L_{11})>0$, bridging the human capital level disparity between rural and urban labors would have an effect that increasing the level of employment of rural labors in the formal sector would generate more total wages than having the labors staying in the rural sector, which can be shown as the following graph (Fig. 2.4). Proposition 3 could be illustrated by the following graph.

From Eqs. (2.18) and (2.19), we get

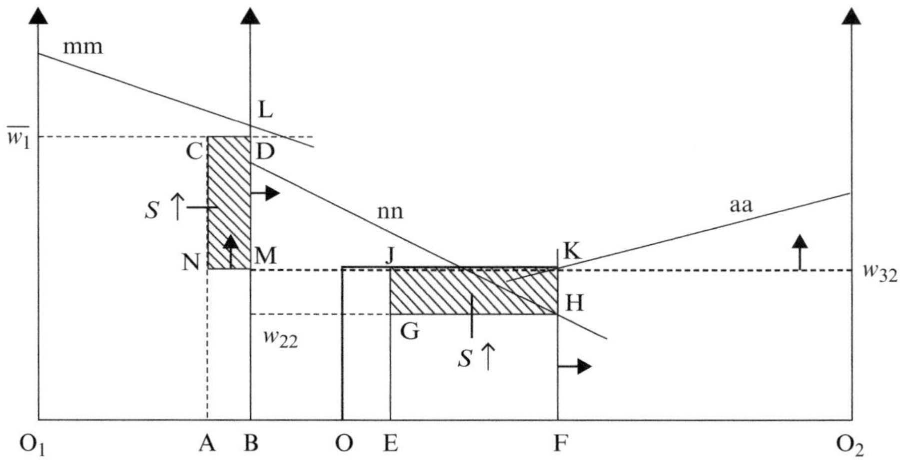

Fig. 2.4 The labor distribution mechanism of the three sectors when $h\downarrow$

$$\begin{aligned}\frac{d(w_{32}-w_{22})}{dh} &= \frac{(L_{12}-L_{11})}{\Delta_1\Delta_2}F_L^1F_{LL}^3\left[p_2F_{LL}^2(L_{22}-L_{21})-(\overline{w_1}-w_{22})\right]\\ &\quad-\frac{(L_{12}-L_{11})}{\Delta_1\Delta_2}F_L^1p_2F_{LL}^2\left[\overline{w_1}-w_{32}+F_{LL}^3(L_R-L_{32})\right]\\ &=\frac{(L_{12}-L_{11})}{\Delta_1\Delta_2}F_L^1\{F_L^1F_{LL}^2F_{LL}^3(L_{22}-L_{21})-F_{LL}^3(\overline{w_1}-w_{22})\\ &\quad-p_2F_{LL}^2\left[\overline{w_1}-w_{32}+F_{LL}^3(L_R-L_{32})\right]\}\end{aligned}$$

It shows that when $\overline{w_1}-w_{32}+F_{LL}^3(L_R-L_{32})>0$, $\frac{d(w_{32}-w_{22})}{dh}<0$. Thus, we derive Proposition 2.4.

Proposition 2.4 When $\overline{w_1}-w_{32}+F_{LL}^3(L_R-L_{32})>0$, reducing the human capital disparity level between rural and urban areas would increase the wage disparity between the rural and informal sectors.

As shown by the arrow in Fig. 2.2, when $h\downarrow$ and $\overline{w_1}-w_{32}+F_{LL}^3(L_R-L_{32})>0$, $(w_{32}-w_{22})\uparrow$, and the rectangular *CDMN* decreases in height, increases in width, and increases in area; the rectangular *GHKJ* increases in height, and the change in width is uncertain, while its area is also enlarged. Similarly, when $h\uparrow$ and $\bar{w}_1-w_{32}+F_{LL}^3(L_R-L_{32})>0$, the rectangular *CDMN* increases in height and decreases in width and area; the rectangular *GHKJ* decreases in height, shows uncertain change in width, and reduces in area.

On the other hand, $(w_{32}-w_{22})\uparrow$ means that the wage level disparity between rural and informal sectors is increasing. As mentioned in the previous parts, the rural labors would be willing to accept relatively low wages of the urban informal sector so as to move to the cities and to wait for the employment and training opportunities in the formal sector. When the urban–rural wage disparity increases, the informal sector is less attractive to the rural labors, and its temporary effect absorbing labor is less effective, and its geographical advantage of being close to the formal sector would be reduced. However, due to narrower gap of urban–rural human capital level, it becomes easier for the rural labors to transfer to the formal sector, even without having to temporarily stay in the informal sector waiting for better opportunities. They could enter into the formal sector directly. Therefore, when $\bar{w}_1 - w_{32} + F^3_{LL}(L_R - L_{32}) > 0$, reducing the urban–rural human capital gap would not harm the rural migrant labors.

4 Conclusion and Policy Suggestions

Based on the Harris–Todaro model of labor distribution, this article establishes a labor transfer model on the formal sector's investment in human capital, deduces the theoretical economic effects on the changes of the urban–rural human capital level disparity, and acquires some useful referential implications. According to the key points of the four propositions, conclusions could be drawn as follows.

As a supplementary measure to the major path of human capital investment by the formal sector, reducing the human capital disparity between the rural and urban labors would improve the effects of formal sector investment in human capital, which are to raise the wage level of the rural sector and to improve social economic welfare. It would also be an effective measure to solve the problem of "structural shortage of technical labor." At current stage, the urban–rural human capital disparity is huge, which would not only affect transfer of rural labor but also have a negative impact on the output and profit of the formal sector. Therefore, active measures should be taken to effectively bridge the human capital disparity between rural and urban labors.

On the other hand, this study shows that all the three sectors could benefit from improved human capital level, which would be reflected in wages, outputs, profits, socioeconomic welfare, etc. Reducing urban–rural human capital disparity could only be achieved through raising rural labors' human capital level. And it had to improve more before the rural labors move to the cities. However, Chinese rural people could hardly afford human capital investment; thus, the effect of personal human capital investment by the farmers themselves is limited. As a macroeconomic policy maker, the government should play a main role in rural human capital investment, making policies to guide and produce incentives for compulsory education and primary education. The quality of rural labor in general could be improved by the government's investment in education. This could lead to improvement of productivity in the rural sector, reduce the investment cost of the formal sector, and even save the entire cost. Based on the government's responsibility, the formal sector should actively take the remaining responsibility in bridging the human capital disparity between hiring transferred labors from the countryside and urban labors. This would improve output and profit of the formal sector, which is also a reasonable solution from the perspective of fairness.

For a long time, as Chinese urban formal sector, urban sectors in developing countries in Asia were not fully aware of the importance of accumulation of human capital of the transferred labors from the rural area. This was mainly because the formal sector did not fully understand the relationship between human capital accumulation and its own development. We further hold that since the development of the formal and rural sectors in developing countries in Asia largely depends on rural labor, while the government is taking active measures to produce incentives for the formal sector to invest in the transferred labors, it should also put more focus on the implementation of compulsory and vocational education in the rural areas, substantiate rural basic education, and compensate for the lacking of human capital investment by the farmers themselves and by the private sector, so that it could ensure the rural human capital level, which is demanded by balanced economic development.

References

Cai, F., & Wang, D. (1999). China's sustainable economic growth and labor contribution. *Economic Research Journal, 10*, 62–68.

Du, Y. (1999). Studies on the impact of education on non-agricultural labor supply in the poor regions. *China Demographic Science, 6*, 26–33.

Grinols, E. L. (1991). Unemployment and foreign capital: The relative opportunity costs of domestic labor and welfare. *Economica, 58*, 107–121.

Harris, J. R., & Todaro, M. P. (1970). Migration, unemployment and development: A two sector analysis. *The American Economic Review, 60*, 126–142.

Hou, F. (2004). Studies on the correlation between benefits to migrant workers and their human capital. *Financial Studies, 4*, 88–100.

Jamison, D., & Gaag, J. (1987). Education and earnings in People's Republic of China. *Economics of Education Review, 6*, 161–166.

Pan, H., & Cheng, P. (2002). The contribution of rural educational investment on rural economic growth. *South Jiangsu Technological Development, 8*, 32–33.

Zhang, Z. (2005). Statistical analysis of migrant worker supply. *China Rural Economy, 1*, 17–25.

Zhao, Y. (1997). Movement of Chinese rural labor and the impact of education. *Economic Research Journal, 2*, 37–42.

Zhou, X., & Zhu, N. (2003). The impact of human capital on economic growth in rural China. *China Demographic Science, 6*, 17–24.

Chapter 3
Economic and Environmental Effects of Rural-Urban Migrant Training

Xiaochun Li and Yu Zhou

Abstract In this chapter, we conduct the simple comparative static analysis of the environmental and economic effects of the government and producer services sector's training of rural-urban migrants. We mainly focus our attention on environmental issues and reach the following conclusions: When the government lowers the interest rate of training loans, environmental conditions will worsen. However, when the producer services sector increases the unit cost of training rural labor, the opposite effect occurs, and environmental conditions will improve. In addition, we discuss the conditions under which a government reduction in the interest rate of training loans will lead to the reduction of pollution damage to agricultural production and a decrease in social utility.

Keywords Environment effects • Low interest rate loan • Employee vocational training • Rural-urban migration

1 Introduction

Harris and Todaro (1970) presented a simple dual-economy model of rural-urban migration with a long-run equilibrium characterized by the existence of urban unemployment. This model corresponds with the existence of persistent urban unemployment in many developing countries. Consequently, the model has attracted the attention of many economists with an interest in the problems of developing countries. Two important issues relating to the Harris-Todaro model are the regulation of environment pollution caused by the production of intermediate goods and the relationship between human capital investment and rural-urban migration.[1]

[1] In the present paper, human capital investment refers purely to the vocational training. Generally speaking, the human capital level is roughly measured by the educational year, and here we treat the vocational training as a way to compensate for the lack of educational year.

X. Li (✉)
Business School, Nanjing University, Nanjing, China
e-mail: xiaochun@nju.edu.cn

Y. Zhou
School of Economics, Nanjing University, 22 Hankou Road, Nanjing, Jiangsu 210093, China

X. Li (ed.), *Labor Transfer in Emerging Economies*, New Frontiers in Regional Science: Asian Perspectives 12, DOI 10.1007/978-981-10-3569-2_3

Of intermediate goods, Dean and Gangopadhyay (1997) used a three-sector model to analyze how limiting the export of intermediate goods would affect environmental pollution, rural-urban migration, and urban unemployment. Chao (2003) also established a three-sector model analyzing the economic effects of imposing a production tax on intermediate goods. Later, Chaudhuri and Mukhopadhyay (2006) analyzed the efficiency of imposing a pollution emission tax on the formal manufacturing sector in a three-sector general equilibrium model that included pollution effects from the informal sector. Earlier empirical researches, such as Papola (1981) and Romatet (1983), suggested that the urban informal sector produced intermediate goods for the formal manufacturing sector and that, in fact, the informal sector was the main source of environmental pollution.

In studies of the relationship between human capital investment and rural-urban migration, Bhagwati and Srinivasan (1977) studied how education affected the job search process of individuals, from which they developed the now-famous job ladder model. Djajic (1985) investigated the relationship between vocational training of employees in the production sector and urban unemployment under the assumption of a minimum wage act. Samanta (2003) analyzed the economic effects of the training of urban sector employees, under the assumption of perfect competition in the agricultural sector and imperfect competition in the urban sector.

However, the abovementioned research is not as relevant in analyzing issues prevalent in developing economies. Currently, developing countries emphasize the development of the producer services sector, and the development of the producer services sector must face problems with differences in human capital originating from rural and urban areas and with environmental pollution.

With the development of the knowledge economy, the producer services sectors in the developing countries have become increasingly technologically intensive and correspondingly demand a higher level of human capital. The development of the producer services sector depends on absorbing the rural-urban migrants, yet the lack of education of many rural migrants is an impediment to sector growth, especially within China. In 2007, the average migrant had approximately 7.7 years of education (up from 6.46 years in 1997) compared to the 13.44 years of education the average urban worker enjoyed (itself an increase from 11.42 ten years prior). The average rural migrant had the equivalent of a junior middle school level education, whereas the average urban resident had an education above the high school level (Xiaochun Li and Xiaoying Qian 2011). This gap in education is thought to be a key reason behind the lagging growth ratio of producer services output value compared to GDP for the past 20 years (Zhibiao Liu 2011).

Compounding the education gap is the environmental issue. In the short run, the expansion of the manufacturing sector will generate more pollution, which is known as the scale effect of environmental pollutions (Grossman and Krueger 1995). Given the vertical linkage between the producer services sector and the manufacturing sector, an expanding services sector will lead to an increase in its output, which is expected to further lead to an increase in manufacturing activity, the consequence of which is the deterioration of the environment. With the development of the producer services sector, the manufacturing sector would generate more pollution. Here, we call such kind of environmental pollution "the producer services sector-induced environmental pollution." Thus, in finding solutions to the development bottleneck of the producer servicers sector, we need to balance out a need to improve the quality of migrant human capital with the need to reduce producer services sector-induced environmental pollution. Given the possibility of a vicious cycle, it is impossible to ignore the confluence of these two factors.

Despite the relative wealth of research about the two aforementioned issues individually, there is still no research attempting to combine the factors of rural-urban migration, employee vocational training (or the human capital investment), and corresponding environmental effects into a unifying framework.

In order to fill the current research gap, the present paper presents a model integrating the rural-urban migration, vocational training of rural-urban migrants employed by the producer services sector, and environmental pollution into the general equilibrium framework of an extended Harris-Todaro model under the profit maximization condition. There are two situations under consideration.

In the first situation, the producer services sector will borrow all money from banks for training rural-urban migrants to meet the minimum human capital required by the production of the producer services sector. The producer services sector will stop training the rural-urban migrants when these migrants meet that human capital level. Given the unit cost of training a rural employee, the government will intervene in the bank system and lower the interest rate of loans for training services (here after in the "low interest rate policy").

In the second situation, the producer services sector will train the rural-urban migrants with their own capital to meet the necessary level of human capital according to the firm's business scale and financial status, given the interest rate of the loan. In this situation, the firms are expected to create a training plan to fulfill their goals, and this plan will decide the unit training cost of transferred labor (here after in "firm's human capital investment").

The present paper is to try to find out the economic and environmental impacts exerted by the government and firms' efforts to raise the human capital level. The reason that we take the government's low interest rate policy is that this policy is not only aimed at increasing the amount of employment of the producer services sector but also this is more applicable in certain Asian countries, such as Japan and Korea that feature the implementation of policy that supports the development of medium-sized and small-sized enterprises. Recently, the Chinese government also has begun using similar policies to encourage medium-scale and small-scale enterprises to develop new energy projects.[2] Thus, we propose that government policies offering low interest rate loans to the producer services sector to train rural employees will probably be implemented by developing countries in the future.

[2]Detailed information can be referred to http://zhcfg.esepworld.com/zhcgch/182795/index.html

Our main result is that environmental effects generated by the producer services sector's employee vocational training of rural-urban migrants depend on the training approach. When the government lowers the interest rate of training loans, environmental conditions will worsen. However, when the producer services sector performs human capital investment, the environment condition will improve.

Besides the theoretical extension of the current researches, in the present paper, we also draw a picture to illustrate the labor allocation mechanism of the three sectors, which can be regarded as an extension of that in Xiaochun Li and Xiaoying Qian (2011) by taking the environment pollution into consideration.

The rest of this chapter is organized as follows: in Sect. 2, we set up a theoretical model in an extended Harris-Todaro framework; in Sect. 3, we conduct a simple comparative static analysis of decreasing the government training loan interest rate and increasing the unit cost of training a rural worker by the producer services sector; and in Sect. 4, we provide concluding remarks.

2 Theoretical Model

We will consider a small and open economy consisting of three sectors: the rural agricultural sector, the urban producer services sector, and the urban manufacturing sector. The agricultural sector utilizes rural labor and sector-specific capital as factors of production, and its wage rate is flexible. The producer services sector produces intermediate goods used as input in the manufacturing sector and utilizes urban labor, trained rural-urban migrants, and sector-specific capital as factors of production. The manufacturing sector utilizes urban labor, rural-urban migration, sector-specific capital, and intermediate goods as factors of production. The wage rate of the manufacturing sector is downward rigid.[3] We furthermore assume that only the production procedure of the agricultural sector depends on environmental factors. That is to say, improvements within the rural environment will create correspondingly higher levels of output. Production from the producer services sector does not generate pollution. However, manufacturing production will generate pollution, which imposes damage to the rural environment through factors such as air and water.

We assume that initially the amount of employment in the urban producer services sector, the urban manufacturing sector, and the rural agricultural sector are $\overline{L_1}, \overline{L_2}$, and $\overline{L_3}$, respectively. The corresponding level of urban unemployment is

[3] In the present paper, we assume that the wage rate of the manufacturing sector is downward rigid because people who are employed in the urban sectors usually receive contractually obligated wage rates or are protected by minimum wage acts or the labor union in urban areas. The same assumption of the downward rigid manufacturing wage rate (especially in the frame of Harris-Todaro model) can be also found in Grinols (1991), Gupta (1993), Tawada and Sunqin (2010), Xiaochun Li and Xiaoying Qian (2011), etc.

$\overline{L_u}$. The price of agricultural good is normalized to be a unit. In the following part, we will only focus our attention to the issues of rural-urban migrants.

2.1 Producer Services Sector

Because of the urban and rural disparity in education, the human capital level of urban workers is higher than that of the rural workers (Xiaochun Li and Xiaoying Qian 2011). We assume that the urban workers could be employed in the producer services sector directly, while the rural labor could enter into the producer services sector only by means of vocational training. The production function of this sector is

$$Y_1 = F^1\left(hL_1, \overline{K_1}\right) \tag{3.1}$$

where Y_1, L_1, and K_1 are the levels of output, labor, and capital employed, respectively. h expresses the efficiency of each worker after vocational training, that is, the minimum per capita human capital level needed by the producer services sector. Here, hL_1 is the human capital stock in that sector. h depends upon the unit cost of training a rural worker:

$$h = h(c) \tag{3.2}$$

Here, c is the unit cost of training a rural labor. $h(.)$ satisfies the conditions $h(0) = 1$, $h' > 0$, and $h'' < 0$. The wage rate of employees in the producer services sector is $h\bar{w}$. The establishment of the wage rate of employees who have a high level of human capital in Eq. (3.2) is in accord with the parameters established by Galor and Moav (2004). If the government gives producer services a loan with interest i, we have

$$p_1 hF_L^1 - (1+i)c = h\bar{w} \tag{3.3}$$

where p_1 is the relative price of the producer services product in terms of agricultural products. From here on, $F_L^i = \frac{\partial F^i}{\partial L_i}$, $i = 1,2,3$.

2.2 Manufacturing Sector

The production function of this sector is given by the equation

$$Y_2 = F^2\left(L_2, T, \overline{K_2}\right) \tag{3.4}$$

where Y_2, L_2, and $\overline{K_2}$ are the levels of output, labor, and capital employed, respectively, and T is the amount of intermediate input. For the sake of simplicity, we assume that $F^2_{LY} = 0$ (Gupta 1993), where $F^2_{LT} = \frac{\partial^2 F^2_L}{\partial L \partial T}$. Profit maximization yields

$$p_2 F^2_L = \bar{w} \tag{3.5}$$

$$p_2 F^2_T = p_1 \tag{3.6}$$

where p_2 is the relative price of manufacturing products in terms of agricultural products and $F^2_T = \frac{\partial F^2}{\partial T}$. Furthermore, we can obtain the following input demand function by rewriting Eq. (3.6) as follows:

$$T = T(p_1) \tag{3.7}$$

where $T' < 0$. In equilibrium, the output of the producer services sector is equal to the demand for its product by the manufacturing sector. Hence,

$$Y_1 = T(p_1) \tag{3.8}$$

2.3 *Agricultural Sector*

The production function of this sector is given by

$$Y_3 = g(E)F^3\left(L_3, \overline{K_3}\right) \tag{3.9}$$

where Y_3, L_3, and $\overline{K_3}$ are the levels of output, labor, and capital employed, respectively, and E is denoted as the quality of the rural environment after pollution. $g(E)$, with the properties of $g > 0$, $g' > 0$, and $g'' < 0$, represents the effect of the rural environment on agricultural productivity. Thus,

$$E = \bar{E} - \lambda Y_2 \tag{3.10}$$

where $\bar{E}$ is the best quality of the rural environment, which is regarded as given. λ expresses the units of local pollution generated by one unit of production of the manufacturing sector. Taking the effect of rural environment on agricultural productivity into consideration, the denotation of Eq. (3.10) here is in accord with Copeland and Taylor (1999) and Tawada and Shuqin Sun (2010). Profit maximization yields

$$gF_L^3 = w_a \tag{3.11}$$

where w_a is the wage rate.

2.4 Labor Market

The full-employment condition can be written as

$$L_1 + L_2 + L_3 + L_u = \bar{L} \tag{3.12}$$

where L_U is the amount of urban unemployment.

The Harris-Todaro labor allocation mechanism in three sectors yields

$$w_a = \frac{L_1 - \overline{L_1}}{\overline{L_3} - L_3} h\bar{w} + \frac{L_2 - \overline{L_2}}{\overline{L_3} - L_3} \bar{w} \tag{3.13}$$

Here, $L_1 - L_1, L_2 - \bar{L}_2$, and $\bar{L}_3 - L_3$ represent the amount of rural-urban migrants employed by the producer services sector, the manufacturing sector, and the total amount of rural transferred labor, respectively. $\frac{L_1 - \bar{L}_1}{\bar{L}_3 - L_3}$ and $\frac{L_2 - L_2}{\bar{L}_3 - L_3}$ can be regarded as the probability of rural-urban migrants to be employed by the producer services sector and of the rural-urban migrants to be employed by the manufacturing sector. This equilibrium migration equation is also used by Xiaochun Li and Xiaoying Qian (2011).

The basic model has been established. Twelve Eqs. (3.1), (3.2), (3.3), (3.4), (3.5), (3.7), (3.8), (3.9), (3.10), (3.11), (3.12), and (3.13) determine 12 endogenous variables, $L_1, L_2, L_3, L_U, w_a, p_1$, $h, E, T, Y_1 . Y_2$, and Y_3. The exogenous variables are i and c.

Now, we will use the following figures to illustrate the rural-urban migration equilibrium and the corresponding environmental impact.

In Fig. 3.1, we first draw the mechanism of labor allocation in the initial phase. According to our pre-assumptions, in the initial phase, the labor employment in the producer services sector, the manufacturing sector, and the agricultural sector are denoted as $\overline{L_1}, \overline{L_2}$, and $\overline{L_3}$, respectively. The amount of the initial urban unemployment is L_U. Here, we assume that in the initial phase, labor has not been transferred from rural areas to urban areas yet, and the government does not offer the loan of low interest rate to the enterprises in the producer services sector. At this time, the environment has not been deteriorated. Equations (3.3), (3.5) and (3.11) will be rewritten as $p_1 F_L^1(\overline{L_1}, \overline{K_{11}}) = \bar{w}$, $p_2 F_L^2(\overline{L_2}, \overline{T_{11}}, \overline{K_{12}}) = \bar{w}$, and $g(\bar{E}) F_L^3(\overline{L_3}, \overline{K_{13}}) = w_{0a}$, respectively. These three equations represent the values of the marginal product of labor in the producer services sector, the manufacturing sector, and the agricultural sector, respectively. Here, $\overline{K_{1i}} (i = 1, 2, 3)$ represents the

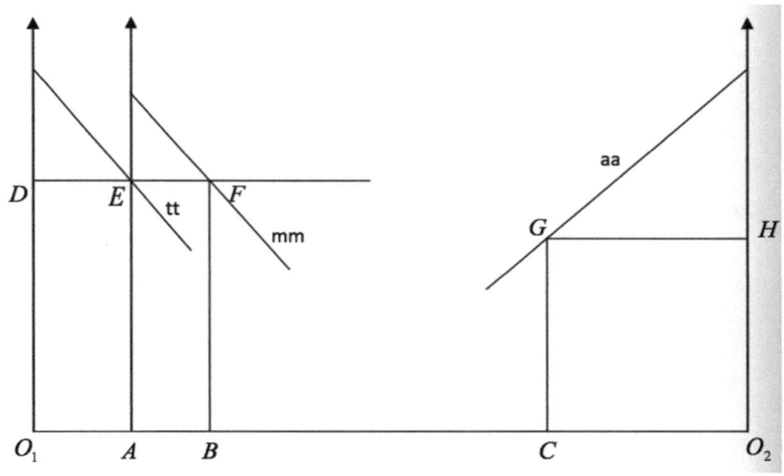

Fig. 3.1 Initial labor allocation mechanisms

sector-specific capital employed by the producer services sector, the manufacturing sector, and the agricultural sector, respectively. $\overline{T_{1i}}$ is the amount of the intermediate input used by the manufacturing sector. w_{0a} is the wage rate of the agricultural sector, satisfying $w_{0a} < \bar{w}$. $\bar{E}$ is the best quality of the environment. Because the production functions satisfy the properties of strict concavity and linear homogeneity, the lines representing the values of the marginal product of labor in the above three sectors have negative slopes. In Fig. 3.1, the horizontal axis is the labor endowment, that is, $O_1O_2 = \bar{L}$. We can find three points, in the horizontal axis, A, B, and C, which satisfy $O_1A = \overline{L_1}, AB = \overline{L_2}, O_2C = \overline{L_3}$, and $BC = \overline{L_U}$. The vertical axis crossing point O_1 represents the wage rate of the producer services sector. We can find a point D that satisfies $O_1D = \bar{w}$ in the vertical axis crossing O_1. Then, drawing a line through D and parallel to O_1O_2 interacts at point E with the axis that is through A and perpendicular to O_1O_2. According to $p_1F_L^1 = \bar{w}$, we can draw a downward sloping line *tt* passing through E, which stands for the value of the marginal labor in the producer services sector. We use the vertical axis through E to represent the manufacturing wage rate. Drawing a line through E and parallel to O_1O_2 interacts at point F with the line that is through B and perpendicular to O_1O_2. From $p_2F_L^2 = \bar{w}$, we can draw a downward sloping line *mm* passing through F to depict the value of the marginal labor in the manufacturing sector. We use the vertical axis through O_2 to represent the agricultural wage rate. Then we can find a point H in the vertical axis crossing O_2, satisfying $O_2H = \bar{w}_a$. Drawing a line through H and parallel to O_1O_2 interacts at point G with the line through C and perpendicular to O_1O_2. From $gF_L^3 = \bar{w}_a$, we can draw a downward sloping line aa passing through G, which stands for the value of the marginal labor in the agricultural sector.

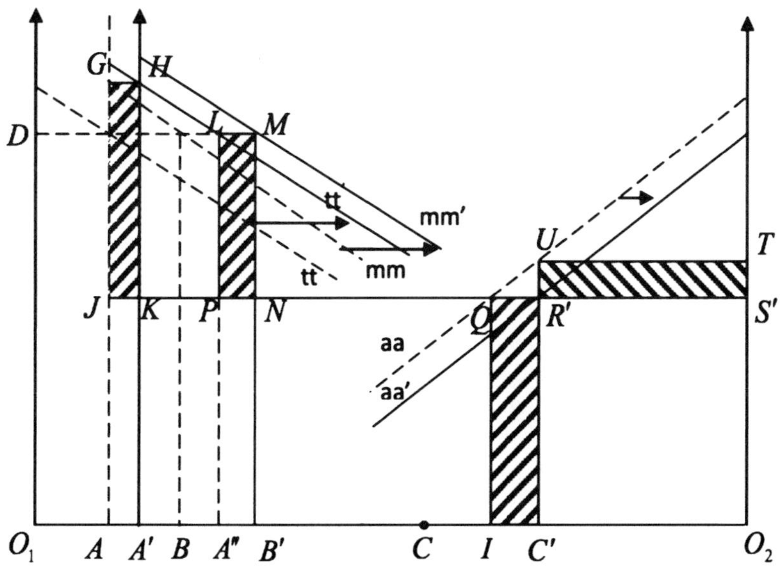

Fig. 3.2 Labor allocation mechanisms of three sectors and the loss of agricultural production

With the help of Fig. 3.1, now we consider the economic and environmental impacts exerted by the rural-urban migration, the low interest rate loan to the producer services sector offered by the government, and the vocational training of rural employees employed by the producer services firms. Figure 3.2 illustrates the labor allocation mechanism of three sectors shown by Eq. (3.13) and the loss of agricultural production due to the environmental pollution. Figure 3.2 can be regarded as an extension of that in Xiaochun Li and Xiaoying Qian (2011) by considering the impact of environmental pollution.

By substituting Eq. (3.12) into Eq. (3.13), we can derive the following equation:

$$(h\bar{w} - w_a)\left(L_1 - \overline{L_1}\right) + (w - w_a)\left(L_2 - \overline{L_2}\right) = w_a\left(L_U - \overline{L_U}\right) \qquad (3.13')$$

Consistent with Fig. 3.1, we have $O_1A = \overline{L_1}, AB = \overline{L_2}, O_2C = \overline{L_3}$, and $BC = \overline{L_U}$ in Fig. 3.2. The dotted lines, tt, mm, and aa, represent the values of the marginal product of labor in the producer services sector, the manufacturing sector, and the agricultural sector, respectively. From Appendix A, we can get the equilibrium values of p_1, L_1, L_U, w_a, and L_3.

At this time, because of the low interest rate loan to the producer services sector offered by the government, and the vocational training to the rural employees employed by the producer services firms, the value of the marginal labor in the producer services sector increases, leading line *tt* to shift rightward to line *tt'*. The derivation of line *tt'* is as follows. Find a point A' on the right side of O_1, such that $O_1A' = L_1$. Thus, $AA' = L_1 - \overline{L_1}$. Given w and c, we can calculate h from equation

$h = h(c)$. We use A as the original point to make a vertical line and find a point G on this line, such that $AG = h\bar{w}$. According to Eq. (3.3), we can derive the value of the marginal product of labor in the producer services sector as line *tt'*.

Furthermore, due to economic development and the increase in the labor employment of the producer services sector attributing to the shift of the vertical axis that represents the wage rate of the manufacturing sector, line mm moves rightward to line *mm'*. Use A' as the original point to make a vertical axis, which interacts with a line passing G and parallel to O_1O_2 at H. Find a point A'' on the right side of A', such that $A'A'' = AB\left(=\overline{L_2}\right)$. Use $A'H$ as the vertical axis, representing the manufacturing wage. From Eq. (3.5), we can draw a downward sloping line *mm'* to represent the value of the marginal product of labor in the manufacturing sector. Drawing a line through D and parallel to O_1O_2 meets the line passing through and perpendicular to A'' at L, which also crosses line *mm'* at M. Drawing a line through M and perpendicular to O_1O_2, it meets O_1O_2 at B', and thus $A'B' = L_2$. It is evident that $A''B' = L_2 - \overline{L_2}$. Use O_2 as the original point and derive C' on the left side of O_1O_2, such that $O_2C' = L_3$. Thus, we have $B'C' = L_U$. We can find a point I on the right side of B', such that $B'I = BC$. Thus, $C'I = L_U - \overline{L_U}$. From Eq. (3.11), we can derive the value of the marginal product of labor *aa'*. Because agricultural production suffers from the deterioration of the rural environment in this phase, the value of the marginal labor in the agricultural sector decreases. Therefore, compared with line *aa*, line *aa'* will shift rightward. We draw a line passing C' and perpendicular to O_1O_2, which meets *aa'* at R'. Hence, $C'R' = w_a$. Furthermore, drawing a line through R' and perpendicular to O_1O_2 meets *aa*, MB', LA'', HA', GA, and the right vertical axis (O_2 the point of origin) at Q, N, P, J, and S'. Thus, $(h\bar{w} - w_a)\left(L_1 - \overline{L_1}\right)$, $(w - w_a)\left(L_2 - \overline{L_2}\right)$, and $w_a\left(L_U - \overline{L_U}\right)$ are represented by the shaded areas, S_{GHKJ}, S_{LMNP}, and $S_{QR'C'D}$, respectively. According to Eq. (3.13′), we have $S_{GHKJ} + S_{LMNP} = S_{QR'C'D}$. Draw a line through C' and perpendicular to O_1O_2. It meets *aa* at U. Draw a line through U and perpendicular to O_1O_2. It meets O_2S' at T. The shaded area $S_{UTS'R'}$ represents the loss of agricultural production due to the environmental pollution.

3 General Equilibrium

Now, we will conduct the comparative analysis of lowering the loan interest rate and increasing the unit investment of training a rural worker.

Total differentiation of Eqs. (3.5), (3.11), (3.12), and (3.13) yields the following equation systems:

Table 3.1 The economic and environmental impacts of low interest rate policy

	dL_1	dL_2	dL_3	dL_U	dp_1	dE
di	−	/	+	[−]	+	+
	dh	dT	dw_a	dY_1	dY_2	dY_3
di	/	−	/	−	−	+

Notes: "−" and "+" indicate that the changes of the exogenous variables will make the endogenous variables change in the opposite and same directions, respectively. "/" means the changes of exogenous variables have an ambiguous impact (or no impact) on endogenous variables; " [−] " must satisfy the condition that $w_a - gF_{LL}^3(\overline{L_3} - L_3) < h\bar{w}$

$$\begin{pmatrix} p_1h^2F_{LL} & 0 & 0 & hF_L^1 \\ hF_L^1 & 0 & 0 & -T' \\ 0 & -gF_{LL}^3 & 1 & \lambda g'F_L^3F_T^2T' \\ h\bar{w} & w_a & -(\overline{L_3} - L_3) & 0 \end{pmatrix} \begin{pmatrix} dL_1 \\ dL_3 \\ dw_a \\ dp_1 \end{pmatrix}$$

$$= \begin{pmatrix} c \\ 0 \\ 0 \\ 0 \end{pmatrix} di + \begin{pmatrix} \frac{h - ch'}{h}(1+i) - p_1hF_{LL}^1h' \\ -F_L^1L_1h' \\ 0 \\ -(L_1 - \overline{L_1})h'\bar{w} \end{pmatrix} dc \tag{3.14}$$

Define the determinant of the above square matrix as Δ and calculate Δ to obtain

$$\Delta = \left[gF_{LL}^3(\overline{L_3} - L_3) - w_a\right]\left[p_1hF_{LL}^1T' + \left(hF_L^1\right)^2\right] < 0$$

Here, $F_{LL}^i = \dfrac{\partial^2F^i}{\partial L_i \partial L_i}, i = 1, 2, 3.$

3.1 The Economic and Environmental Impacts of Low Interest Rate Policy

The producer services sector will borrow all money from banks for training rural-urban migrants to meet the minimum human capital needed by the production of the producer services sector. The producer services sector will stop training the rural-urban migrants when they meet that human capital level. In this time, the unit cost of training a rural employee is given, that is, $dc = 0$. According to Cramer's rule with respect to di in Eq. (3.14), we can solve the above equation system and get Table 3.1.

According to Table 3.1, we establish the following results.

Proposition 3.1 In our assumed economy, government lowering of the interest rate of loans will contribute to the deterioration of the rural environment and exert the following economic impacts:

- The number of workers employed in the agricultural sector decreases, the number of rural-urban migrants employed in the producer services sector increases, and urban unemployment increases on the condition that $w_a - gF_{LL}^3(\overline{L_3} - L_3) < \bar{w}$.
- The outputs of the producer services and manufacturing sectors increase, while the output of agricultural sector decreases.
- The price of the producer services sector's product falls, and the demand of the intermediate input by the manufacturing sector increases.

The mechanism of Proposition 3.1 can be described as follows. When the government lowers the interest rate of the training loan, the cost of the producer services sector making loans will decrease. Thus, more transferred labor will take the opportunity to be trained, and the producer services sector will increase the employment of transferred rural labor, resulting in an increase in the output of the producer services sector. Then the manufacturing sector will increase the intermediate input and generate more output, which will deteriorate the rural environment. It is demonstrated that the government lowering the interest rate in order to support the human capital investment performed by the producer services sector does not solve the environmental problem, which should be noticed by the policy makers. Other subsidy policies leading to an increase in the amount of the employment of the producer services sector, as well as the human capital stock, will also attribute to the deterioration of the environment. The precondition of Proposition 3.1 is worth noting: "all money for training rural-urban migrants to meet the required minimum human capital level are borrowed by the producer services sector from banks. The producer services sector will stop training the rural-urban migrants when these migrants meet that human capital level." If this precondition cannot be met, the situation discussed in Proposition 3.1 will change.

3.2 The Economic and Environmental Impacts of Firm's Human Capital Investment

Now, we discuss the economic and environmental impacts exerted by the firm's autonomous human capital investment. In this time, the interest rate of the loan is given, that is, $di = 0$. The producer services sector will use the self-owned capital to train the rural-urban migrants to meet the necessary level of human capital according to their amount of business and financial status. Under the second plan, the firms are expected to create a training plan to fulfill their goals, and this plan will

Table 3.2 The economic and environmental impacts of firm's human capital investment

	dL_1	dL_2	dL_3	dL_U	dp_1	dE
di	–	/	/	/	+	+
	dh	dT	dw_a	dY_1	dY_2	dY_3
di	+	–	/	/	–	/

Notes: "–" and "+" indicate that the changes of the exogenous variables will make the endogenous variables change in the opposite and same directions, respectively. "/" means the changes of exogenous variables have an ambiguous impact (or no impact) on endogenous variables

decide the unit training cost of transferred labor. According to Cramer's rule with respect to *dc* in Eq. (3.14), we can solve the above equation system and get Table 3.2.

According to Table 3.2, we establish the following results.

Proposition 3.2 In our assumed economy, the increased unit cost in the producer services sector of training a rural worker will improve the quality of the rural environment and exert the following economic impacts:

- The number of rural-urban migrants employed in the producer services sector decreases.
- The output of the manufacturing sector decreases.
- The price of the producer services sector's product rises, and the demand of the intermediate input by the manufacturing sector decreases.

Differently from the government's subsidy policies aimed at increasing the amount of employment, the enterprises increase the per capita human capital level according to their amount of business and financial status. When the enterprises use higher per capita human capital level and reduce the amount of the employees being trained, this does not mean that the human capital stock will increase. Thus, the output of the producer services sector does not necessarily increase and so does the output of the manufacturing sector (and pollution). Proposition 3.2 claims that an increase in the unit cost of training a rural employee will result in a reduction of the human capital stock. The reason can be shown as follows: when the producer services sector increases the unit cost of training a rural labor, the unit cost of hiring a migrant by the producer services sector will increase. Thus, less transferred workers will take the opportunity to be trained, and the producer services sector will decrease the employment of rural workers. The decrease of employment will also decrease the output of the producer services sector, and the manufacturing sector will correspondingly decrease intermediate inputs. Hence, the decrease of the output of manufacturing sector will improve the rural environment.

Comparing Proposition 3.1 with Proposition 3.2, we can conclude that when the producer services sector increases the unit cost of training a rural worker will improve the rural environment, which should be put in the top priority for the policy makers.

3.3 The Low Interest Rate Policy, the Loss of the Agricultural Sector Due to the Environmental Pollution, and the Social Welfare

Now we will discuss the effects of government lowering of the interest rate of training loans on the loss of agricultural production due to the environmental pollution and the social welfare.[4]

The shaded area $S_{UTS'R'}$ in Fig. 3.1 can be illustrated by the following equation:

$$S_{UTS'R'} = F^3 - g(E)F^3 \tag{3.14}$$

Substituting Eqs. (3.8) and (3.10) into Eq. (3.14), and total differentiation of Eq. (3.14), we can get

$$\frac{dS_{UTS'R'}}{di} = (1-g)F_L^3\frac{dL_3}{di} + g'F^3\lambda F_T^2 T'\frac{dp_1}{di} \tag{3.15}$$

According to Table 3.1 and summarizing the above, we establish the following results.

Proposition 3.3 When $(1-g)F_L^3\frac{dL_3}{di} > -g'F^3\lambda F_T^2 T'\frac{dp_1}{di}$, the government lowering of the loan interest rate will reduce the loss of agricultural production due to the environmental pollution; when $(1-g)F_L^3\frac{dL_3}{di} < -g'F^3\lambda F_T^2 T'\frac{dp_1}{di}$, the government lowering of the loan interest rate will increase the loss of agricultural production due to the environmental pollution.

From Eq. (3.15), we know that the increase of the loss of agricultural production due to the environmental pollution is determined by two factors, the change of the employment in the agricultural sector and the change of the market price of producer services sector output. On the one hand, when the government lowers the interest rate of the loan, the producer services sector will increase the employment of rural transferred workers, leading to the number of workers employed in the agricultural sector decreasing. On the other hand, the government lowering the interest rate of the loan will decrease the market price of producer services sector output, meaning that the manufacturing sector will increase the production of intermediate inputs. Hence, the increase of the output of the manufacturing sector will decrease the quality of the rural environment and lower the marginal production value of the agricultural sector. The first term of Eq. (3.15), $(1-g)F_L^3\frac{dL_3}{di}$, represents the positive effect of reducing the loss of agricultural production from environmental pollution, since the decrease of the employment of the agricultural sector reduces the loss. The second term of Eq. (3.15), $g'F^3\lambda F_T^2 T'\frac{dp_1}{di}$, which satisfies

[4]The change of c has ambiguous impacts on the loss of agricultural production due to the environmental pollution and the social utility level.

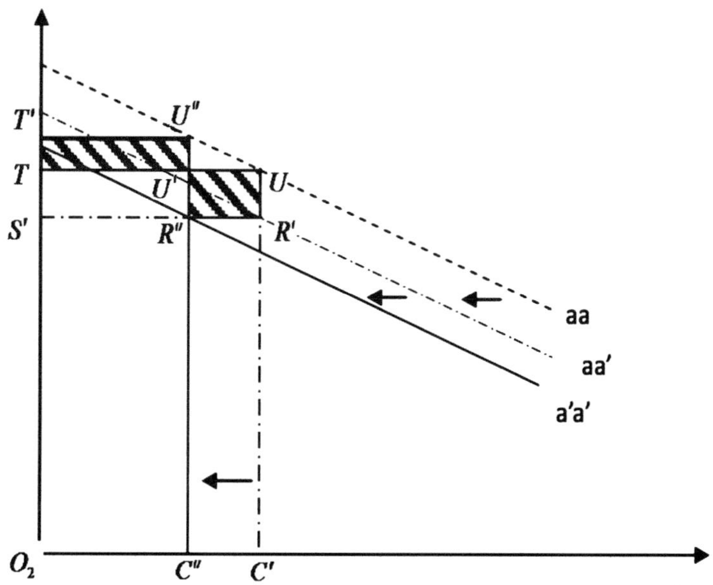

Fig. 3.3 The effects of the government lowering the interest rate of training loan on the loss of agricultural production

the equation $g'F^3\lambda F_T^2T'\frac{dp_1}{di} = -g'F^3\frac{dE}{di}$, represents the negative effect of increasing the loss of agricultural production from environmental pollution, since a decrease in market price of producer services sector output leads to the deterioration of rural environment. If $(1-g)F_L^3\frac{dL_3}{di} > -g'F^3\lambda F_T^2T'\frac{dp_1}{di}$, that is, if the positive effect outweighs the negative effect, then the government's lowering of the loan interest rate will reduce the loss of agricultural production. Conversely, if $(1-g)F_L^3\frac{dL_3}{di} < -g'F^3\lambda F_T^2T'\frac{dp_1}{do}$, the positive effect is less than the negative effect and the opposite occurs. Proposition 3.3 can be illustrated by the following figure.

The illustration of proposition can also be shown by Fig. 3.3 with the help of the right side of Fig. 3.2 to evaluate the effects of lowering the interest rate on the loss of agricultural production. The government lowering the interest rate of the loan will decrease the employment of the agricultural sector, which is shown by a leftward shift of line $C'U$ to the point C'' in Fig. 3.3. According to Proposition 3.1, lowering the interest rate of the loan will also lead to the deterioration of rural environment, the consequence of which is further damage to agricultural production. These can be shown in Fig. 3.3 by a leftward shift of the marginal production curve of agricultural sector, *aa'*. Here, we denote the new marginal production curve of agricultural sector as *a'a'*. We draw a line from C'' and perpendicular to the horizontal axis. It meets *a'a'*, *TU*, and *aa* at R'', U', and U'', respectively. Draw a line passing U'' and parallel to the horizontal axis. It meets the vertical axis at T'. Thus, the shaded area, $S_{UR'R''U''}$, expresses the reduced loss of the agricultural production due to decrease of the employment of the agricultural sector. The shaded area, $S_{U''U'T'T}$, expresses the additional loss of the agricultural production due to the further deterioration of the rural environment by the increase of the output of the manufacturing sector. If $S_{UR'R''U''} > S_{U''U'T'T}$, the first half of Proposition 3.3 can be established; if $S_{UR'R''U''} < S_{U''U'T'T}$, then the second half of Proposition 3.3 can be established.

The demand side of the economy is represented by the expenditure function, which is defined as $e = e(p_2, U)$, where U is the social utility level. Let G equal the national income. Hence, the country's budget constraint can be stated as

$$e(p_2, U) = G \tag{3.16}$$

The welfare effect can be obtained by totally differentiating Eq. (3.16) to yield

$$e_U dU = dG = p_2 dY_2 + dY_3.$$

Furthermore, we have

$$e_U \frac{dU}{dk} = \frac{dG}{dk} = \left(p_2 - \lambda g' F^3\right) F_T^2 T' \frac{dp_1}{dk} + g F_L^3 \frac{dL_3}{dk}, k = i, c \tag{3.17}$$

We build the results as follows.

Proposition 3.4 When $\left(p_2 - \lambda g' F^3\right) F_T^2 T' > -g F_L^3 \frac{dL_3}{di} / \frac{dp_1}{di}$, the government lowering of the interest rate of the loan will lead to the decrease of the social utility level, while when $\left(p_2 - \lambda g' F^3\right) F_T^2 T' < -g F_L^3 \frac{dL_3}{di} / \frac{dp_1}{di}$, the opposite occurs on the social utility.

From Eq. (3.17), we know that the change of the social utility level is determined by two factors, the change in employment of the agricultural sector and the change in the market price of producer services sector output. On the one hand, when the government lowers the loan interest rate, the producer services sector will increase the employment of rural transferred workers, in turn decreasing the number of workers employed in the agricultural sector. Therefore, the output of agricultural sector decreases. On the other hand, the government lowering of the interest rate of the loan will decrease the market price of producer services sector output, the consequence of which is that the manufacturing sector will increase the intermediate input. Hence, the increase of the output of manufacturing sector will generate more pollution, and the agricultural sector will suffer from the deterioration of the rural environment. It is through this mechanism that the government lowering the interest rate of the loan will lead to the decrease of the social utility level on the condition $\left(p_2 - \lambda g' F^3\right) F_T^2 T' > -g F_L^3 \frac{dL_3}{di} / \frac{dp_1}{di}$. It is worthwhile to note that, if the government's efforts make the increase of the manufacturing production value less than the pollution damage to agricultural production, that is, when

$(p_2 - \lambda g' F^3) F_T^2 T' > -g F_L^3 \frac{dL_3}{di} / \frac{dp_1}{di}$, the level of social utility will decrease. However, if the increase of the manufacturing production value is more than the total loss of the agricultural production value from environmental deterioration and the decrease of employment in the agricultural sector, the government lowering of the interest rate of the loan will increase the social utility level.

4 Conclusion

The environmental effects of rural-urban migration and the relationship between human capital investment and rural-urban migration have been two popular issues in economic research. However, there is still no research attempting to combine rural- urban migration, vocational training of employees (or human capital investment), and the corresponding environmental effects into a unified framework. Integrating the above three factors into a unified theoretical framework will contribute to addressing the issues that prevail in the developing countries. The present paper presents a model involving rural-urban migration, vocational training of the rural-urban migrants employed by the producer services sector, and environmental pollution into a general equilibrium framework. This is a necessary and crucial extension of the current researches, and the obtained results have significant implications to the real economy.

We conduct the comparative static analysis of lowering the training loan interest rate by the government and increasing the unit cost of training a rural worker by the producer services sector. There are several notable results. When the government lowers the interest rate of training loans, environmental conditions will worsen. The increase in the producer services sector unit cost of training a rural worker will increase the level of human capital of the rural people employed by this sector and improve rural environmental quality. That is, increasing the level of human capital will improve environmental quality. Thus, the governments in developing countries should make policies that guide enterprises to increase the unit cost of training an employed rural worker. In addition, some other economic results can be also derived. Under certain conditions, lowering the interest rate of the loan by the government will reduce pollution damage to agricultural production, but might decrease the social utility level as well. The above results can be used to implement development polices by policy makers.

It is clear that further analysis should consider the role of capital mobility and foreign direct investment. As it currently stands, other similar subsidy policies aimed at encouraging the enterprises for the human capital investment like the tax rebate and wage subsidy, and the comprehensive comparison among the different subsidy policies would be taken into consideration for the future studies. The present paper is an attempt to provide a foundation for future research.

Appendix

The determination of p_1, L_1, L_3, w_a, and L_U:

The derivations of the equilibrium can be shown as follows: given that the values of the exogenous variables are i and c, we can derive p_1, L_1, L_3, w_a, and L_U. When given $\bar{w}$ and exogenous variables i and c, we can derive L_2 by solving Eq. (3.5). By solving Eqs. (3.3) and (3.8), we also know p_1 and L_1. Substituting p_1 into Eq. (3.7), we know factor T. Substituting L_2 and T into Eq. (3.4), Y_2 is derived. Given Y_2, from Eq. (3.10), we can know factor E. Substituting E into Eq. (3.11) and L_1, L_2 into Eq. (3.13), only wa and L_3 are unknown variables. By solving the system of equations, we can derive w_a and $L_{3.}$ Finally, L_U can be derived by substituting w_a and L_3 into Eq. (3.12).

The conclusion drawn from this chapter is meaningful for the Asian developing countries. Environment of developing countries is generally worrying, especially in Asia. And training aiming at those farmers who transferred from rural area to urban area is an important option to optimize developing Asia economy. According to the conclusion of this chapter, choosing suitable ways of human capital training on the basis of the very economic environment can save developing costs which means killing two birds with one stone.

References

Bhagwati, J. N., & Srinivasan, T. N. (1977). Education in a job ladder model and the fairness-in-hiring rule. *Journal of Public Economics, 7*(1), 1–22.

Chao, C.-C. (2003). Jobs, production linkages, and the environment. *Journal of Economics, 79*, 113–122.

Chaudhuri, S., & Mukhopadhyay, U. (2006). Pollution and informal sector: A theoretical analysis. *Journal of Economic Integration, 21*(2), 363–378.

Copeland, B. R., & Taylor, M. S. (1999). Trade, spatial separation, and the environment. *Journal of International Economics, 47*(1), 137–168.

Dean, J. M., & Gangopadhyay, S. (1997). Export bans, environmental protection, and unemployment. *Review of Development Economics, 1*, 324–336.

Djajic, S. (1985). Human Capital, Minimum wage and unemployment: A Harris-Todaro model of developed open economy. *Economica, 52*, 491–508.

Galor, O., & Moav, O. (2004). From physical to human capital accumulation: Inequality in the process of development. *Review of Economic Studies, 71*(4), 1001–1026.

Grinols, E. L. (1991). Unemployment and foreign capital: The relative opportunity costs of domestic labor and welfare. *Economica, 62*, 59–78.

Grossman, G. M., & Krueger, B. A. (1995). Economic growth and the environment. *Quarterly Journal of Economics, 110*(2), 353–377.

Gupta, M. R. (1993). Rural-urban migration, informal sector and development policies. *Journal of Development Economics, 41*, 137–151.

Harris, J. R., & Todaro, M. (1970). Migration, unemployment and development: A two sector analysis. *American Economic Review, 40*, 126–142.

Li, X., & Qian, X. (2011). Economic analysis on the urban-rural disparity in human capital in China. *South African Journal of Economics, 79*(2), 146–160.

Liu, Z. (2011). Why is service share so small in China's developed region? *Journal of Nanjing University (Philosophy, Humanities and Social Sciences), 3*, 13–19 (in Chinese).
Papola, T. (1981). *Urban informal sector in a developing economy*. New Delhi: Vikus Publishing House.
Romatet, E. (1983). Calcutta's informal sector: Theory and reality. *Economic and Political Weekly, 18*(50), 2115–2128.
Samanta, S. (2003, November). *Training, unemployment and fiscal subsidy: A Harris-Todaro approach* (SSRN Working Paper Series). http://ssrn.com/abstract=471981 or doi:10.2139/scorn.471981
Tawada, M., & Sun, S. (2010). Urban pollution, unemployment and national welfare in a dualistic economy. *Review of Development Economics, 14*(2), 311–322.

Chapter 4
Minimum Wage on Migrant Workers and Its Employment Effect: A Case Study of the Yangtze River Delta Region before and after the Financial Crisis

Xiaochun Li, Ping He, Yu Zhou, and Zheyu Dong

Abstract Based on the model of buyer's monopoly, this article takes the Yangtze River Delta region as an example to analyze the employment effect of minimum wage on migrant workers. Empirical study of statistical data from seven cities in the region demonstrates that minimum wage could contribute to employment of migrant workers. With the impact of the financial crisis, market adjustment could disturb and destabilize the positive effect of minimum wage policies. Therefore, government should take active measures and interfere in the labor market to maintain targeted employment level and economic growth.

Keywords Minimum wage • Migrant workers • Yangtze River Delta • Buyer's monopoly • Financial crisis

1 Posing of the Problem

The minimum wage refers to the minimum reward that the employer pays to workers for their labor during the legal work time according to the law or to their agreement. In early twentieth century, the minimum wage system first appeared in New Zealand and Australia. Today, 80% of all countries have established the minimum wage system. The Chinese government announced the regulations on minimum wage in the enterprises in 1993 and started the minimum wage system. In the real economic life today, one of the goals of the establishment and adjustment of the minimum wage system is to protect the migrant workers' rights. In fact, the labor market in China could be divided into the primary market and the secondary market. In the secondary labor market, jobs usually involve hard, dirty, and

---

X. Li (✉)
Business School, Nanjing University, Nanjing, China
e-mail: xiaochun@nju.edu.cn

P. He • Y. Zhou • Z. Dong
School of Economics, Nanjing University, 22 Hankou Road, Nanjing, Jiangsu 210093, China

X. Li (ed.), *Labor Transfer in Emerging Economies*, New Frontiers in Regional Science: Asian Perspectives 12, DOI 10.1007/978-981-10-3569-2_4

exhausting work, while wages are close to, or even below, the required minimum wage level. The migrant workers are the major suppliers in the secondary labor market; nevertheless, in some region, economic development is achieved at the expense of the migrant workers' rights, and the majority of them have been earning relatively low wages for a long time. Needless to say, the establishment of the minimum wage system is conducive to increasing migrant workers' incomes. However, the employment effect of the minimum wage on migrant workers has always been a great concern in both the Chinese academia and the Chinese society.

In fact, scholars worldwide have never ceased studying the employment effect of minimum wage. Traditional Keynesians believe that the minimum wage is a reflection of the inelasticity of wages at low level. It is harmful to the expansion of job opportunities and thus is a crucial factor in causing unemployment. Stigler (1946) also opposes to minimum wage. He brings about the unemployment effect model in 1946 and argues that, in a perfect competition market, if the minimum wage is not higher than the market equilibrium wage, it will have no effect on the labor market. But otherwise, it will lead to reduced demand for labor by the enterprises and, thus, cause unemployment. A different opinion in the academia holds that the minimum wage does not necessarily lead to unemployment. For example, Reynolds and George (1965) argue that the minimum wage could have an impact by stimulating the firms to improve management, enhancing technological innovation, and increasing productivity, which could counterbalance the increased cost due to the minimum wage. Therefore, it does not necessarily lead to unemployment. Brown (1988) discusses the relationship between minimum wage and unemployment by presenting empirical research. He finds that increasing the minimum wage has small or even ambiguous effects of decreasing the low-wage workers' employment; Stephen and Stanley (1990), Card (1992), and Card and Kruger (1994) all employ cross-sectional comparisons to investigate the employment effects of minimum wage. According to their estimation, minimum wage has negligible or even positive effects of low-wage workers' employment; Deere et al. (1995) reexamine the methods of estimating the employment effects of minimum wage. It is shown that whether the increase of minimum wage will lead to the decrease of low-wage workers' employment depends on the how the researchers divide the population, such as by age or by gender. However, the above researches fail to focus on the employment effects of minimum wage in developing countries, especially for China, and their findings, in some degree, make no sense when we investigate how the minimum wage will effect migrant workers' employment in a buyer's monopoly market in China's urban areas.

In China's economic transition, there has only been 16 years since the adoption of the minimum wage standard. However, scholars have shown great interest in studying its effect. Similar to the situation in the international academia, the Chinese scholars have contrary opinions on this issue. Zhang Wuchang (2000) is among the first scholars in China to argue against the minimum wage standard. He states that the minimum wage would lead to unemployment of lower-class workers as well as capital outflows. Ping Xinqiao (2005) also questions the idea of minimum wage, as he believes that it would raise the real cost of labor and cost of violation of laws for the employers and would actually reduce employment in the cities. On the other hand, Wang Yanmin and Zhang Deyin (2004) hold an opposite view and emphasize the practicality of minimum wages. Zhang Zhiyong (2007) argues against the position that minimum wage is harmful to employment of migrant workers and affirms its practicality. He mentions that implementation of the minimum wage standard could not eradicate the problem of unemployment, but it could avoid further exacerbation of the problem and protect the migrant workers' rights. In addition to the polarized opinions, there are also balanced studies combining the two views. Luo Xiaolan (2007b) thinks that the employment effect of the minimum wage standard on migrant workers has a turning point. Before reaching the point, the minimum wage standard would promote employment of migrant workers, while it would hinder employment after reaching the point. Further analysis dividing into regions and industries shows that the minimum wage standard has a positive effect in the eastern and western regions and negative in the middle part of the country. It has a positive effect in manufacturing industries and negative in the construction industry. Therefore, these opinions provoke our inquiry into the characteristics of minimum wage in China's socialist market economy. What the employment effect of minimum wage on migrant workers in China is will be the central concern of this article. Moreover, the authors will focus on the Yangtze River Delta region and study the employment effect of minimum wage on migrant workers in this region, which is due to the following reasons:

1. The Yangtze River Delta region is China's manufacturing base and the new engine of China's economic development. Output from the second and third industries composes a major part of total output in this region. In 2007, the average ratio is 94.7% among 16 cities in this region. Rapid development in manufacturing and construction industries attracts the most migrant workers to work here. Therefore, the employment effect of minimum wage on migrant workers in this region is more typical of the phenomenon compared to that in other places.
2. In the Yangtze River Delta region, Shanghai started its minimum wage standard in 1993, followed by Zhejiang Province and Jiangsu Province in 1994 and 1995, respectively. They are among the earliest cities and provinces to adopt this policy. In addition, the adjustment of the minimum wages in this region is timely; thus, it makes a good case for the authors' observation of the employment effect.

When the authors are working on this article, the global financial crisis since late 2008 started to have huge impact in China. A lot of enterprises reduced production scale, stopped production temporarily, or even closed down, while many migrant workers lost their jobs and had to return home for a living. The Ministry of Human Resources and Social Security of China announced in November 2008, "Because of the current economic environment and the enterprises' situation, adjustment of the minimum wage in the enterprises will be postponed."[1] During the meetings of the National People's Congress and the National Committee of the Chinese People's

[1]Xinhua Net: http://bt.xinhuanet.com/2008-11/18/content_14949267.htm

Political Consultative Conference in March 2009, some representatives suggested suspension of the minimum wage adjustment, which is believed to exert a lot of burden on the small- and medium-sized enterprises. Particularly, under the circumstances of the financial crisis, migrant would worry or care about whether they can hold their jobs more than about their wage standard.[2] Therefore, minimum wage has again become the concern of the society. Then, under the impact of the financial crisis, should the minimum wage policy in China be canceled? Admittedly, as economic policy, the minimum wage would have different effect in different economic situations. However, currently there have not been many studies on this issue in China, and the impact of minimum wage on migrant workers in the financial crisis is not clear. Therefore, this article will study into the employment effect of minimum wage under the circumstance of the financial crisis, which will be conducive to better understanding of the problem.

The second and third parts below are analyses of the employment effect of minimum wage on migrant workers before the financial crises. In the second part, the authors will start with a theoretical analysis of the employment effect of minimum wage and then continue with empirical studies with data of the Yangtze River Delta region in the third part. In the fourth part, the authors will analyze theoretically the situation under the impact of the financial crisis.

2 Wage and Employment Decision in the Buyer's Monopoly Market

In the labor market (sometimes being referred to as the "migrant workers' market" below), buyer's monopoly means that, in the employment of migrant workers, the decision power on their wage is on the buyer's side. The migrant workers' market in China, including that in the Yangtze River Delta region, shows typical characteristics of buyer's monopoly. Liu Jiangfeng and Zhang Xiaohui (2004) argue that the shortage of migrant workers in Guangdong and Fujian provinces in 2004 is one of the phenomena of buyer's monopoly. The advantage of the employers and excess supply of labor led to a market equilibrium price that is below the price of labor, so that the migrant workers cannot afford their lives and are forced to return home in the countryside. Luo Xiaolan (2007a) argues that buyer's monopoly often happens in a divided labor market in real economic life. In the secondary labor market in China, excess supply of labor and the difference in bargaining and negotiating power of the two parties all show typical characteristics of a buyer's monopoly market. Bai Baoli and Cong Li (2007) think that the asymmetric power of the labor market is one of the features of China's labor market. Each migrant worker is in a disadvantaged position, and their dispersed distribution leads to their disadvantaged

[2]CPC Member from Guangdong Suggested Cancellation of the Minimum Wage Standard. Xinhua Net: http://news.21cn.com/guangdong/yaowen/2009/02/15/5869440.shtml

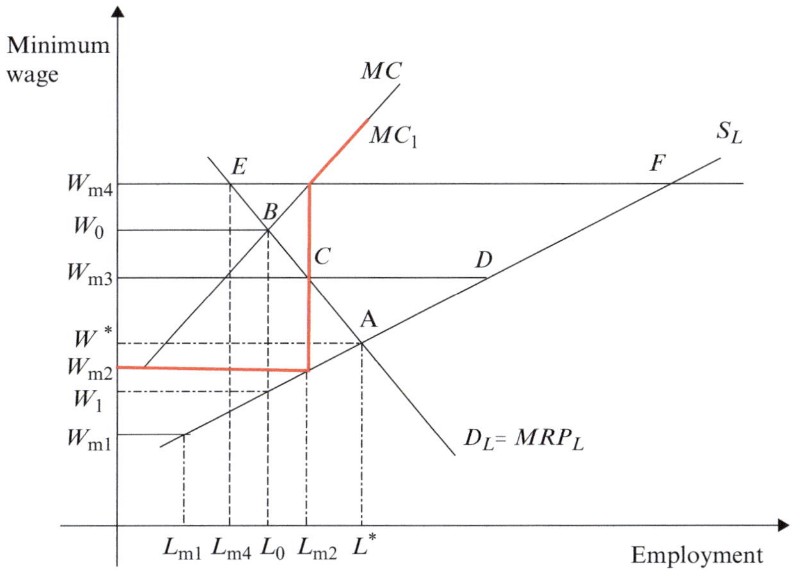

Fig. 4.1 Employment and wage in a buyer's monopoly market

position as a whole. Compared to individual workers, employers are in the monopolist's position.

In general, because the migrant workers often are not well educated and their working skills are low, they are only able to participate in hard, dirty, and tedious work. Most migrant workers lack the capability and condition to negotiate with their employers. In addition, most migrant workers work in medium- and small-sized private enterprises and joint ventures, which are usually labor-intensive. As wages take a large part of the cost of those enterprises, they often try to control cost by lowering wages. As the economy grows in recent years, the government promotes establishment of industrial zones, whose constellation effect puts the employers into an even better position. It is more likely for the employers to unify and determine labor's price than for the migrant workers to unify and ask for a pay raise. Therefore, the migrant workers' market in China is showing typical characteristics of buyer's monopoly.

In the following, the authors will analyze the employment effect of minimum wage under the circumstance of buyer's monopoly in the following graphs. The model assumes homogeneity of labor, which is low-skilled labor force. As in Fig. 4.1, in a perfect competition market, the labor market equilibrium is at A (L^*, W^*). In a buyer's monopoly market without other interference, the employers have to pay the existing workers the same wage level when they hire each extra labor unit with a relatively high wage rate in order to maintain all workers' motivation; thus, the marginal cost of hiring an extra worker exceeds the supply price of labor at any point. The employment level and wage level in this situation are decided by B (L_0, W_0) in $MPR_L = MC$. However, at a lower wage level W_1, the employers are able to recruit enough workers already. Therefore, W_1 is the real wage paid by the employers under the employment level of L_0. When the government regulations put the minimum wage at W_m, employment level will increase to $L_m(L_m>L_0)$. Meanwhile, the MC curve on the employers' side also changes: Before L_m, the MC curve is a horizontal line at the level of W_m; after that it returns to an upward sloping curve, as shown by MC_1 in Fig. 4.1. (We assume $W_m= W_{m2}$).

However, a different minimum wage level will lead to huge differences in its employment effect:

1. When the minimum wage is below W_1, the employers' optimum employment point is still at (W_1, L_0), which is not affected by the minimum wage regulations. Therefore, the wage and employment level remains at W_1 and L_0, and the minimum wage has no effect on migrant workers' employment, as shown by W_{m1} in Fig. 4.1.
2. When the minimum wage is between W_1 and W^*, the minimum wage will have a positive effect on employment of migrant workers without causing their unemployment. As shown by W_{m2} in the figure, the employment level rises to L_{m2}, without causing other unemployment.
3. When the minimum wage level is between $W^*$and W_0, quantity of employment of migrant workers will be increased. However, the increase in quantity will be counterbalanced by increase of unemployment as the minimum wage level rises. As shown by W_{m3} in Fig. 4.1, when the employment level increases to L_{m2}, CD is the amount of jobs lost.
4. When the minimum wage is beyond W_0, not only the quantity of employment of migrant workers decreases but also more unemployment is created. As shown by W_{m4} in the figure, the employment quantity reduces to L_{m4}, and EF is the amount of unemployment derived.

Considering that migrants' move to the cities does not affect their contract rights to the rural land, these workers have the option to return to their land when they encounter difficulty in finding jobs in the cities. That is, to say, the unemployment of migrant workers is transferrable. As long as promoting employment of migrant workers is the goal to be considered, the wage level between W_1 and W_0 can all be acceptable. Particularly, considering stability of urban employment and harmonious development, government should target at maintaining the minimum wage level between W_1 and W_0. The employment effect is most positive at this level, as it increases employment without causing unemployment. In the following, we would refer to this range as the "appropriate" wage level.

The above is the authors' theoretical analysis. When applied in the real economic life in the Yangtze River Delta region, is the current minimum wage at an appropriate market level before the economic crisis? Is it having a positive employment effect on the migrant workers, as concluded in theory? The authors will solve these problems by empirical studies.

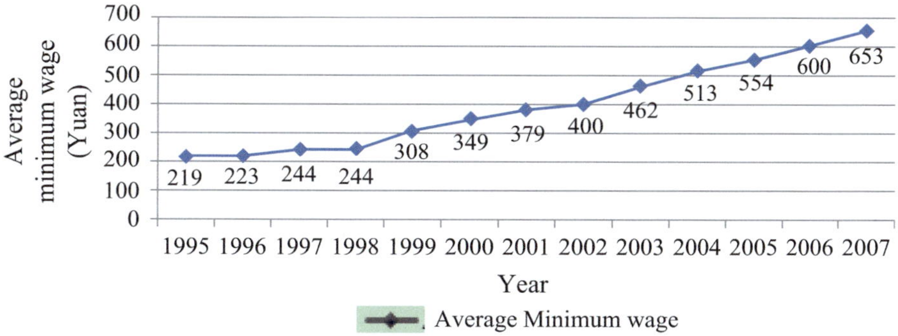

Fig. 4.2 Trend of the average minimum wage in the Yangtze River Delta region (Source: calculations based on data from the governmental websites of Shanghai, Hangzhou, Jiaxing, Nanjing, Wuxi, Changzhou, and Xuzhou, as well as the statistical yearbooks of relevant years). Note: the average minimum wage in seven cities in each year, using baseline of 1995 level in RMB, withholding inflation

3 Empirical Studies of the Employment Effect of Minimum Wage on Migrant Workers

1. *The current situation of the minimum wage in the Yangtze River Delta region*

The authors would first take a brief review on the trend of the minimum wage standard in the Yangtze River Delta region between the years 1995 and 2007. As shown in the following figure, the minimum wage level in this region, withholding inflation of prices, shows a continuously rising trend. This means that the real purchasing power of the minimum wage is also increasing, as shown in Fig. 4.2.

Then, considering the average ratio of the minimum wage to local average wage in different cities at the same period of time, the minimum wage level in the Yangtze River Delta region is relatively low in this regard. According to the "Social Average Rule" commonly used in those countries with minimum wage standard, the minimum wage should take 40–60% of local average wage.[3] However, there were only 2 years in which the Yangtze River Delta region met the standard among 13 years. Moreover, the minimum wage standard selected in the study is the highest level in those cities. When taking different levels of minimum wages into consideration, the ratio would be even lower, and it even shows a descending trend since 2000, as shown in Fig. 4.3.

In general, the two said indicators show that the minimum wage in the Yangtze River Delta region is still at a relatively low level. In addition, as the minimum wage increases, the average proportion of country residents who work in the second and third industries in this region increases from 52 to 72% during the year 1998–2007. It appears that the minimum wage is having a positive effect on

[3]Tencent News: http://news.qq.com/a/20060509/001110.htm

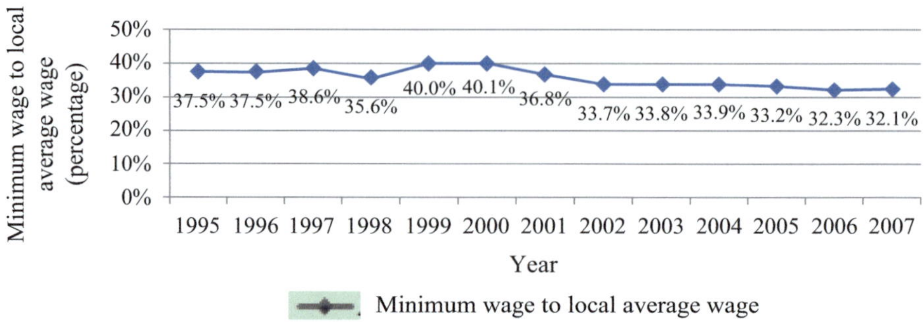

Fig. 4.3 Trend of the average ratio of the minimum wage to the average wage in the Yangtze River Delta (Source: calculations based on data from the governmental websites of Shanghai, Hangzhou, Jiaxing, Nanjing, Wuxi, Changzhou, and Xuzhou, as well as the statistical yearbooks of relevant years). Note: In this figure, minimum wage and average wage both are prices of the current periods

employment of migrant workers. Still, no conclusion could be drawn about its real effect without further quantitative analysis.

3.1 Selection of Data

In order to enlarge the sample base, this article uses panel data for econometrical test. Due to limit of date, the authors take data of seven cities, namely, Shanghai, Hangzhou, Ningbo, Nanjing, Wuxi, Changzhou, and Xuzhou, between the years 1995 and 2007, instead of testing all 16 cities in the Yangtze River Delta region. The variables include the following five ones:

Explained variable: the employment of migrant workers (JY). In theory, it ideally should include both local farmer workers and migrant workers from outside. But the data of migrant workers from outside is too difficult to obtain. Firstly, migrant worker is not clearly defined currently in statistics. Secondly, we lack statistical data about migrant workers' employment in general. Since the base number of rural labor varies greatly among different regions, this article uses the proportion of regional farm workers who work in the second and third industries to indicate employment of migrant workers.

Explanatory variable: the minimum wage (GZ). Since 80% of the migrant workers receive monthly salaries in China[4], the authors use monthly minimum wage data of the highest local standard.

Controlled Variables: (1) Income from agricultural business (SR) is used to indicate the migrant workers' willingness of employment in the cities. Farmers'

---

[4]Life and Education Situations of Migrant Workers in the Cities—Report on Quality of Life of Urban Migrant Workers II. Jiangsu Labor and Social Security Net: http://www.js.lss.gov.cn/pub/ldbzw/nmggz/dcbg/t20061225_10263.htm

agricultural income is the opportunity cost of their work in cities. We can assume that, with increasing income from agriculture, farmers will be less willing to go to the cities for jobs. (2) As for the practicality of employment of migrant workers, the bigger the production value of the second and third industries gets, the more nonagricultural work opportunities they can provide for the migrant workers under the theoretical circumstance of intermediate skill level. Since GDP varies greatly in different regions, the authors use the ratio of production value of the second and third industries to overall GDP (FNGDP) to indicate development of local second and third industries. (3) Registered unemployment rate in cities and township (SYL). This is an indicator of unemployment rate of the city and township residents. However, it largely reflects the general tendency of employment. The authors assume that unemployment rate (SYL) will have a negative effect on migrant workers' employment.

The minimum wage data is from the websites of the department of human resources and social security in various cities, and other data are from local statistical yearbooks or are estimated from other statistics available.

3.2 Model and Analytical Results

The authors use 1995 income level as baseline to calculate the minimum wage and agricultural incomes, withholding inflation. In order to reduce heteroskedasticity, the authors take natural logarithms of the statistics for analysis. The analysis is based on the fixed effect model, which is as follows:

$$\ln JY_{it} = \alpha_{1i} + \alpha_2 \ln ZDGZ_{it} + \alpha_3 \ln SR_{it} + \alpha_4 \ln FNGDP + \alpha_5 \ln SYL_{it} + u_{it}.$$

In the above formula, α_{1i} is the intercept item that changes with the cases; α_2,α_3, α_4, and α_5, respectively, refer to minimum wage, agricultural incomes, flexibility of local GDP, and urban registered unemployment rate on employment of migrant workers. α_{1i},α_2,α_3,α_4,and α_5 all are constants.

Since different places have different minimum wages, economic structures, and maturity of the labor market, the authors will first make a regression analysis of data of the Yangtze River Delta region and then discuss in detail the employment effect in Jiangsu, Zhejiang, and Shanghai, respectively. Please refer to the attachment for detailed data.

It shows in Table 4.1 that the minimum wage coefficient is positive and statistically significant; however, it is only 0.17 and inelastic. This means that, though minimum wage has a positive effect on migrant workers' employment, the effect is relatively weak. It could be possibly explained by the low minimum wage level. According to the theoretical analysis above, the employment effect of minimum wage largely depends on the minimum wage level. The authors have mentioned previously that the minimum wage level in the Yangtze River Delta region is relatively low, judged by either the absolute value or its ratio to local

Table 4.1 The result of regression analysis of the employment effect on migrant workers in the Yangtze River Delta region

	Coefficient	T-value
C	−1.24	−3.10***
Minimum wage	0.17	4.40***
Agricultural income	0.01	−0.01
Ratio of second and third industries	3.34	6.22***
Unemployment rate	−0.10	−4.38***
Fixed effect	First 2s: Jiaxing 0.16 Wuxi 0.07	
	Last 2s: Nanjing −0.17 Xuzhou −0.05	
Adjusted R^2	0.94	
F-value	134.74***	

Note: *, **, *** refer to at 10, 5, and 1% level, respectively; the result is statistically significant

average wage. Therefore, such low wage itself can only have limited effect on migrant workers' employment. In addition, despite its low level, implementation of the minimum wage policy faces many obstacles in reality.

The first obstacle comes from the migrant workers who are direct beneficiaries of the policy. Some migrant workers do not even know about the minimum wage regulations and merely accept what is given by their employers. Some other migrant workers accept the price offered by their employers "rationally" even when knowing their wage is below standard because of their high substitutability, low opportunity cost, and the inelasticity of their future expenses.

The second obstacle comes from the direct "victims" of the policy, the employers, since the policy, to some extent, increases their labor cost. The enterprises will take the cost of punishment into consideration as regards whether to obey the regulations. If the cost is below the increased labor cost, the employers will "rationally" violate the laws, and vice versa. Nevertheless, even "obedience" to the law could be achieved at the expense of deducted wages or longer working time for the migrant workers.

The third obstacle comes from the regulators and supervisors of the policy, the government. Because of the prevalent local protectionism and the current evaluation standard of local government, local GDP growth and urban residents' employment are often deemed more important than migrant workers' employment and their right. Since the minimum wage regulation will increase firms' labor cost, especially for those in the labor-intensive industries, the regulations will lead to outflow of the enterprises and less revenue for the local government. In addition, while the policy will promote the migrant workers' employment, it will, to some extent, diminish local residents' employment opportunities. Though some scholars argue that local residents' unemployment is largely voluntary[5], migrant workers do crowd out some local residents in the secondary labor market. Judging by their own

[5]Yuan Zhigang 1997. Unemployment Economics. Shanghai People's Publishing House, p. 152.

interest, local government will not be willing to make all efforts to implement the policy.

Although the minimum wage does not have significant effect on migrant workers' employment, it is still more elastic and statistically more significant than agricultural income. Agricultural income, the most fundamental opportunity cost of working in the cities for the migrant workers, has always been considered one of the most significant factors affecting their employment. The current fact that the employment effect of the minimum wage has greatly exceeded the impact of agricultural income implies that minimum wage has become an important factor in influencing migrant workers' employment as well. The coefficient of the ratio of production value of the second and third industries to total GDP is positive and larger than 1, which means that migrant workers' employment is sensitive to development of the second and third industries. The agricultural income has a positive coefficient, which is contrary to the assumption. However, comparing the wage and agricultural income in the Yangtze River Delta region withholding inflation, the authors discover that the average annual wage of the migrant workers is 852 yuan higher than their annual agricultural income. With further economic development, the gap is even getting larger. This implies that agricultural income, as opportunity cost, is too low to attract the migrant workers to stay on their land. The unemployment rate has a negative coefficient, which is in accordance with the authors' assumption. In the following, the authors will further analyze the employment effect of the minimum wage on migrant workers in different regions by dividing the Yangtze River Delta region into Jiangsu, Zhejiang, and Shanghai in the regression analysis below.

The analysis of Table 4.2 is as follows.

Table 4.2 Regression analysis of regional employment effect of minimum wage on migrant workers

Variable	Jiangsu	Zhejiang	Shanghai
C	−1.47	−2.58	9.22
	(−4.97)***	(−4.97)***	(1.03)**
Minimum wage	0.17	0.26	0.40
	(5.22)***	(5.16)***	(−2.8)**
Agricultural income	−0.001	0.10	0.17
	(−0.03)	(1.74)*	(−1.37)
Proportion of the second and third industries	1.27	1.67	−12.22
	(3.00) ***	(2.67)**	(−1.30)
Unemployment rate	−0.09	−0.04	−0.02
	(−3.57)***	(−0.78)	(−0.19)
Fixed effect	Max.:Wuxi 0.09	Max.:Jiaxing 0.03	
	Min.:Nanjing −0.07	Min.:Hangzhou-0.03	
Adjusted R2	0.95	0.93	0.46
F-value	139.67***	66.02***	3.52

Note: *, **, *** refer to at 10, 5, and 1% level, respectively; the result is statistically significant

The minimum wage of migrant workers all has a positive effect in Jiangsu, Zhejiang, and Shanghai, which means that increase in the minimum wage has positive employment effect on migrant workers in all three regions. Nevertheless, none of the values are larger than 1, meaning employment is not very sensitive to the increase of the minimum wage in all three regions. The causes of this phenomenon have been discussed in the previous part of the paper. Similarly, in all three regions, the minimum wage is more elastic and statistically more significant than agricultural income. This implies that the minimum wage has become an important factor in influencing migrant workers' employment in these regions. However, their elasticity is different across region, with the lowest of 0.17 in Jiangsu, followed by 0.26 in Zhejiang, and the highest is 0.40 in Shanghai. This could be possibly explained by the following two reasons. Firstly, as for elasticity, the minimum wage level in Shanghai is always the highest in the region, and adjustments of the standard in Shanghai are frequent and timely. Since the policy was made, the minimum wage standard has been adjusted almost every year. To the migrant workers, this is a positive signal and incentive for them to take nonagricultural jobs. In addition, in regard to average range of adjustment, it is about 10% between 1996 and 2007. Compared to the annual GDP growth of 14%, the minimum wage level should not exert a heavy burden on the employers. Secondly, as for the economic structure, privately owned business is most developed in this region. Most of them are medium- and small-sized firms, where a majority of the migrant workers are employed. Therefore, implementation of the minimum wage standard should be helpful to promote migrant workers' employment in this region. However, since the employees are at a disadvantaged position in the negotiation of wages with their employers, their wages and working conditions are mainly decided by their employers single-sided.[6] Meanwhile, the medium- and small-sized enterprises usually face great pressure for survival and profit-making. Therefore, it could be expected that a few enterprises would violate the minimum wage regulations, which limits the effect of minimum wage. Thus, its elasticity is low.

The coefficient of agricultural income is negative in Jiangsu, but positive in both Zhejiang and Shanghai, which is on the contrary to the authors' assumption. After comparing the wage income and agricultural income in both regions (withholding inflation), the authors find that the average annual wage income of the farmers is 572 yuan more than their annual agricultural income in Zhejiang, yet the difference is 3313 yuan in Shanghai. With the development of economy, the gap is getting even larger. This means that agricultural income, as opportunity cost, is too low to attract the farmers to stay on their land.

[6]Xia Xiaolin 2007: The Labor Capital Relationship and Coordination Mechanism in the Privately Owned Sectors—Research Report of the Unions of the Private Businesses in Zhejiang. Management World, Vol. 6.

The ratio of the second and third industries has a positive effect on migrant workers' employment in Jiangsu and Zhejiang, in accordance with the authors' assumption that "the production value of the second and third industries is positively proportional to migrant workers' employment." It has a negative effect in Shanghai, however, contrary to the assumption. A possible explanation is that, as urban economy develops and the production structure is upgraded, Shanghai has put high-technology industries as a privilege of their industrial upgrading target. By the end of 2007, production of high-tech industries composes of 24.4% of all industrial production in Shanghai. As traditional industries are upgraded into new technology-intensive industries, they increasingly require high-skilled workers. The migrant workers, however, usually have low education level and simple working skills and hence cannot meet the requirement of new job opportunities. The development of the third industries focuses on modern service industries, such as finance, insurance, foreign trade, and tourism, which exclude most of the migrant workers with limited human capital. In general, the negative effect of the production ratio of the second and third industries to total GDP in Shanghai is appropriate reflection of structural unemployment of the migrant workers who do not possess the human capital to meet the job requirements.

The unemployment coefficient in all three regions is negative, which is in accordance with the assumption.

In sum, the minimum wage standard has a positive employment effect on migrant workers, both locally and in the region as a whole. Their elasticity is somewhat different across provinces, yet the commonality is that the employment effect is relatively weak. Based on the previous theoretical analysis, the authors imply from the data of positive employment effect that the current minimum wage level is possibly at an appropriate market level, meaning it is between W_1 and W_0 as shown in Fig. 4.1. Further, taking into consideration the previous analysis of the current minimum wage level in the Yangtze River Delta region, the authors would argue that it is still at a relatively low level and is unlikely to cause unemployment by exceeding the equilibrium wage W^* in a perfect competition market. In other words, before the economic crisis, the employment effect of minimum wage on the migrant workers is positive and conducive, which also has large room for further upward adjustment.

4 The Employment Effect of Minimum Wage on Migrant Workers Under the Impact of the Financial Crisis

The analysis above demonstrates that minimum wage, since its implementation, has a positive effect on migrant workers' employment in the Yangtze River Delta region. However, the global financial crisis since late 2008 has had severe impact on China's economy, in which the Yangtze River Delta region also suffered. Many small- and medium-sized enterprises closed down or reduced demand for labor.

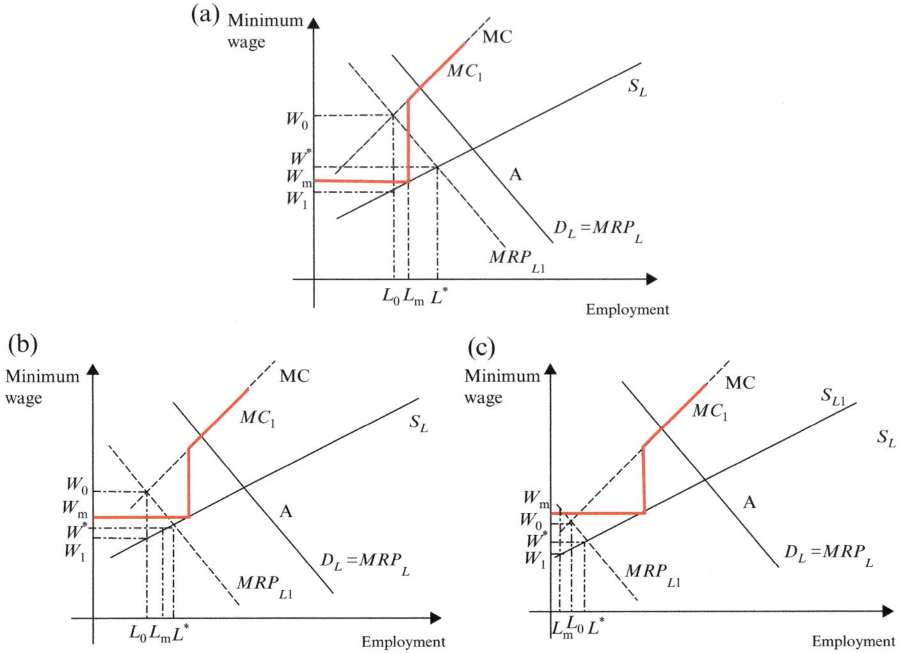

Fig. 4.4 (**a**) Economy is less affected by the crisis, the market demand curve shift rightward slightly. (**b**) Economy is almost not affected by the economic crisis, the market demand curve shift rightward sharply. (**c**) Economy affected by the crisis, the market demand curve shift leftward sharply

Accordingly, many migrant workers flowed back to their homes in the countryside. With the impact of the financial crisis, the demand and supply in the labor market change, together with the employment effect of the minimum wage on migrant workers. Based on Fig. 4.1, the authors further analyze as follows.

With the impact of the financial crisis, many firms reduced or stopped production, or even closed down, resulting in decreased demand for labor. As shown in the figure, this is indicated as move of D_L to the lower left. Assuming that the minimum wage is unadjusted in the financial crisis (in real economic life, most regions, including the Yangtze River Delta region, did not adjust the minimum wage in response to the crisis), MC curve maintains its shape due to unchanged supply of labor: Before L_m there is a horizontal line of W_m, and after it is an upward sloping curve to the right. That is, to say, in the crisis, the equilibrium wage and employment level are $W^*$and L^*, respectively. In a monopoly condition free of interference, the equilibrium wage and employment are W_1 and L_0, respectively; the minimum wage is W_m; and the employment level with the minimum wage is L_m. As shown in Fig. 4.4, market adjustment could have three possible results relating to employment effect.

1. After market adjustment, W^* is higher than W_m, while it does not lead to unemployment, and L_m is still higher than L_0. That is, to say, in the new market condition, the minimum wage still has a positive effect on migrant workers' employment. At this point, there is still room for the minimum wage to increase, as shown in Fig. 4.4a.
2. After market adjustment, W^* is lower than W_m. Although L_m is still higher than L_0,the minimum wage is high enough to cause excess supply of labor and hence unemployment of some migrant workers. Considering downward adjustment of the minimum wage standard usually is not appropriate, the wage would be kept at the original level, so that further unemployment of migrant workers could be avoided, as shown in Fig. 4.4b.
3. After adjustment, W_m is beyond the level of W_0, while L_m is below L_0. At this level, excess supply of labor would cause unemployment. If necessary, the government should consider reducing the minimum wage to an appropriate level. Admittedly, this could attract strong opposition from the low-income group; thus, it requires careful deliberation, as shown in Fig. 4.4c.

To sum up, affected by the financial crisis and the market adjustment thereof, the previously optimum level of minimum wage could become no longer appropriate, and thus its employment effect on migrant workers could become uncertain. As seen in Fig. 4.4, whether the minimum wage can maintain a positive effect on employment relies on the degree of change in the market. Therefore, the government should take active measures to adjust the minimum wage within the appropriate range in times of market change. This requires the government to analyze the changing situation of the appropriate range of minimum wage corresponding to the market changes and adjust the level of minimum wage accordingly. Theoretically, this means that the government should target at moving the labor demand curve D_L in Graph 1 rightward in order to ensure that the minimum wage is staying between W_1 and W^*. Practically, various measures to expand investment in enterprises, particularly medium- and small-sized enterprises, should be studied and tried. In fact, in order to maintain employment in economic crises, the local governments in the Yangtze River Delta region have taken some measures, such as to solve the financing problems of medium- and small-sized enterprises, to lower start-up barriers for firms, to increase investment and employment opportunities, and to avoid large-scale unemployment of migrant workers. On the labor suppliers' side, the government provides favorable policies for the migrant workers to start new business, improves rural infrastructure to prepare for the migrants' return, and provides vocational training for the farmers to improve human capital and to become better prepared for a new job, etc.

5 The Persistence of the Buyer's Monopoly on the Minimum Wage Line: A Study of Employment Effects in Jiangsu, Zhejiang, and Shanghai

Jiangsu Province, Zhejiang Province, and Shanghai Municipality are three parallel administrative areas in the Yangtze River Delta region. Although they share many similarities in regard to economy and geography, each area has its own characteristics that influence regional economic trends. This section provides a comparative analysis of these three area's minimum wage lines' employment effects.

It is well recognized that an important reason for setting a minimum wage line is that a result of the labor supply and the balanced market wage agreed upon by workers and their employment units cannot meet those workers' basic living standards. Therefore, the minimum wage line is, in theory, higher than the balanced market wage. Although raising the minimum wage can improve workers' incomes, it may also increase labor supply, reduce labor demand, and increase unemployment. So in order to reduce possible negative impacts on unemployment, many developed countries that implement a minimum wage should make minor adjustments to the minimum wage, which generally amount to less than 10%. Even if there may be a substantial upward adjustment, continued adjustment over several consecutive years is rarely seen. Please refer to Table 4.3.

However, in terms of minimum wage adjustments, Jiangsu, Zhejiang, and Shanghai are a different story; they have witnessed substantial growth in this regard for consecutive years. From 2008 to 2015, the average minimum wage growth rate was 13.3% in Shanghai, 11.1% in Jiangsu, and 9.9% in Zhejiang. In the same

Table 4.3 Annual growth rate of the minimum wage in the six countries: 2006–2015

Year	China (Shanghai minimum monthly wage)	USA (Federal minimum hourly wage)	France (minimum monthly wage)	Britain (minimum hourly wage)	Japan (national weighted average amount per hour)
2007	12.00%	8.35%	1.61%	3.18%	–
2008	14.29%	17.38%	1.59%	3.80%	–
2009	0	10.69%	3.13%	1.22%	–
2010	16.67%	0	1.52%	2.24%	–
2011	14.29%	0	0.75%	2.53%	2.38%
2012	13.28%	0	1.48%	1.81%	0.96%
2013	11.72%	0	4.38%	1.94%	1.63%
2014	12.35%	0	0.70%	3.01%	2.00%
2015	10.99%	0	0.69%	3.08%	2.09%

Data source: trading economics.com

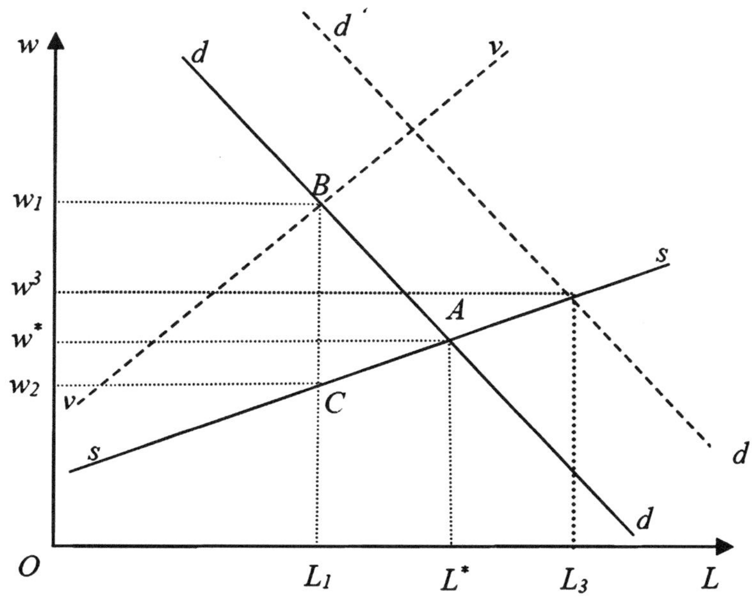

Fig. 4.5 Labor demand curve shifts to the right

period, employments in these three places increased. This got us thinking: Have continuous substantial increases to the minimum wage in Jiangsu, Zhejiang, and Shanghai affected unemployment? As the Yangtze River Delta has rid itself of the impact of financial crisis of 2010, is the labor market still subject to a buyer's monopoly?

This section examines labor markets in rapidly growing economies, as shown in Fig. 4.5. As the economy grows, there is an increased producer surplus, and companies can employ more workers under the same wage conditions. The demand curve *dd* moves to *d′d′*. The new balanced wage rises to w^3, widening the space signifying a minimum wage that promotes employment. Even if the minimum wage is higher than w^*, it can promote employment as long as it is no more than w^3. In recent years, the industrial enterprise producer surplus in the Yangtze River Delta region has been increasing (please refer to Fig. 4.6). We can therefore deduce that the minimum wage line space that promotes employment in Jiangsu, Zhejiang, and Shanghai continues to expand. This is why the Yangtze River Delta can continuously and significantly raise the minimum wage. This conclusion is more innovative than the one in the previous section, where the conclusion is static and cannot explain why continuously and sharply raised minimum wages are able to promote employment. It should be noted that this effect is obvious in rapidly developed economies. If the economy is in a stable development stage, the producer surplus

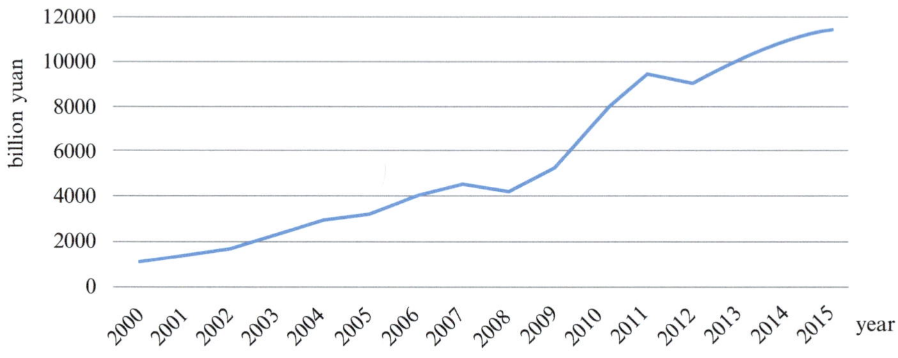

Fig. 4.6 The industrial enterprise producer surplus of enterprises above designated size in the Yangtze River Delta region

will not change much. The effect of the *dd* curve shifting rightward will be less obvious, and there might even be increased unemployment.

Next, we empirically analyze the employment effect of the minimum wage in Jiangsu, Zhejiang, and Shanghai. Econometric model is as follows:

$$\ln l_{it} = \alpha_{1i} + \alpha_2 \ln w_{it} + \alpha_3 \ln X_{it} + u_{it}$$

where i means sector i, t means years, X_{it} are control variables, l_{it} is the employment in sector i, and w_{it} is the minimum wage in sector i of the year t. In order to reduce variance, we adopt the natural logarithm from the variables corresponding to the data. We select the following indicators:

1. Minimum wage, w

Jiangsu, Zhejiang, and Shanghai have been developing rapidly as a whole, but their respective economic growths still differ. The minimum wage levels should be set in accordance with local economic situations. Shanghai has one minimum wage level, while Jiangsu has three levels and Zhejiang has four levels. This article uses the highest level from each of these three places as the three minimum wage standards and calculates workers' real purchasing power, with the minimum wages from 2005 used as the constant prices for these three places, respectively.

2. The proportion of secondary and tertiary industries in the GDP, gdp

The section examines the proportion of secondary and tertiary industries in the GDP, rather than the total GDPs, of the three aforementioned places. This is because the migrant labor force is mainly employed in secondary and tertiary industries; the former exerts a larger influence on labor inflow than the total GDP and the per capita GDP. The higher the proportion of secondary and tertiary industries in GDP, the greater the industry scale that can attract labor employment;

the greater the industry scale, the more workers needed. Therefore, there should be a positive relationship between the proportion of secondary and tertiary industries in employment and the GDP.

3. Per capita fixed asset investment in urban areas, k

This section measures the aforementioned factor of the investment ratio of fixed assets with respect to the populations of Jiangsu, Zhejiang, and Shanghai. Per capita fixed asset investment can be used as a representative indicator of per capita capital stock and can reflect the size of capital intensity. If the per capita investment in fixed assets is large, then capital intensity is high, and vice versa. Higher capital intensity means that capital is more abundant, whereas continuously increasing per capita capital stock may have a negative impact on employment. Conversely, increasing the per capita capital stock of industries with lower capital intensity may have a positive impact on employment. Therefore, per capita fixed asset investment is expected to be inversely related to employment.

Note: The data sets for 2000, 2001, and 2015 are estimated by the author based on the proportion of fixed asset investment in urban areas compared to total fixed asset investment in other years.

4. Per capita consumption expenditure in urban areas, c

The number of workers attracted by a region is affected by not only its wage level but also its cost of living. Net income is the true key indicator of labor force attraction. Therefore, per capita consumption expenditure is expected to be inversely related to employment.

5. Registered unemployment rate in urban areas, u

Registered unemployment rates in urban areas reflect the probability that workers may fail to find a job. Before finding their ultimate workplaces, workers are considered unemployed. If the unemployment rate of a given area is high, workers will be less willing to work in that area. If an area has a low unemployment rate, workers will be more willing to work there. Of course, registered unemployment rates in urban areas are generally lower than actual unemployment rates, but can reflect the general unemployment situation of those areas.

Source: The data above all comes from the official website of the National Bureau of Statistics; statistical reports on human resources and social security development of Jiangsu, Zhejiang, and Shanghai; statistical reports on national economy and social development; and the official website of the Shanghai Municipal Human Resources and Social Security Bureau unless otherwise specified.

The empirical results are as follows (Table 4.4).

Table 4.4 Empirical results

	Shanghai labor	Jiangsu labor	Zhejiang labor
lnw	1.118***	0.167	0.862*
	(5.15)	(0.47)	(2.55)
lngdp	−6.995	−0.490	3.325
	(−0.37)	(−0.14)	(1.19)
lnk	0.651	0.154	0.0669
	(1.53)	(0.62)	(0.71)
lnc	−0.558	0.578	−0.0730
	(−1.54)	(1.24)	(−0.21)
lnu	0.0285	−0.792**	−0.817***
	(0.31)	(−4.51)	(−4.86)
Constant	−1.942	0.400	2.660
	(−0.55)	(0.13)	(1.35)
R^2	0.9874	0.9799	0.9935

Notes: *t* statistics in parentheses
* $p<0.05$; ** $p<0.01$; *** $p<0.001$

According to the analysis above, we can summarize the impacts of minimum wages in Jiangsu, Zhejiang, and Shanghai on employment as follows:

(1) Similarities:

1. The coefficients of minimum wages in Jiangsu, Zhejiang, and Shanghai are all positive, indicating that official minimum wages generally promote employment. This is especially notable in Shanghai and Zhejiang, as the minimum wage coefficient in Shanghai is significantly positive at the 1% level, and Zhejiang's is significantly positive at the 10% level; the positive impact of Jiangsu is not significant. Generally speaking, the low-end labor market of the Yangtze River Delta is still in a buyers' monopoly and has not undergone substantive changes.
2. In most years from 2001 to 2015, the growth rate of minimum wages in Jiangsu, Zhejiang, and Shanghai was higher than that of unemployment rates, which showed a downward trend in most years, as shown in Fig. 4(7). It can be determined that the minimum wage levels in Shanghai and Zhejiang are between w_2 and w_3 in Fig. 4(5), which has some distance from w_3, meaning that there is considerable room for minimum wage growth in those two locales. The minimum wage in Jiangsu may be close to w_3. Therefore, even if its minimum wage increases, it will not cause a significant increase in unemployment (Fig. 4.7).

(2) Differences:

There is a major difference between the respective impacts of minimum wages in each of the three examined places when it comes to employment intensities.

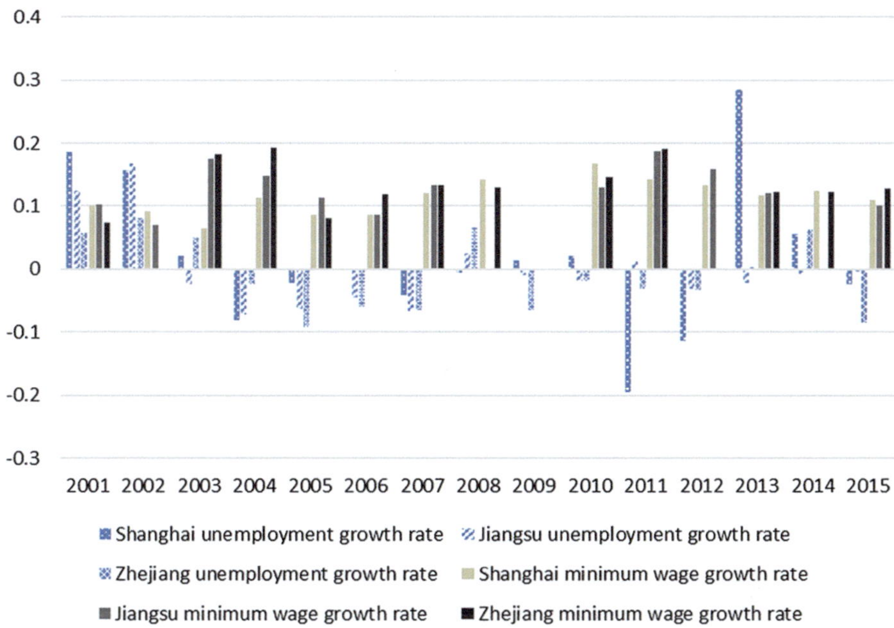

Fig. 4.7 Minimum wage growth rate and unemployment growth rate in Shanghai, Jiangsu, and Zhejiang: 2001–2015 (Data source: statistical reports on human resources and social security development of Jiangsu, Zhejiang, and Shanghai and statistical reports on national economy and social development of Jiangsu, Zhejiang, and Shanghai)

The impact of Shanghai is the most obvious. When the minimum wage there increases by 1% point, employment is expected to increase by 1.118%. As for Zhejiang, when its minimum wage increases by 1% point, its employment will increase by 0.862%. There is a lot of room for Shanghai to raise its minimum wage, followed by Zhejiang. However, it is difficult to judge how much room Jiangsu has to raise its minimum wage.

As a buyer's monopoly in labor market can dynamically persist, the minimum wage lines in Jiangsu, Zhejiang, and Shanghai are still expected to rise continuously. However, with the ongoing deepening of industrial restructuring and the formation of a new normal in economic development, the future expansion rates of production surplus of enterprises in Jiangsu, Zhejiang, and Shanghai are expected to slow down. The effects of increasing minimum wages on employment will therefore decline, and the growth rate of minimum wages will be lower than it was 10 years ago. Jiangsu will enter a non-buyer's monopoly with a low-end labor market earlier than either Shanghai or Zhejiang.

Among developing Asian countries, some are similar to Jiangsu, Zhejiang, and Shanghai in terms of economic growth. In other words, under a dual economic environment, these three places have high developmental levels. The conclusions of this section should be useful for those three locales.

6 Conclusion

Since the majority of the migrant workers hold jobs that are lowly paid and unstable, the employment of this group of people would be greatly affected by the minimum wage standard. Before the economic crisis, in a labor market of buyer's monopoly, the employment effect of minimum wage on the migrant workers would be determined by the "level" of the minimum wage. When it is kept at an appropriate level – meaning beyond the wage decided by the employers but below that of the equilibrium labor price in a perfect competition market – it could generate a positive impact on migrant workers' employment, in other words, creating new jobs while not eliminating existing ones. According to the econometric analysis, the minimum wage level in the Yangtze River Delta region is conducive to increasing quantity of employment of migrant workers. Referring to the real economic situation, it is highly unlikely that the current minimum wage exceeds the equilibrium wage level in a perfect competition market. Therefore, the current minimum wage is probably at an appropriate level, with large room for upward adjustment. The financial crisis resulted in adjustment of the labor market. Accordingly, the government should take all effective measures to guide adjustment of local market so that it could maintain the minimum wage within an appropriate range, as well as its positive effect. Based on the general principle of "no downward adjustment," the government could reduce the rate of minimum wage growth or hold it back temporarily when the minimum wage appears to be beyond the appropriate level.

Finally, the authors would make a few suggestions to the migrant workers who intend to look for jobs in the cities: They should actively participate in vocational trainings in order to build up their competitiveness. Their low skills largely determine that their jobs are easily substitutable, lowly paid, and often unstable. There has been severe structural problem in the employment of migrant workers, which was only exacerbated by the financial crisis. Therefore, the fundamental way for the migrant workers to improve their employment opportunities and wage-negotiating power is to improve their vocational skills.

Economic realities in the China's Yangtze River Delta region have provided valuable experience for labor transfer in Asian developing countries. One characteristic of labor market in those underdeveloped countries of Asia is monopsony. Though raising the minimum wage can expand employment, improving labor quality is the ultimate way to enhance bargaining power of workers and finally solve the employment problem. As a matter of fact, relevant government departments must give full attention to the human capital training of immigrant labor force.

Appendix

City	Year	Minimum wage (1995=100)	Ratio of labor in the second and third industries	Ratio of production of the second and third industries to total GDP	Agricultural income (yuan) 1995=100	Unemployment rate
Shanghai	1995	270.00	0.715	0.976	1183.00	2.70
	1996	274.81	0.699	0.977	1170.68	2.70
	1997	280.65	0.684	0.979	1092.32	2.80
	1998	289.56	0.634	0.981	1055.79	2.90
	1999	324.81	0.649	0.982	815.53	3.10
	2000	381.15	0.669	0.984	799.99	3.50
	2001	419.69	0.674	0.985	828.25	4.30
	2002	455.87	0.679	0.986	659.53	4.80
	2003	485.12	0.713	0.988	691.94	4.90
	2004	529.33	0.737	0.990	738.56	4.50
	2005	569.65	0.757	0.990	669.55	4.40
	2006	611.90	0.679	0.991	624.96	4.40
	2007	664.39	0.763	0.992	596.37	4.30
Hangzhou	1995	230.00	0.470	0.909	1141.00	2.80
	1996	208.14	0.482	0.907	1410.86	2.30
	1997	229.00	0.486	0.912	1315.48	2.70
	1998	224.95	0.489	0.915	1193.91	2.90
	1999	340.23	0.500	0.920	1106.17	3.40
	2000	337.53	0.530	0.925	1234.87	3.50
	2001	364.05	0.552	0.929	1281.62	4.48
	2002	368.47	0.580	0.936	1142.26	4.40
	2003	437.65	0.605	0.940	1227.96	4.39
	2004	509.09	0.639	0.948	1474.72	4.33
	2005	540.95	0.667	0.950	1932.89	3.71
	2006	598.36	0.685	0.955	1125.72	3.46
	2007	655.21	0.700	0.960	1150.09	3.21
Jiaxing	1995	230.00	0.486	0.817	2734.00	1.20
	1996	212.57	0.502	0.834	2658.04	3.00
	1997	230.36	0.499	0.845	3249.95	3.20
	1998	232.69	0.492	0.862	2395.77	3.18
	1999	373.07	0.514	0.880	2298.67	3.40
	2000	369.01	0.565	0.885	2580.23	3.44
	2001	389.88	0.600	0.892	2513.31	3.45
	2002	389.88	0.635	0.910	2043.55	4.00
	2003	453.27	0.669	0.920	2249.37	4.10

(continued)

City	Year	Minimum wage (1995=100)	Ratio of labor in the second and third industries	Ratio of production of the second and third industries to total GDP	Agricultural income (yuan) 1995=100	Unemployment rate
	2004	511.93	0.707	0.923	2840.28	4.10
	2005	549.39	0.725	0.927	3190.36	3.80
	2006	596.28	0.740	0.935	3135.91	3.70
	2007	643.67	0.755	0.939	3810.52	3.60
Nanjing	1995	210.00	0.454	0.923	1876.59	2.24
	1996	217.59	0.461	0.933	1970.08	2.30
	1997	254.62	0.472	0.936	2341.57	2.10
	1998	254.62	0.464	0.939	1305.82	2.30
	1999	295.12	0.470	0.943	1299.46	2.50
	2000	359.68	0.475	0.946	1663.77	3.10
	2001	396.97	0.497	0.949	1679.45	3.60
	2002	433.77	0.554	0.953	1721.34	4.10
	2003	502.18	0.595	0.959	1334.59	4.20
	2004	559.78	0.648	0.964	1387.24	4.03
	2005	610.17	0.663	0.968	1250.15	3.35
	2006	652.14	0.698	0.970	1271.06	3.33
	2007	712.73	0.721	0.974	1179.37	3.26
Wuxi	1995	210.00	0.759	0.947	1974.00	1.47
	1996	214.67	0.748	0.948	1647.58	1.45
	1997	242.92	0.697	0.953	1519.10	1.92
	1998	240.75	0.679	0.956	1295.75	1.96
	1999	275.42	0.674	0.959	1354.71	1.96
	2000	335.67	0.682	0.960	1447.67	2.30
	2001	369.35	0.689	0.960	1651.74	3.60
	2002	398.31	0.716	0.964	1760.88	3.80
	2003	462.95	0.756	0.972	1725.78	3.86
	2004	511.09	0.786	0.980	1781.41	3.48
	2005	557.64	0.788	0.983	2017.22	3.27
	2006	596.00	0.802	0.984	1957.28	3.18
	2007	650.74	0.810	0.986	2094.63	3.28
Changzhou	1995	210.00	0.599	0.892	3050.13	1.08
	1996	217.79	0.605	0.894	3057.26	1.20
	1997	249.35	0.596	0.906	2971.14	1.40
	1998	245.42	0.594	0.912	2383.32	1.90
	1999	285.33	0.590	0.918	2143.84	2.46
	2000	349.49	0.603	0.925	2565.41	2.98
	2001	384.95	0.610	0.930	2556.50	3.20

(continued)

City	Year	Minimum wage (1995=100)	Ratio of labor in the second and third industries	Ratio of production of the second and third industries to total GDP	Agricultural income (yuan) 1995=100	Unemployment rate
	2002	418.08	0.634	0.936	2304.57	3.40
	2003	487.38	0.692	0.948	2206.70	3.50
	2004	536.51	0.727	0.953	2496.26	3.60
	2005	584.24	0.746	0.957	2981.89	3.58
	2006	624.42	0.760	0.962	3143.06	3.40
	2007	680.46	0.770	0.967	3301.03	3.21
Xuzhou	1995	175.00	0.275	0.750	2240.22	1.60
	1996	218.18	0.284	0.763	2281.55	1.50
	1997	223.04	0.284	0.786	2557.77	1.62
	1998	223.04	0.278	0.791	2429.80	1.30
	1999	263.46	0.368	0.803	2551.48	1.52
	2000	308.89	0.306	0.808	2594.36	1.89
	2001	326.08	0.328	0.815	2794.11	2.40
	2002	337.84	0.364	0.797	2885.50	3.58
	2003	404.81	0.423	0.842	2893.61	4.30
	2004	433.74	0.458	0.843	3174.40	4.03
	2005	466.85	0.481	0.860	3305.35	3.44
	2006	518.49	0.503	0.873	3525.44	3.03
	2007	560.72	0.534	0.885	3612.08	2.80

Source of data: The authors derived them from the governmental websites of Shanghai, Hangzhou, Jiaxing, Nanjing, Wuxi, Changzhou, and Xuzhou, as well as the statistical yearbooks from 1995 to 2007

References

Bai Baoli, & Cong Li. (2007). Establishment of modern property rights system to increase consumers' demand. *Economics Jingwei, 2*.

Brown, C. (1988). Minimum wage laws: Are they overrated. *The Journal of Economic Perspectives, 2*(3), 133–145.

Card, D. (1992). Using regional variation in wages to measure the effects of the federal minimum wage. *Industrial and Labor Relations Review, 46*(1), 22–37.

Card, D., & Krueger, A. (1994). Minimum wages and employment: A case study of the fast-food industry in New Jersey and Pennsylvania. *The American Economic Review, 84*(4), 772–793.

Deere, D., Murphy, K. M., & Welch, F. (1995). Employment and the 1990–1991 minimum-wage hike. *The American Economic Review, 85*(2), 232–237.

Liu Jianfeng, & Zhang Xiaohui. (2004). Low wage and unprotected rights, the migrant drought of the Zhujiang river delta region. *China Industrial and Commercial Times*. October 5.

Luo Xiaolan. (2007a). Analysis of the employment effect of the minimum wage in the condition of the Buyer's monopoly labor market in China. *Financial and Trade Studies, 4.*

Luo Xiaolan. (2007b). The employment effect of the minimum wage standard on migrant workers in China—Country-wise, regional and industrial empirical analyses. *Fiancial Studies, 11.*

Ping Xinqiao. (2005). Focus on the labor and capital relationship in privately owned business. *The View of Privately-Owned Business, 6.*

Reynolds Lloyd, & Peter George. (1965). *Productivity, and industrialization in Puerto Rico.* Homewood: Richard D, Irwin.

Stephen, B., & Stanley, T. D. (1990). A meta-analysis of the union-nonunion wage gap. *Industrial and Labor Relations Review, 44*(1), 54–67.

Stigler, G. (1946). The economics of minimum wage legislation. *American Economic Review, 36* (3), 58–365.

Wang Yanmin, & Zhang Deyin. (2004). Who caused the root of the problem? *Cooperative Economics and Technology, 7.*

Xia Xiaolin. (2007). Labor and capital relationship and its coordination, mechanism in privately-owned sectors – Research report on unions in private businesses in Zhejiang. *Management World, 6.*

Yuan Zhigang. (1997). *Unemployment economics.* Shanghai: Shanghai People's Publishing House.

Zhang Wuchang. (2000). The root of the problem: Minimum wages. *Baidu Economics.* http://tieba.baidu.com/f?kz=500768

Zhang Zhiyong. (2007). Will the minimum wage standard discourage migrant workers' employment? *Financial Science, 10.*

Part II
Migrants Remittances

This portion is made up of two chapters. Most of this study report on migrant remittances consists of empirical studies, but thus far, theoretical research has produced little in the way of results. Two papers in this book analyzing migrant remittance are all theoretical research. Chapter 5 investigates the economy effect of migrant remittance from unskilled labor working in urban sector in the case of skilled-unskilled wage inequality. Chapter 6 investigates the influence of migrant remittance on the urban economy, and for the first time, theoretical analysis has been conducted with respect to the theoretical field.

Chapter 5
An Economic Analysis of Remittance of Unskilled Migration on Skilled–Unskilled Wage Inequality in Labor Host Region

Xiaochun Li and Yu Zhou

Abstract The present paper establishes a two-sector general equilibrium model and conducts the comparative static approach to investigate the impact exerted by an increase in the remittance rate of the unskilled migrants on the skilled–unskilled wage inequality in the labor host region. We find that the unskilled migrants increase their remittance rate to the labor-outsourcing regions that will decrease the skilled–unskilled wage inequality in the labor host region.

Keywords Unskilled migrants • Remittance • Skilled–unskilled wage inequality • Labor host region

1 Introduction

The migrant remittance has captured lots of attention to the development economists during the last decades. World Bank (2001) estimates that the Indian immigrant remittance occupied 2.6% of GDP in 1999 and the Pakistan immigrant remittance took 1.8% of GDP in 1999. Rodriguez (1996) points out that 17% of Philippine citizens received the immigrant remittance, which occupied 8% of the Philippine's national income. Cox et al. (1998) show that 25% of households in Peru received the immigrant remittance, which took 22% of Peru's national income. Furthermore, Cox and Ureta (2003) use the data collected from Salvatore and show that 14% of rural people and 15% of urban citizens in Salvatore received the overseas immigrant remittance in 1997. In addition to the economic impacts of the international migration on the labor-outsourcing regions or countries, the rural–urban migrant remittance in developing countries also exerts lots of economic impacts. For example, China's rural–urban migrants send or take home (or the

X. Li (✉)
Business School, Nanjing University, Nanjing, China
e-mail: xiaochun@nju.edu.cn

Y. Zhou
School of Economics, Nanjing University, 22 Hankou Road, Nanjing, Jiangsu 210093, China

X. Li (ed.), *Labor Transfer in Emerging Economies*, New Frontiers in Regional Science: Asian Perspectives 12, DOI 10.1007/978-981-10-3569-2_5

labor-outsourcing region) part of their income obtained from the labor host region, and the family members of the migrant workers in the labor-outsourcing region could benefit a lot from the rural migrant remittance. This is a common phenomenon among nearly 200 million rural–urban migrants in China. It has been estimated by the Chinese government that the rural–urban migrant remittance reached nearly 330 billion RMB (around 55 billion US dollars) in 2010, which almost took 20–50% of the income of the households who receive the remittance.[1] Chen (2006) estimated that the total amount of rural migrant remittance could reach billions and the rural migrant remittance also alleviates the financial pressures in rural areas and becomes an important source of financing for education and medical expenses.

From the above typical facts, we know that the migrant remittance generates great impacts on the labor-outsourcing regions or countries, which arouse the interests of both the empirical and theoretical economists. The theoretical studies mainly consider the economic impacts of the migrant remittance on the price level, production activities, and social welfare in the labor-outsourcing regions or countries. The typical studies can be referred to Lundahl (1985), Kirwan and Holden (1986), Djajic (1986, 1998), Rivera-Batiz (1986), Quibria (1997), and McCormick and Wahba (2000). The current empirical studies mainly center on the contributions of the migrant remittance to the economic growth and the impacts of the migrant remittance on the citizens' income and income inequality in the labor-outsourcing regions or countries. The representative empirical literatures can be referred to Taylor and Wyatt (1996), Lucas (2005), Rodriguez (1996), Cox et al. (1998), World Bank (2001), Glytsos (2002), and Cox and Ureta (2003).

On the other hand, enormous empirical studies show that both developed and developing countries have suffered from the increased skilled–unskilled wage inequality. The representative empirical literatures can be referred to Lawrence (1994), Feenstra and Hanson (1996), Wood (1997), Feenstra and Hanson (2003), and Banga (2005). The current theoretical studies try to address the issues relating to the growing skilled–unskilled wage gap from the perspectives of the trade and investment liberation (Anwar 2006; Anwar and Rice 2009; Beladi et al. 2008; Chaudhuri 2004, 2008; Chaudhuri and Yabuuchi 2007; Marjit and Kar 2005; Marjit et al. 2004; Yabuuchi and Chaudhuri 2007, 2009) and the technical progress (Fang et al. 2008; Moore and Ranjan 2005). However, the academia seldom relates the enlarging skilled–unskilled wage inequality to the migrant remittance.

However, the impact exerted by an increase in the remittance of unskilled migrants on the skilled–unskilled wage inequality is largely ignored. Such problem cannot be avoided in reality and exists in practice. In order to fill the current research gap, the present paper establishes a two-sector general equilibrium model and conducts the comparative static approach to investigate the impact exerted by an increase in the remittance of the unskilled migrants on the skilled–unskilled wage inequality in the labor host region. We find that the unskilled migrants increase their remittances to the labor-outsourcing regions that will decrease the skilled–unskilled wage inequality in the labor host region.

---

[1]Detailed information can be referred to: http://www.npc.gov.cn/npc/xinwen.rdlt/sd/2010-03/16/content_1564113.htm (Yuanqian Li Yuanqian 2010).

The rest of this chapter is organized as follows: in Sect. 2, we set up the theoretical model; in Sect. 3, we conduct the theoretical analysis of the established model; and we draw a conclusion in Sect. 4.

2 Theoretical Model

Consider a typical closed urban economy of developing countries, which absorbs the rural–urban migrants. There are two kinds of labor in this economy, the urban citizens and the rural–urban migrants. Generally speaking, for developing countries, the human capital level of the urban citizens is higher than that of the rural people. Therefore, in our assumed economy, it is reasonable for us to treat the urban citizens as the skilled labor and the rural–urban migrants as the unskilled labor. Because the rural–urban migration control policies prevail in the developing countries (Lall et al. 2006; Zhao 2005), we set the number of the rural people who transfer to urban areas as given.

The urban economy consists of two sectors, sector 1 and sector 2. Sector 1 is the skilled labor-intensive sector, using the local skilled labor and capital as factors of production. Sector 2 is the unskilled labor-intensive sector, employing rural–urban migrants, capital, and the local skilled labor who cannot find the job in sector 1 as factors of production. In developing countries, sector 2 can be represented by architecture industries, catering services, and other physical labor industries. These sectors are typically unskilled labor-intensive. However, in sector 2, due to the technical limitation, the productivity of skilled labor is the same as that of the unskilled one. It is reasonable to see that in this situation, the skilled labor will receive a wage rate same as that of unskilled labor. Similar notions can be referred to McCormick and Wahba (2000).[2] Sector 2 belongs to the unskilled-intensive industries, and the labor employed in that sector is protected by minimum wage law or receives the contractual wage rate. The situation prevails in developing countries (see Yabuuchi and Chaudhuri 2007). For example, the Chinese rural–urban migrants can neither enter the urban state-owned enterprises nor high-tech industries (see Li and Qian 2011).

The production functions of sector 1 and sector 2 are given by:

$$X_1 = F^1(L_{U1},\ K_1) \tag{5.1}$$

$$X_2 = F^2(L_{U2} + \bar{L}_{TR},\ K_2) \tag{5.2}$$

where X_1 and X_2 are the outputs of sector 1 and sector 2, respectively. L_{U1} and L_{U2} are the urban labor employed by sector 1 and sector 2, respectively. K_1 and K_2 are

[2]It is commonly seen in reality that if a technician cannot find a job in the tech-sector, and if he/she would like to find a job in the clean industry, the technician has to receive a wage rate as a common cleaner (the unskilled labor).

the capital utilized by sector 1 and sector 2, respectively. $\bar{L}_{TR}$ is the amount of the unskilled migrants. F^1 and F^2 are the strictly quasiconcave and linearly homogenous functions of sector 1 and sector 2, respectively.[3]

The profit maximization condition yields

$$pF_L^1 = w_S \tag{5.3}$$

$$F_L^2 = \bar{w}_U \tag{5.4}$$

$$pF_K^1 = r \tag{5.5}$$

$$F_K^2 = r \tag{5.6}$$

where $F_L^i = \partial F^i / \partial L \ (i = 1, 2)$ and $F_K^i = \partial F^i / \partial K \ (i = 1, 2)$. Here we normalize the price of the output of sector 2 into unit. p is the relative price of the output of sector 1 in terms of the output of sector 2. r is the interest rate. w_S is the wage rate of the skilled labor employed by sector 1. $\bar{w}_U$ is the wage rate of the unskilled labor used by sector 2, which satisfies $w_S > \bar{w}_U$.

The full employment condition of factor markets is shown as follows:

$$L_{U1} + L_{U2} = \bar{L}_U \tag{5.7}$$

$$K_1 + K_2 = \bar{K} \tag{5.8}$$

where $\bar{L}_U$ and $\bar{K}$ are the labor and capital endowments in the labor host region.

If we assume that a ($0< a <1$) represents the unskilled migrant remittance rate, that is, the unskilled migrant worker will send a proportional of his income back to the region where the migrant worker comes from, then we can get the total amount of the consumption expenditure of the labor host region, I, which is described as

$$I = w_S L_{U1} + \bar{w}_U L_{U2} + (1 - a)\bar{w}_U \bar{L}_{TR} + r\bar{K} \tag{5.9}$$

The assumed economy only produces two products. By virtue of Walras law that one good market clearing means the other product market will be cleared up, we know that the market-clearing condition can be demonstrated by:

$$D^1(p, I) = X_1 \tag{5.10}$$

where D^1 is the indirect demand of the output produced by sector 1 in our assumed economy. Now the basic model has been constructed. We have ten equations, from

[3]Generally speaking, the skilled labor-intensive sector (sector 1) has a higher per capita capital stock than that of the unskilled labor-intensive sector (sector 2). The per capita capital stock of the skilled labor-intensive sector (sector 1) has a threshold value. In this situation, it is not hard to see that there exists no corner solution of our established model (the skilled labor cannot be fully employed by sector 1).

Eqs. (5.1), (5.2), (5.3), (5.4), (5.5), (5.6), (5.7), (5.8), (5.9), and (5.10), which determine ten endogenous variables, X_1, X_2, L_{U1}, L_{U2}, K_1, K_2, p, r, w_S, and I. The exogenous variable is a.

3 Comparative Static Analysis

Analyzing the established economy system, we know that given the value of p, from Eqs. (5.1), (5.2), (5.3), (5.4), (5.5), (5.6), (5.7), and (5.8), we can solve for the equilibrium values of X_1, X_2, L_{U1}, L_{U2}, K_1, K_2, r, and w_S. Therefore, X_1, X_2, L_{U1}, L_{U2}, K_1, K_2, r, and w_S can be shown as the functions of p. From Eq. (5.9), we can know that I is also the function of p. Finally, we substitute I and X_1 into Eq. (5.10) and then solve for the value of p.

First, we build Lemma 5.1 to investigate the impact of an increase in the remittance of the unskilled migrant labor on the price of the output produced by sector 1.

Lemma 5.1 In our assumed economy, an increase in the remittance of the unskilled migrant labor will decrease the price of the output produced by sector 1.

Proof Total differentiation of Eq. (5.10) yields

$$\frac{dp}{da} = \frac{D_I^1 \bar{w}_U \bar{L}_{TR}}{D_p^1 + D_I^1 \frac{\partial I}{\partial p} - \frac{dX_1}{dp}}$$

where $D_p^1 = \frac{\partial D^1}{\partial p} < 0$ and $D_I^1 = \frac{\partial D^1}{\partial I} > 0$. The Walras price adjustment process can be established by the following excess demand function:

$$\dot{p} = D^1(p,\ I) - X_1(p)$$

where $\dot{p} = \frac{dp}{dt}$. It is necessary for us to get a stable solution of the established economic system when conducting the comparative static analysis. The above price adjustment process must satisfy the following condition to guarantee the existence of the equilibrium solutions:

$$D_p^1 + D_I^1 \frac{\partial I}{\partial p} - \frac{dX_1}{dp} < 0$$

Therefore, we can get $\frac{dp}{da} < 0$.

Q.E.D.

Then, we will investigate the impacts on the reallocation of production factors between two production sectors generated by an increase in the remittance of the unskilled migrant labor, which could be summarized by Lemma 5.2.

Lemma 5.2 In our assumed economy, if sector 1 is more capital-intensive than sector 2, an increase in the remittance of the unskilled migrant labor will increase the employment of the skilled labor and capital, as well as the output in sector 1. At the same time, the employment of the skilled labor and capital, as well as the output in sector 2, will decrease. If sector 1 is less capital-intensive than sector 2, an increase in the remittance of the unskilled migrant labor will reduce the employment of the skilled labor and capital, as well as the output in sector 1. At the same time, the employment of the skilled labor and capital, as well as the output in sector 2, will increase.

Proof Substitute Eqs. (5.6), (5.7), and (5.8) into Eqs. (5.4) and (5.5), and then total differentiation of Eqs. (5.4) and (5.5) yields

$$\begin{pmatrix} pF^1_{KL} + F^2_{KL} & pF^1_{KK} + F^2_{KK} \\ -F^2_{LL} & -F^2_{LK} \end{pmatrix} \begin{pmatrix} dL_{U1} \\ dK_1 \end{pmatrix} = \begin{pmatrix} -F^1_K \\ 0 \end{pmatrix} dp$$

The determinant of the coefficient matrix of the above equation system is denoted as Δ, and from the linearly homogenous features of F^2, we know

$$\Delta = -pF^1_{KL}F^2_{KL} + pF^1_{KK}F^2_{LL}$$

Because $-pF^1_{KL}F^2_{KL} < 0$ and $pF^1_{KK}F^2_{LL} > 0$, the sign of Δ is ambiguous. We denote that $k_1 = \frac{K_1}{L_{U1}}$ and $k_2 = \frac{K_2}{L_{U2}+L_{TR}}$, which represent the per capita amount of capital in sector 1 and sector 2, respectively. From the linearly homogenous features of F^1 and F^2, we know that if $k_1 > k_2$, $\Delta < 0$; if $k_1 < k_2$, $\Delta > 0$. We use Cramer's rule to solve the above equation system and get

$$\frac{dL_{U1}}{dp} = \frac{F^1_K F^2_{LK}}{\Delta}$$

$$\frac{dK_1}{dp} = \frac{-F^1_K F^2_{LL}}{\Delta}$$

If $k_1 > k_2$, we have $\frac{dL_{U1}}{dp} < 0$ and $\frac{dK_1}{dp} < 0$. From Eq. (5.1), we can get $\frac{dX_1}{dp} < 0$. From Eqs. (5.7) and (5.8), we know $\frac{dL_{U2}}{dp} > 0$ and $\frac{dK_2}{dp} > 0$. From Eq. (5.2), $\frac{dX_2}{dp} > 0$ is achieved. Combining with the proof of Lemma 5.1, we have that if $k_1 > k_2$, then $\frac{dL_{U1}}{da} > 0$, $\frac{dK_1}{da} > 0$, $\frac{dL_{U2}}{da} < 0$, $\frac{dK_2}{da} < 0$, $\frac{dX_1}{da} > 0$, and $\frac{dX_2}{da} < 0$, which is demonstrated by the previous part of Lemma 5.2.

If $k_1 < k_2$, we have $\frac{dL_{U1}}{dp} > 0$ and $\frac{dK_1}{dp} > 0$. From Eq. (5.1), we can get $\frac{dX_1}{dp} > 0$. From Eqs. (5.7) and (5.8), we have $\frac{dL_{U2}}{dp} < 0$ and $\frac{dK_2}{dp} < 0$. From Eq. (5.2), we have $\frac{dX_2}{dp} < 0$.

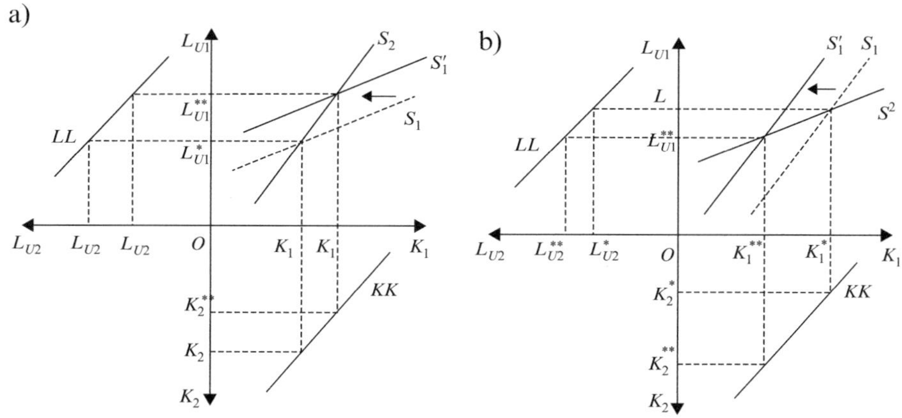

Fig. 5.1 Economic mechanism of Lemma 5.2

Combining with the proof of Lemma 5.1, we have that if $k_1 > k_2$, then $\frac{dL_{U1}}{dp} < 0$, $\frac{dK_1}{dp} < 0, \frac{dL_{U2}}{dp} > 0, \frac{dK_2}{dp} > 0, \frac{dX_1}{dp} < 0$, and $\frac{dX_2}{dp} > 0$, which is described by the latter part of Lemma 5.2.

Q.E.D.

Lemma 5.2 can be also illustrated by Fig. 5.1. O is the original point. The left half the horizontal axis is L_{U2}, and its right half represents K_1. The upper half of the vertical axis is L_{U1}, and the lower half of the vertical axis is K_2. Substituting Eqs. (5.6), (5.7), and (5.8) into Eqs. (5.4) and (5.5), we can get the following rearrangement of Eqs. (5.4) and (5.5):

$$F_L^2(\bar{L}_U + \bar{L}_{TR} - L_{U1}, \bar{K} - K_1) = \bar{w}_U$$
$$pF_K^1(L_{U1}, K_1) = F_K^2(\bar{L}_U + \bar{L}_{TR} - L_{U1}, \bar{K} - K_1)$$

In the first quadrant of Fig. 5.1, we use line S_1 and line S_2 to represent the relation between L_{U1} and K_1 depicted in Eqs. (5.4) and (5.5), respectively. It is easy to verify that L_{U1} and K_1 move in the same direction. In the second quadrant of Fig. 5.1, line LL shows the relation between L_{U1} and L_{U2} in Eq. (5.7). In the fourth quadrant of Fig. 5.1, line KK describes the relation between K_1 and K_2 given by Eq. (5.8). Without generality, we assume the initial equilibrium values of L_{U1}, L_{U2}, K_1, and K_2 are L_{U1}^*, L_{U2}^*, K_1^*, and K_2^*, respectively.

If $k_1 > k_2$, after analyzing equations $pF_K^1(L_{U1}, K_1) = F_K^2(\bar{L}_U + \bar{L}_{TR} - L_{U1}, \bar{K} - K_1)$ and $F_L^2(\bar{L}_U + \bar{L}_{TR} - L_{U1}, \bar{K} - K_1) = \bar{w}_U$, we can get that the location of line S_1 and line S_2 in the first quadrant of Fig. 5.1 can be described by Fig. 5.1 (a). In this situation, the slope of line S_1 is less steady than that of line S_2. When the unskilled migrant labor increases the remittance, from Lemma 5.1 we know that p will decrease. According to $pF_K^1(L_{U1}, K_1) = F_K^2(\bar{L}_U + \bar{L}_{TR} - L_{U1}, \bar{K} - K_1)$, we can get that line S_1 will shift leftward to S_1'. In this situation, it can be directly obtained from Fig. 5.1 (a) that L_{U1}^* will increase to L_{U1}^{**} and K_1^* will increase to K_1^{**}. From line LL and line KK, we know that L_{U2}^* will decrease to L_{U2}^{**} and K_2^* will reduce toK_2^{**}.

If $k_1 < k_2$, after analyzing equations $pF_K^1(L_{U1}, K_1) = F_K^2(\bar{L}_U + \bar{L}_{TR} - L_{U1}, \bar{K} - K_1)$ and $F_L^2(\bar{L}_U + \bar{L}_{TR} - L_{U1}, \bar{K} - K_1) = \bar{w}_U$, we can get that the location of line S_1 and line S_2 in the first quadrant of Fig. 5.1 can be described by Fig. 5.1 (a). In this situation, the slope of line S_1 is more steady than that of line S_2. When the unskilled migrant labor increases the remittance, from Lemma 5.1 we know that p will decrease. According to $pF_K^1(L_{U1}, K_1) = F_K^2(\bar{L}_U + \bar{L}_{TR} - L_{U1}, \bar{K} - K_1)$, we can get that line S_1 will shift leftward to S_1'. In this situation, it can be directly obtained from Fig. 5.1 (a) that L_{U1}^* will decrease to L_{U1}^{**} and K_1^* will decrease to K_1^{**}. From line LL and line KK, we know that L_{U2}^* will increase to L_{U2}^{**} and K_2^* will increase to K_2^{**}.

In our assumed economy, if sector 1 employs the skilled labor, sector 1 should be capital-intensive. Thus, the former part of Lemma 5.2 is more in accordance with our assumptions. Therefore, the unskilled labor increasing the remittance rate will raise the labor and capital employment, as well as the output, in sector 1. At the same time, the unskilled labor increasing the remittance rate will reduce the labor and capital employment, as well as the output, in sector 2. Such result will lead to a reduction of the output in sector 2 and an increase in that of sector 1. However, according to Lemma 5.1, the unskilled labor increasing the remittance rate will decrease the price level of its output, and the enterprises in sector must decrease the output in order to maintain the original price. This runs in contrast to the former part of Lemma 5.2. Therefore, what is the relation between an increase in the production factor employment and a reduction of the price level?

Now, on the basis of Lemma 5.1 and Lemma 5.2, we will turn attention to the analysis that how an increase in the remittance of the unskilled migrant labor influences the skilled–unskilled wage inequality in the labor host region.

Proposition In our assumed economy, an increase in the remittance of the unskilled migrant labor will narrow down the skilled–unskilled wage inequality in the labor host region.

Proof Total differentiation of Eq. (5.3) yields

$$\frac{dw_S}{dp} = pF_{LL}^1 \frac{dL_{U1}}{dp} + pF_{LK}^1 \frac{dK_1}{dp} + F_L^1$$

If $k_1 > k_2$, from the proof of Lemma 5.2, we substitute the values of $\frac{dL_{U1}}{dp}$ and $\frac{dK_1}{dp}$ into the above equation and get

$$\frac{dw_S}{dp} = k_1 F_K^1 + F_L^1 > 0$$

If $k_1 < k_2$, from the proof of Lemma 5.2, we substitute the values of $\frac{dL_{U1}}{dp}$ and $\frac{dK_1}{dp}$ into the above equation and also get

$$\frac{dw_S}{dp} = k_1 F_K^1 + F_L^1 > 0$$

Thus, we can conclude $\frac{dw_S}{da} < 0$. At the same, we can also find that the impact exerted by an increase in the remittance of the unskilled migrant labor on the skilled–unskilled wage gap in the labor host region is irrelevant to the factor intensity of the production sectors in the labor host region.

Q.E.D.

The migrant remittance comes from the wages of unskilled labor working for the urban sector. When the unskilled labor increases the migrant remittance rate, they will reduce their consumption in the labor host regions. Generally, the unskilled labor will both reduce the consumption of the product produced by sector 2 and that by sector 1. According to the analysis of Lemma 5.2, the output in sector 1 increases. In order to avoid the reduction of the consumption of the output produced by sector 1, decreasing the price is a reasonable choice for sector 1. This explains the establishment of Lemma 5.1 and Lemma 5.2. Especially for sector 1, on the condition of the increases in the output, the labor, and capital employment, firms in sector 1 will decrease the employee's wage rate to obtain the profit. On the other hand, the wage rate of sector 2 is protected by the minimum wage law and downward rigid. Therefore, only sector 1 decreases its employee's wage rate, the consequence of which is the reduction of the skilled–unskilled wage gap.

4 Concluding Remarks

The present paper establishes a two-sector general equilibrium model and conducts the comparative static approach to investigate the impact exerted by an increase in the remittance of the unskilled migrants on the skilled–unskilled wage inequality in the labor host region. We find that the unskilled migrants increase their remittances to the labor-outsourcing regions that will decrease the skilled–unskilled wage inequality in the labor host region. In developing countries, a reduction of the skilled–unskilled wage inequality has both the political and economic significance. Although guiding the unskilled labor increasing their remittance rate may decrease the liquidity of the labor host regions, the unskilled labor increasing their remittance rate also has the positive impact. Especially for discussing the regional economy, the government guiding the unskilled labor increasing their remittance rate will not only benefit the labor-outsourcing regions but also contribute to the labor host regions, which is the economic development.

A reduction of the skilled–unskilled wage inequality in the labor host regions doesn't necessarily show the positive impact exerted by an increase in the migrant remittance rate. The labor host regions should also pay attention to the accompanied increase in the migrant remittance rate, which kills two birds with one stone.

In this chapter, we just investigate the impact exerted by an increase in the remittance of the unskilled migrants on the skilled–unskilled wage inequality in the framework of a closed urban economy, rather than an open economy. Taking an open economy into account is a potential extension of the present paper. Obviously, introducing a third sector producing the non-traded intermediate input for sector 2 in our established model and investigating its wage inequality impacts are also a good avenue for future research.

It should be pointed out that this chapter is particularly meaningful for the Asian developing countries. This is because many Asian developing countries, such as Vietnam, Thailand, India, and Indonesia, have massive internal immigrants, as well as wage gap between skilled and unskilled labor, affecting economic development. This chapter may help to formulate suitable economic policy, which cannot only encourage unskilled workers' remittances but also reduce the wage gap, achieving fair economic effects.

References

Anwar, S. (2006). Factor mobility and wage inequality in the presence of specialization- based external economies. *Economics Letters, 93*(1), 88–93.

Anwar, S., & Rice, J. (2009). Labour mobility and wage inequality in the presence of endogenous foreign investment. *Economic Modelling, 26*(6), 1135–1139.

Banga, R. (2005, March). Liberalisation and wage inequality in India (ICRIER Working Paper, Vol. 156).

Beladi, H., Chaudhuri, S., & Yabuuchi, S. (2008). Can international factor mobility reduce wage rate inequality in a dual economy? *Review of International Economics, 16*(5), 893–903.

Chaudhuri, S. (2004). International migration of skilled and unskilled labour, welfare and skilled–unskilled wage inequality: A simple model. *Journal of Economic Integration, 19*(4), 726–741.

Chaudhuri, S. (2008). Wage inequality in a dual economy and international mobility of factors: Do factor intensities always matter? *Economic Modelling, 25*, 1155–1164.

Chaudhuri, S., & Yabuuchi, S. (2007). Economic liberalization and wage inequality in the presence of labor market imperfection. *International Review of Economics and Finance, 16* (4), 592–603.

Chen, E. (2006). *Domestic money transfer services for migrant workers in China – A report to CGAP*. http://www.bwtp.org/asiamicrofinanee

Cox, E. A., & Ureta, M. (2003). International migration, remittances and schooling: Evidence from El Salvador. *Journal of Development Economics, 72*, 429–461.

Cox, D., Eser, Z., & Jimenez, E. (1998). Motives for private transfers over the life cycle: An analytical framework and evidence for Peru. *Journal of Development Economics, 55*, 57–80.

Djajic, S. (1986). International migration, remittance and welfare in a development economy. *Journal of Development Economics, 21*, 229–234.

Djajic, S. (1998). Emigration and welfare in an economy with foreign capital. *Journal of Development Economics, 56*, 433–445.

Fang, C., Huang, L., & Wang, M. (2008). Technology spillover and wage inequality. *Economic Modelling, 25*(1), 137–147.

Feenstra, R. C., & Hanson, G. H. (1996). Foreign investment, outsourcing and relative wages. In F. Robert, G. Gene, & I. Douglas (Eds.), *Political economy of trade policies: Essays in honor of Jagdish N. Bhagwati*. Cambridge, MA: MIT Press.

Feenstra, R. C., & Hanson, G. H. (2003). Global production sharing and rising wage inequality: A survey of trade and wages. In E. K. Choi & J. Harrigan (Eds.), *Handbook of international trade*. London: Basil Blackwell.

Glytsos, N. P. (2002). The role of migrant remittances in development: Evidence from Mediterranean countries. *International Migration, 40*(1), 5–25.

Kirwan, F., & Holden, D. (1986). Emigrants remittance, non-traded goods and economic welfare in the source country. *Journal of Economic Studies, 13*(2), 52–58.

Lall, S. V., Selod, H., & Shalizi, Z. (2006). *Rural–urban migration in developing countries, World Bank policy research working paper 3915*. Washington, DC: The World Bank.

Lawrence, R. Z. (1994). *Trade, multinationals, and labor, NBER Working Paper 4836*. Cambridge, MA: National Bureau of Economic Research.

Li, X., & Qian, X. (2011). Economic analysis on the urban–rural disparity in human capital in CHINA. *South African Journal of Economics, 79*(2), 146–160.

Lucas, R. E. B. (2005). *International migration and economic development. Expert group on development issues*. Stockholm: Swedish Ministry for Foreign Affairs.

Lundahl, M. (1985). International migration, remittance and real incomes: Effects on the source country. *The Scandinavian Journal of Economics, 87*(4), 647–657.

Marjit, S., & Kar, S. (2005). Emigration and wage inequality. *Economics Letters, 88*(1), 141–145.

Marjit, S., Beladi, H., & Chakrabarti, A. (2004). Trade and wage inequality in developing countries. *Economic Inquiry, 42*, 295–303.

McCormick, B., & Wahba, J. (2000). Overseas employment and remittances to a dual economy. *The Economic Journal, 110*(463), 509–534.

Moore, M., & Ranjan, P. (2005). Globalization vs. skill biased technical change: Implications for unemployment and wage inequality. *The Economic Journal, 115*(503), 391–422.

Quibria, M. G. (1997). International migration, remittance and income distribution in the source country: A synthesis. *Bulletin of Economic Research, 49*(1), 29–46.

Rivera-Batiz, F. (1986). International migration, remittance and economic welfare in the source country. *Journal of Economic Studies, 13*(3), 3–19.

Rodriguez, E. R. (1996). International migrants' remittances in the Philippines. *Canadian Journal of Economics, 29*(2), 427–432.

Taylor, J. E., & Wyatt, T. J. (1996). The shadow value of migrant remittances, income and inequality in a household-farm economy. *Journal of Development Studies, 32*(6), 899–912.

Wood, A. (1997). Openness and wage inequality in developing countries: The Latin American challenge to East Asian conventional wisdom. *World Bank Economic Review, 11*(1), 33–57.

World Bank. (2001). *World tables*. Washington, DC: The World Bank.

Yabuuchi, S., & Chadhuri, S. (2009). Skill formation, capital adjustment cost and wage inequality. *Review of Urban and Regional Development Studies, 21*(1), 2–13.

Yabuuchi, S., & Chaudhuri, S. (2007). International migration of labor and skilled–unskilled wage inequality in a developing economy. *Economic Modelling, 24*(1), 128–137.
Yuanqian, L. (2010). Detailed information can be referred to http://www.npc.gov.cn/npc/xinwen/rdlt/sd/201003/16/content_1564113.htm
Zhao, Z. (2005). Migration, labor market flexibility, and wage determination in China: A review. *The Developing Economies, 43*(2), 285–312.

Chapter 6
The Impacts of Rural–Urban Migrants' Remittances on the Urban Economy

Xiaochun Li and Dianshuang Wang

Abstract Much literature finds that migrants' remittances have positive effects on the labor-outsourcing region; however, it should be noted that the massive funds outflow from the labor host region poses an impact on that region as well. Moreover, the existing literature sheds little light on the theoretical study of remittances within one economy. This article theoretically analyzes the economic impact of migrants' remittances on the labor host region, the urban region, and establishes a three-sector general equilibrium model to investigate the impacts of an increase in remittances on wage, employment, and welfare level in the urban region from the short- and long-term perspectives. We find that an increase in remittances will reduce the output of the informal sector and decrease urban residents' welfare in the short term, while it will increase the output of the informal sector and promote urban residents' welfare in the long term.

Keywords Remittances • Labor migration • Urban welfare • Economic impact

1 Introduction

The majority of migrants move from developing to developed countries internationally, or intercountry migrants move from rural to urban regions within developing countries, while remittances flow in the opposite way. Previous academic studies, particularly empirical research, on migrants' remittances concentrated on the economic contribution of remittances to the labor-outsourcing countries or rural regions. Theoretical research has been sparse compared to empirical research in the area. Among the existing theoretical studies, Lundahl (1985) and Djajic (1986) assume that remittances are used for consumption purposes in the labor-outsourcing countries and construct a two-by-two theoretical model to analyze the impacts of remittances on economic development and welfare level. The former finds that the

X. Li (✉)
Business School, Nanjing University, Nanjing, China
e-mail: xiaochun@nju.edu.cn

D. Wang
School of Economics, Nanjing University, 22 Hankou Road, Nanjing, Jiangsu 210093, China

X. Li (ed.), *Labor Transfer in Emerging Economies*, New Frontiers in Regional Science: Asian Perspectives 12, DOI 10.1007/978-981-10-3569-2_6

share of income migrants remit back home affects nonmigrants' gain. The latter shows that if the flow of remittances exceeds a certain critical amount, the remaining residents benefit from migration, even if they do not receive any of the remittances themselves. Kirwan and Holden (1986) assume that the remittances are used solely for consumption and consider the impact of the magnitude of remittances on the welfare of the labor-outsourcing region. Within this framework, the welfare effect of emigration is indeterminate, depending on the magnitude of remittances. Welfare will fall where remittances merely maintain source country nominal income at its pre-emigration level. Where remittances are sufficiently large, they can compensate for the emigration-induced disruption of internal trade in internationally non-traded goods. Rivera-Batiz (1986) examines the impact of remittances of the temporary and permanent migrants on changes in prices, income distribution, and social welfare in the source country. Remittances reinforce the following impacts: emigration tends to raise home (non-traded) goods prices, and emigration turns income distribution in favor of labor and against capital. Quibria (1997) discusses the impact of remittances on welfare of different social classes within the source country. It is shown that pure emigration can be beneficial to the non-emigrants in the source country, irrespective of the welfare criteria adopted, if accompanied by sufficient remittances. Djajic (1998) integrates foreign capital into his analytical framework and examines the welfare implications of remittances when they flow back to the source country and are used to finance consumption and manufacturing. The study concludes that when foreign capital is present in the economy, remittance-financed capital accumulation by returning emigrants in the source country necessarily improves the welfare of the remaining residents. In contrast, remittance-financed consumption of the returning migrants may be beneficial or detrimental to the remaining residents, depending on relative factor intensities of traded and non-traded goods. It is worth noting that Li and Zhou (2013) shift their focus to the labor host region. They establish a two-sector general equilibrium model to investigate the impact of remittances of the unskilled migrants on the skilled and unskilled wage inequality. They find that if the unskilled migrants increase their remittance rate to the labor-outsourcing regions, then the skilled–unskilled wage inequality in the labor host region decreases.

On the other hand, there is a strand of the Harris–Todaro literature that considers the urban economy. Previous research concentrates on aspects such as urban output, unemployment and welfare, etc. Typical studies include Gupta (1997), Yabuuchi and Beladi (2001), Chaudhuri (2007), and Kar and Marjit (2001). Though the above research discusses effects of various factors on the urban economy during the movement of labor, they do not incorporate migrants' remittance. For example, Gupta (1997) considers a Harris–Todaro framework, with special consideration to the urban informal sector, to investigate policy effects in this economy and conclude that an increase in formal sector prices would decrease the wage rate in the informal sector, raise the interest rate of formal sector, and lower the unemployment rate. Yabuuchi and Beladi (2001) analyze the effects of wage subsidy policies on unemployment and welfare in a model that is characterized by the existence of both open unemployment and the informal sector that produces final goods. They conclude that wage subsidies to the agricultural and informal sectors increase welfare and decrease urban unemployment. The effects of a wage subsidy in the manufacturing sector on welfare and unemployment are conditional. Chaudhuri (2007) establishes a three-sector Harris–Todaro model with agricultural dualism and a non-traded final commodity. In the given setup, an inflow of foreign capital is likely to improve welfare and does not necessarily worsen the problem of unemployment.

As mentioned above, we make the following two comments on existing research: first, most of the existing theoretical research focuses on the impacts of remittances on the labor-outsourcing region (developing countries or rural regions). However, we should also note their impacts on the labor host region (developed countries or urban regions) when massive funds flow out from that region. Second, theoretical research sheds little light on the impact of migrants' remittance on labor in the urban region within one economy. Though Li and Zhou (2013) investigate the impact exerted by an increase in the remittance rate of the unskilled migrants within one economy, their research is limited to wage inequality and fails to address the impact of remittances on the urban region. Therefore, the economic impact of remittances on the urban region is not clear.

Though current theoretical research analyzing migrants' remittances within developing countries is rare, this economic phenomenon cannot be ignored in the developing economy. Emerging economies, like China and India, experience the most extensive internal migration today. According to national statistics, by the end of 2013, China had a total of 269 million rural migrant workers.[1] However, rural people in urban labor markets are generally relegated to dirty, dangerous, and poorly paid occupations that offer few prospects for advancement to more comfortable and stable working and living conditions. Because of the precarious living and working conditions, most migrants leave their family members, especially children, in the villages. Indeed, in 2013, only 13% of the rural–urban migration was family migration. In such circumstances the migrants commonly perceive their stay in the city as temporary. Many migrants, therefore, remit sizeable amounts of money. According to national statistics and by the authors' estimation, remittances reached nearly 1 trillion RMB (around 160 billion US dollar) in 2013. With the development of China's economy and the growing number of migrant workers, the flow of remittances to the rural region is expected to accelerate, and these remittances play an increasingly important role in China's economy. Similarly, internal migrants in India constitute a large population: 309 million internal migrants or 30% of the population (Census of India 2001) and by more recent estimates 326 million or 28.5% of the population (NSSO 2007–2008). The domestic remittance market was estimated to be $10 billion in 2007–2008, 80% directed toward rural households (Tumbe 2011). With rising incomes, huge migrant remittances can encourage the development of labor-outsourcing regions, and there are reasons to think that such remittances have influences on labor host regions.

[1]Source: http://www.stats.gov.cn/tjsj/zxfb/201405/t20140512_551585.html

This chapter builds a theoretical framework to address the relative economic issues of the urban region and establishes a three-sector general equilibrium model to investigate the impacts of an increase in remittances on wage, employment, and welfare level in the urban region from the short-term and long-term perspectives (in order to express the remittance within one economy, which is the subject of this chapter, we define "migrants' remittance" as "rural–urban migrants' remittance" or "remittance" for short). We find that an increase in remittances will reduce the output of the informal sector and decrease urban residents' welfare in the short term, while it will increase the output of the informal sector and promote urban residents' welfare in the long term. In the following, we will establish a theoretical model in the second section, present a theoretical analysis in the third section, and state conclusions in the last section.

2 The Theoretical Model

This article uses a model of the economy with conditions similar to the traditional three-sector Harris–Todaro model, that is, a small, open, developing economy with three sectors: urban formal sector, urban informal sector, and agricultural sector. We begin by examining the short term, when capital is sector specific. The urban informal sector refers to the urban small service sector. The informal sector employees provide domestic services to urban residents. Included in this sector are newsstand owners, street vendors, shoeshine boys, and so forth. The economy uses two factors of production, labor, and capital, and factors do not move internationally. The urban formal sector employs labor L_1 and sector-specific capital K_1 to produce tradable goods X_1. The urban informal sector only uses labor L_2 to produce non-tradable goods X_2, which are totally consumed by people living in the urban area. The agricultural sector produces tradable agricultural commodity X_3 using labor L_3 and sector-specific capital K_3. The production functions of the formal, informal, and agricultural sector are given by

$$X_1 = F^1(L_1, K_1) \tag{6.1}$$

$$X_2 = F^2(L_2) \tag{6.2}$$

$$X_3 = k(\beta)F^3(L_3, K_3) \tag{6.3}$$

where F^1, F^2, and F^3 are production functions increasing with each factor, satisfying linear homogeneity, and are strictly quasi-concave. k is a parameter expressing the impact of remittances on the agriculture sector. We assume that k is a diminishing rate of growth function of the amount of remittances. Expressed mathematically $k = k(\beta)$, $k(0) = 1$, $k'(\beta) > 0$, and $k''(\beta) < 0$. β is a parameter expressing the amount of remittances sent by rural–urban migrants working in the urban formal sector.

Under the condition that the market is perfectly competitive, we could obtain the following:

$$p_1 = a_{L1}\bar{w} + a_{K1}r_1 \tag{6.4}$$

$$p_2 = a_{L2}w_2 \tag{6.5}$$

$$k(\beta) = a_{L3}w_3 + a_{K3}r_3 \tag{6.6}$$

where $a_{ij}(i = L, K; j = 1, 2)$ represents factor i used in producing one unit of goods in the jth sector and a_{i3} ($i = L, K$) represents factor i used in producing one unit of goods (without remittance effect) in agricultural sector (e.g., $a_{K3} = K_3/F^3$). $\bar{w}$ is the wage rate of the urban formal sector, which is downward rigid due to labor unions. w_2 is the wage rate of labor in the informal sector, which is fully elastic. w_3 is the elastic wage rate of labor in the agricultural sector. r_1 and r_3 are the interest rates of capital in the formal sector and agricultural sector, respectively. We normalize the price of the agricultural product as the unit. p_1 and p_2 are the price of the formal sector and informal sector goods relative to that of agriculture goods. p_1 is assumed to be given and constant in a small open economy.

We assume that an urban resident who fails to find a formal sector job takes up informal sector employment.

Informal goods market-clearing condition can be demonstrated by

$$p_2X_2 - g(p_1X_1 + p_2X_2 - \beta) = 0 \tag{6.7}$$

where p_1X_1 and p_2X_2 represent the gross product in the formal sector and informal sector, which equal the total income of workers in the two sectors. The urban residents (including rural–urban migrants) will spend g ($0 < g < 1$) of their income on consumption of informal output, and g is urban residents' average propensity to consume informal sector goods.

According to the Harris–Todaro model, the allocation mechanism between sectors can be shown as

$$w_3 = \frac{a_{L1}X_1}{a_{L1}X_1 + a_{L2}X_2}\bar{w} + \frac{a_{L2}X_2}{a_{L1}X_1 + a_{L2}X_2}w_2 \tag{6.8}$$

From Eq. (6.8), the wage rate of the informal sector is lower than that of the agricultural sector. Migrant workers choose to work in the urban informal sector because then there is a better chance of finding a formal sector job than there would have been from working in the agricultural sector. This has been pointed out by Li and Qian (2011). Due to the low wage, we assume that the migrants working in the informal sector do not send money back. The market-clearing conditions of the three factors, namely, labor, formal sector capital, and agricultural sector capital, could be shown as follows:

$$a_{L1}X_1 + a_{L2}X_2 + a_{L3}F^3 = L \tag{6.9}$$

$$a_{K1}X_1 = K_1 \tag{6.10}$$

$$a_{K3}F^3 = K_3 \tag{6.11}$$

where L, K_1, and K_3 represent the endowment of labor, formal sector-specific capital, and agricultural sector-specific capital, respectively.

β is an endogenous variable in the paper, and it is obvious that $\beta < p_1X_1$. Furthermore, β is the amount of remittances sent from urban formal sector to rural region exactly. In China, family of the rural–urban migrants accounts for over 80% of total rural family[2]; according to Hu and Wang (2007), rural–urban migrants' remittances take up 65% of their household income, with most of the remainder shared by agricultural income and other nonagricultural income, and the share of remittances sent by nonmigrants should be very low; thus, the overwhelming majority of remittance outflow from urban to rural area is sent by rural–urban migrants. In India, migrants' remittances accounted for over 81% of remittance outflow from urban to rural area.[3] Therefore, the main attribute of β is rural–urban migrants' remittances. The basic theoretical model thus consists of eight equations: (6.4), (6.5), (6.6), (6.7), (6.8), (6.9), (6.10), and (6.11). Eight endogenous variables are determined: w_2, w_3, r_1, r_3, X_1, X_2, X_3, and p_2.

3 Comparative Statics

3.1 The Economic Impact of an Increase in Remittances in the Short Run

We assume that there are no changes of price in the international market and factor endowments in the short term. An increase in remittances will have no impact on the urban formal sector due to the downward rigid wage rate and specific capital. Differentiating Eqs. (6.4), (6.5), (6.6), (6.7), (6.8), (6.9), (6.10), and (6.11) and writing in a matrix notation, we can obtain the following equation:

$$\begin{pmatrix} 0 & \theta_{L3} & \theta_{K3} & 0 & 0 \\ F & 0 & 0 & F & 0 \\ B & C & 0 & D & 0 \\ \frac{L_2}{L_3}S^2_{LL} & S^3_{LL} & S^3_{LK} & \frac{L_2}{L_3} & 1 \\ 0 & S^3_{KL} & S^3_{KK} & 0 & 1 \end{pmatrix} \begin{pmatrix} \widehat{w}_2 \\ \widehat{w}_3 \\ \widehat{r}_3 \\ \widehat{X}_2 \\ \widehat{X}_3 \end{pmatrix} = \begin{pmatrix} A \\ -g\beta \\ 0 \\ A \\ A \end{pmatrix} \widehat{\beta} \tag{6.12}$$

[2]Data source: http://finance.sina.com.cn/money/lccircle/20060329/11092457244.shtml

[3]Calculation by authors according to estimated data in Tumbe (2011).

where "$\widehat{\ }$" represents the rate of change, S_{ij}^{h} is the partial elasticity of substitution between factors i and j in the hth sector (e.g., $S_{KL}^{3}=\frac{\vartheta a_{K3}}{\vartheta w_3}\frac{w_3}{a_{K3}}$), $S_{ij}^{h}>0(i\neq j)$ and $S_{ij}^{h}<0(i=j)$, $i=L, K$, and $j=1, 2, 3$. We also have $\theta_{K3}=a_{K3}r_3/k$, $\theta_{L3}=a_{L3}w_3/k$, $A=\frac{k'\beta}{k}>0$, $B=L_2\left[(w_3-w_2)S_{LL}^{2}-w_2\right]<0$, $C=(L_1+L_2)w_3>0$, $D=L_2(w_3-w_2)>0$, and $F=g(p_1X_1-\beta)>0$.

Define the determinant of the matrix in Eq. (6.12) as Δ, and calculate Δ to obtain

$$\Delta=F\left\{\theta_{K3}\left[(B-D)\left(S_{LL}^{3}-S_{KL}^{3}\right)-C\frac{L_2}{L_3}\left(S_{LL}^{2}-1\right)\right]+\theta_{L3}\left(S_{LK}^{3}-S_{KK}^{3}\right)(D-B)\right\}$$
$$>0$$

By Cramer's rule with respect to $\widehat{\beta}$ from Eq. (6.12), we get following results:

$$\Delta\frac{\widehat{X}_2}{\widehat{\beta}}=ACF\left(S_{KK}^{3}-S_{LK}^{3}\right)-g\beta B\left[\theta_{L3}\left(S_{KK}^{3}-S_{LK}^{3}\right)-\theta_{K3}\left(S_{KL}^{3}-S_{LL}^{3}\right)\right]$$
$$+\theta_{K3}g\beta CS_{LL}^{2}\frac{L_2}{L_3}<0$$

Since the only input factor is labor in the urban informal sector, we also obtained the following results:

$$\frac{\widehat{w}_2}{\widehat{\beta}}>0,\ \frac{\widehat{p}_2}{\widehat{\beta}}>0$$

We can also get the following results by solving Eq. (6.12):

$$\Delta\frac{\widehat{X}_3}{\widehat{\beta}}=AF(D-B)\left[\theta_{L3}\left(S_{LK}^{3}-S_{KK}^{3}\right)+\theta_{K3}\left(S_{KL}^{3}-S_{LL}^{3}\right)\right]$$
$$+AFC\frac{L_2}{L_3}\left(S_{LL}^{2}-1\right)\left(S_{KK}^{3}-\theta_{K3}\right)+\left(\theta_{L3}S_{KK}^{3}-\theta_{K3}S_{KL}^{3}\right)g\beta\frac{L_2}{L_3}\left(B-DS_{LL}^{2}\right)$$
$$>0$$

$$\Delta\frac{\widehat{r}_3}{\widehat{\beta}}=AF\left[C\frac{L_2}{L_3}\left(1-S_{LL}^{2}\right)+(B-D)\left(S_{LL}^{3}-S_{KL}^{3}\right)\right]-\theta_{L3}g\beta\frac{L_2}{L_3}\left(B-DS_{LL}^{2}\right)>0$$

The above results are summarized as Proposition 6.1.

Proposition 6.1 An increase in remittances will not change the amount of labor employed by the formal sector and the interest rate of that sector but will generate the following impacts:

Fig. 6.1 Economic impacts of an increase in remittances

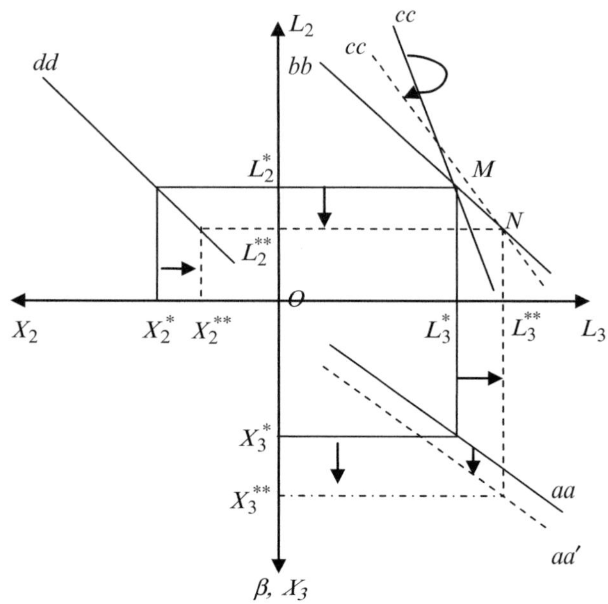

1. The output of the informal sector and the amount of labor employed by that sector will decrease. The wage rate of the informal sector as well as goods price will increase.
2. The output of the agricultural sector and the interest rate of capital in that sector will increase.

In the short term, capital is sector specific. As shown in the established model, production in the urban formal sector is an independent subsystem, irrelevant to other economic activities. Therefore, an increase in remittances does not affect the formal sector. An increase in remittances generates part of the urban funds outflow to the rural area. As a result, the demand for the urban sectors' goods falls, which reduces the incentive of the enterprises in that sector, resulting in a decline of output of the informal sector. Since the only input factor is labor in the urban informal sector, the decline of output of informal sector produces two results: the wage rate of the informal sector and the amount of labor employed will be decreased.

Since the wage of the informal sector is the lowest among the three sectors, it is difficult to reduce the wage further; therefore, reducing the amount of labor employed will be the first choice by the informal sector. As a consequence, the marginal productivity of labor will be increased in the informal sector, which leads to an increase of the wage as well as price. On the other hand, due to an increase in remittances from urban region, production condition in the rural area improves, which attracts labor in informal sectors to migrate back to the rural area, causing the employment of agricultural sector to rise. Given that capital is sector specific to agricultural sector, the output of that sector and the interest rate will increase.

The partial economic impacts of Proposition 6.1 could be illustrated by Fig. 6.1. O is the original point in Fig. 6.1. The left half of the horizontal axis is the output of informal sector (X_2), and its right half represents the amount of employment by agricultural sector (L_3). The upper half of the vertical axis is the amount of employment by informal sector, and the lower half of the vertical axis is the remittances and the output of agricultural sector. We use line *bb* and line *cc* to represent the relation between L_3 and L_2, line *aa* to represent the relation between L_3 and X_3, and line *dd* to represent the relation between L_2 and X_2, respectively.

From Eq. (6.3), it is easy to verify that L_3 and X_3 move in the same direction because capital is specific in the short term. Seeing that an increase in remittances does not affect the employment of formal sector, we could obtain that the slope of line *bb* is -1 from Eq. (6.9). In the second quadrant of Fig. 6.1, line *cc* shows the relation between L_3 and L_2 in Eq. (6.8), and the slope of line *cc* is less steady than that of line *bb*. Line *dd* describes the relation between X_2 and L_2 given by Eq. (6.2). The initial equilibrium values of L_3, L_2, and X_2 are L_3^*, L_2^*, and X_2^*, respectively. When remittances are rising, we obtain that line *aa* shifts downward to *aa'* according to Eq. (6.3). In this situation, it can be obtained that the output of the agricultural sector will increase to X_3^{**} and the employment of that sector will increase to L_3^{**}. While the line *bb* does not change, the slope of line *cc* would become less steady and shift rightward due to an increase in remittances, which is shown by a move from line *cc* to line *cc'* eventually (intersection point from *M* to *N*). Thus, in the new equilibrium, the amount of and the output of informal sector decreases to L_2^{**} and X_2^{**}, respectively.

An increase in the remittances will change the welfare of urban residents. Next, we examine the changes from remittances on urban residents' welfare. For urban residents, they consume goods of the formal sector, informal sector, and agricultural sector. The minimum expenditure function of urban residents is given by $E(p_1, p_2, 1, U)$ and their income $\bar{w}L_1 + Kr + w_2L_2 - \beta$. Income–expenditure equilibrium of urban residents is given by

$$E(p_1, p_2, 1, U) = \bar{w}L_1 + K_1r_1 + w_2L_2 - \beta \tag{6.13}$$

where U is the urban residents' social utility. To analyze the welfare implication of remittances, totally differentiating Eq. (6.13), we could obtain the following by solving Eq. (6.12):

$$\begin{aligned}
\Delta E_U U\frac{\widehat{U}}{\widehat{\beta}} &= \Delta w_2 L_2\left(\frac{\widehat{X}_2}{\widehat{\beta}} + \frac{\widehat{w}_2}{\widehat{\beta}} + S_{LL}^2\frac{\widehat{w}_2}{\widehat{\beta}}\right) - \Delta E_{p_2}p_2\frac{\widehat{p}_2}{\widehat{\beta}} - \Delta\beta \\
&= \beta g(B-D)\left[\theta_{L3}\left(S_{LK}^3 - S_{KK}^3\right) - \theta_{K3}\left(S_{LL}^3 - S_{KL}^3\right)\right] \\
&\quad + \beta gC\theta_{K3}\frac{L_2}{L_3}\left(S_{LL}^2 - 1\right) - FCA\theta_{K3} + \Delta w_2L_2S_{LL}^2\frac{\widehat{w}_2}{\widehat{\beta}} - \Delta E_{p_2}p_2\frac{\widehat{p}_2}{\widehat{\beta}} - \Delta\beta \\
&< 0
\end{aligned}$$

where $E_U = \frac{\partial E}{\partial U} > 0$, $E_{p_2} = \frac{\partial E}{\partial p_2} > 0$.

According to $E_U > 0$ and $\Delta > 0$, we could get

$$\widehat{U}/\widehat{\beta} < 0$$

Proposition 6.2 An increase in remittances will decrease urban residents' welfare in the short term.

Seeing that an increase in remittances will not change the output of the formal sector, it exerts an influence on urban residents' welfare by changing the informal sector. As remittances increase, part of the urban funds outflow will be transferred to the rural sectors, causing the income of urban residents to reduce. According to Proposition 6.1, an increase in remittances will decrease the output of the informal sector. Though the wage rate will increase, the total income of informal sector will decrease due to the decline of employment. Meanwhile, the price of informal sector will go up, leading to an increase in expenditure and a decrease of welfare. The combined impact is a decline in the welfare level of urban residents.

3.2 *The Economic Impact of an Increase in Remittances in the Long Run*

In this section, we examine the impact of increased remittances on the economy in the long term. The price of formal sector changes, and capital is perfectly mobile between the formal sector and the agricultural sector. Since capital is perfectly mobile between sectors, equilibrium in the capital market requires that the rate of return to capital is equal, that is, $r_1 = r_3 = r$. The market for capital is cleared when

$$a_{K1}X_1 + a_{K3}F^3 = K \tag{6.11'}$$

In the long run, there are seven equations in the general equilibrium model, namely, (6.4), (6.5), (6.6), (6.7), (6.8), (6.9), and (6.11′), along with seven endogenous variables, w_2, w_3, r, X_1, X_2, X_3, and p_2. Differentiating Eqs. (6.4), (6.5), (6.6), (6.7), (6.8), (6.9), and (6.11′) and writing in a matrix notation, we can obtain the following equation:

$$\begin{pmatrix} 0 & \theta_{L3} & 0 & 0 & 0 \\ F & 0 & -gp_1X_1 & F & 0 \\ B & w_3L_U & (w_3-\bar{w})L_1 & G & 0 \\ L_2S_{LL}^2 & L_3S_{LL}^3 & L_1 & L_2 & L_3 \\ 0 & K_3S_{KL}^3 & K_1 & 0 & K_3 \end{pmatrix} \begin{pmatrix} \widehat{w}_2 \\ \widehat{w}_3 \\ \widehat{X}_1 \\ \widehat{X}_2 \\ \widehat{X}_3 \end{pmatrix} = \begin{pmatrix} A \\ -g\beta \\ 0 \\ L_3A \\ K_3A \end{pmatrix} \widehat{\beta} \tag{6.12'}$$

where $L_U = L_1 + L_2$, $G = (w_3 - w_2)L_2 > 0$.

Δ_1 is the determinant of the matrix in Eq. (6.12′); by solving the determinant, we obtain the following expression:

$$\Delta_1 = \theta_{L3}L_1L_2L_3\left\{gp_1X_1k_3\frac{L_2}{L_1}w_2 - F\left[k_1\left(w_3 - (w_3 - w_2)S_{LL}^2\right)\right.\right.$$
$$\left.\left. -k_3\left(\bar{w} - (\bar{w} - w_2)S_{LL}^2\right)\right\}.$$

Obviously, only after determining the sign of Δ_1 can we conduct relevant economic analysis. Thus, we make the following assumption.

Assumption $\frac{w_2-(\bar{w}-w_2)S_{LL}^2}{w_2-(w_3-w_2)S_{LL}^2} < \frac{k_1}{k_3} < \frac{\bar{w}-w_2}{w_3-w_2}$, namely, the rate of per capita capital of the formal to the agricultural sector lies in a certain interval.

The per capita capital of the formal sector is bigger than that of agricultural sector in most developing countries, namely, $k_1/k_3 > 1$. Though the assumption is made from the mathematical point of view, the assumption is not against the real-world situation. In developing countries with great gap between urban and rural areas, rural–urban migrants desire to enter urban formal sector, and they accept low wages in the urban informal sector, waiting for a chance to find a formal sector job; therefore, S_{LL}^2 is the extreme lack of elasticity; and the wage of urban formal sector $\bar{w}$ is much greater than that of the agricultural sector w_3. Thus, the left side of inequality $\frac{w_2-(\bar{w}-w_2)S_{LL}^2}{w_2-(w_3-w_2)S_{LL}^2}$ is slightly greater than 1 and $\frac{\bar{w}-w_2}{w_3-w_2}$ considerably greater than 1. Thus, even under the assumption, k_1/k_3 still have a large selection range, so the assumption also has wide representation in the real-world situation.

According to the assumption, we could obtain $\Delta_1 > 0$, and we could obtain results by solving Eq. (6.12′):

$$\frac{\widehat{w}_3}{\widehat{\beta}} = \frac{A}{\theta_{L3}} > 0$$

$$\Delta_1\frac{\widehat{X}_1}{\widehat{\beta}} = AFK_3\left\{L_3\left(S_{LL}^3 - S_{KL}^3\right)[B - L_2(w_3 - w_2)] - w_3L_UL_2\left(S_{LL}^2 - 1\right)\right\}$$
$$+ \theta_{L3}g\beta K_3L_2L_2w_2$$
$$> 0$$

$$\Delta_1\frac{\widehat{X}_2}{\widehat{\beta}} = \theta_{L3}g\beta\left[B(L_1K_3 - L_3K_1) - (w_3 - \bar{w})L_1K_3L_2S_{LL}^2\right]$$
$$+ Agp_1X_1\left[BL_3K_3\left(S_{LL}^3 - S_{KL}^3\right) - w_3L_UL_2K_3S_{LL}^2\right]$$
$$- A\beta F\left[w_3L_U(L_1K_3 - L_3K_1) - (w_3 - \bar{w})L_1K_3L_3\left(S_{LL}^3 - S_{KL}^3\right)\right]$$
$$> 0$$

Following $\frac{\widehat{X}_2}{\widehat{\beta}} > 0$, we could obtain that

$$\frac{\widehat{w}_2}{\widehat{\beta}} < 0, \quad \frac{\widehat{p}_2}{\widehat{\beta}} < 0$$

Summarizing the above results, we get Proposition 6.3.

Proposition 6.3 In the long term, under the assumption that the rate of per capita capital of the formal to the agricultural sector lies in a certain interval, an increase in remittances will generate the following impacts:

1. The output of the urban formal sector and informal sector increases.
2. The wage rate and goods price of the informal sector decrease.
3. The wage rate of the agricultural sector increases.

The impacts of remittances on the informal sector prove to be different between the short and long run: the output of the informal sector will decrease in the short term, while it will increase in the long term. In the long term, as long as the dual economic structure does not change, Harris–Todaro labor transfer mechanism will take effect: migrant workers will migrate to the urban, increasing the labor force and output in the informal sector, decreasing the wage and goods price in that sector. Due to the downward rigid wage, the employment of formal sector will not change. However, the output of the formal sector increases according to calculation. A possible situation is that remittances turn into capital of agricultural sector and flow into the formal sector, which leads to an increase in the formal sector.

Next, we will investigate the impact of remittances on welfare of urban residents in the long run. Totally differentiating Eq. (6.13), we could obtain the following by using the assumption and solving Eq. (6.12′):

$$\begin{aligned}\Delta_1 E_U U \frac{\widehat{U}}{\widehat{\beta}} = \Delta_1(\bar{w}L_1 + rK_1)\frac{\widehat{X}_1}{\widehat{\beta}} + \Delta_1 w_2 L_2\left(\frac{\widehat{X}_2}{\widehat{\beta}} + \frac{\widehat{w}_2}{\widehat{\beta}} + S_{LL}^2\frac{\widehat{w}_2}{\widehat{\beta}}\right) - \Delta_1 E_{p_2} p_2 \frac{\widehat{p}_2}{\widehat{\beta}} \\ - \Delta_1 \beta \\ > 0\end{aligned}$$

Owing to $E_U > 0$ and $\Delta_1 > 0$, we get

$$\widehat{U}/\widehat{\beta} > 0$$

Proposition 6.4 An increase in remittances will increase urban residents' welfare in the long term.

The effect on urban residents' welfare from the increase of remittance proves to be drastically different between the short and long run. There are two reasons to account for this occurrence in the long-run case: from Proposition 6.3, the goods price of the informal sector decreases, which means that the real income of urban residents grows; moreover, an increase in remittances will cause the output of the urban formal sector and informal sector to increase; though an increase in remittances will bring part of the urban funds outflow to the rural area and decrease the wage of informal sector, the combined impact will promote urban residents' welfare eventually.

4 Concluding Remarks

This article analyzes theoretically the economic impact of migrants' remittances on labor host region, urban region, within one economy. Since similar analysis has been sparse, the main contents of this chapter are new perspectives to the best of our knowledge. Though part of the urban funds outflow to the rural area through remittances, these impacts are not all negative, and an increase in remittances of the migrants will increase urban residents' welfare in the long term. Considering that the impacts of remittances in the short term differ vastly from that in the long term, the implication of this chapter is that people should pay more attention to the impacts of remittance and adopt corresponding measures according to economic situation and minimize the negative impacts of remittances when capital is immobile between sectors.

Like Chap. 5, this chapter is particularly important for developing countries in Asia, for these countries themselves have large internal immigrants. In the past, the government and the scholars paid more attention to the overseas remittance. Given the fact that economic internal immigrant remittances have positive significance to both city and countryside, we suggest that Asian policy authorities attach greater importance and note the differences between the long-term and short-term political effects, promoting the common development of urban and rural areas.

References

Chaudhuri, S. (2007). Foreign capital, welfare and urban unemployment in the presence of agricultural dualism. *Japan and the World Economy, 19*, 149–165.

Djajic, S. (1986). International migration, remittances and welfare in a dependent economy. *Journal of Development Economics, 21*(2), 229–234.

Djajic, S. (1998). Emigration and welfare in an economy with foreign capital. *Journal of Development Economics, 56*, 433–445.

Gupta, M. R. (1997). Informal sector and informal capital market in a small open less-developed economy. *Journal of Development Economics, 52*, 409–428.

Hu, F., & Wang, Q. (2007). An analysis of determinants of remittances of China's rural migrants–Application of interval regression model. *Statistical Research, 24*(10), 20–25. (in Chinese).

Kar, S., & Marjit, S. (2001). Informal sector in general equilibrium: Welfare effects of trade policy reforms. *International Review of Economics & Finance, 10*(3), 289–300.

Kirwan, F., & Holden, D. (1986). Emigrants' remittances, non-traded goods and economic welfare in the source country. *Journal of Economic Studies, 13*(2), 52–58.

Li, X. C., & Qian, X. Y. (2011). Economic analysis on the urban–rural disparity in human capital in China. *South African Journal of Economics, 79*(2), 146–160.

Li, X. C., & Zhou, Y. (2013). An economic analysis of remittance of unskilled migration on skilled–unskilled wage inequality in labor host region. *Economic Modelling, 33*, 428–432.
Lundahl, M. (1985). International migration, remittances and real incomes: Effects on the source country. *The Scandinavian Journal of Economics, 87*(4), 647–657.
Quibria, M. G. (1997). International migration, remittances and income distribution in the source country: A synthesis. *Bulletin of Economic Research, 49*(1), 29–46.
Rivera-Batiz, F. (1986). International migration, remittances and economic welfare in the source country. *Journal of Economic Studies, 13*(3), 3–19.
Tumbe, C. (2011). *Remittances in India: Facts and issues, MPRA working paper series no. 331*. Bangalore: Indian Institute of Management.
Yabuuchi, S., & Beladi, H. (2001). Urban unemployment, informal sector and development policies. *Journal of Economics, 74*(3), 301–314.

Part III
Environmental Protection

This portion comprises three chapters. Chapter 7 serves as a connecting link between the preceding and the following, researching the effect of migrant remittances on the environment, which is a new perspective. This paper is based on the fact that rural-urban migrants motivated by altruism are striving to send more remittance home to improve the quality of lives for their families, which will lead to an enlargement in the scale of production in the urban sector; the result of which is an increase in pollution during the production process. Chapter 8 investigates the impact of the heterogeneous labor transfer between sectors on the environment under the international skilled and unskilled labor movements and the price change of the agricultural products. Chapter 9 mainly investigates the problem of transboundary pollution. Investigating transboundary pollution in theory is helpful to solve the problem of transboundary pollution in practical economic activities. This chapter integrates intra-region labor migration and inter-region labor migration into Harris-Todaro model in the presence of unidirectional transboundary pollution, analyzing the environmental and regional economic effects of reducing the transfer cost of inter-region labor migration and increasing the capital subsidy to the less regions. Additionally, we compare the environmental and regional economic effects of the improvement of pollution abatement technology in different regions.

Chapter 7
Environmental Effects of Remittance of Rural–Urban Migrant

Xiaochun Li and Jing Zhou

Abstract In this chapter, we investigate the environmental effect of the migrant remittance. The rural–urban migrant is an extremely important component of immigrant. Although they work and live in the city, the altruistic remittance affects the production scale of urban sector and then exerts impact on the environment. We mainly reach the following conclusions: the increase of the migrant remittance can improve the environment in the short term while worsen the environment in the long run.

Keywords Rural–urban migrants • Remittance • Environment

1 Introduction

Migrant remittance refers to the part of their income that migrants send home. In 1999, remittance in India, the Philippines, and Mexico formed 2.6%, 8.9%, and 1.7% of their GDPs, respectively (Stalker 2002). Hoyos (2008) and Zarate-Hoyos (2004) showed that nearly 1.3 million households in Mexico received migrant remittance in 2000, which formed almost 48.9% of the Mexican national monetary income. It is also shown that over 10% of rural households and over 4% of urban households received remittance. So far, most papers merely studied the effect of international migrant remittance on the labor-outsourcing countries. The typical studies that could be referred to are Bhagwati and Srinivasan (1977), and Djajić (1985). However, the remittance of rural–urban migrants in the developing countries, particularly in nations with a dual economy, is an extremely important component of national income. For example, Chinese rural–urban migrants, nearly 260 million in number, send or take part of the income obtained from the labor-host region to the labor-outsourcing region. It has been estimated by the writer that the rural–urban migrant remittance in China was more than 1000 million RMB

X. Li (✉)
Business School, Nanjing University, Nanjing, China
e-mail: xiaochun@nju.edu.cn

J. Zhou
School of Economics, Nanjing University, 22 Hankou Road, Nanjing, Jiangsu 210093, China

X. Li (ed.), *Labor Transfer in Emerging Economies*, New Frontiers in Regional Science: Asian Perspectives 12, DOI 10.1007/978-981-10-3569-2_7

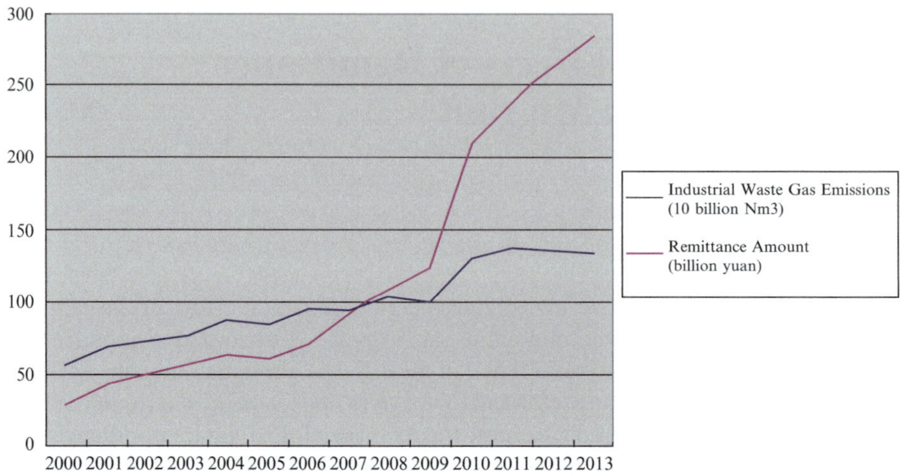

Fig. 7.1 The total amount of migrant remittance and of industrial waste gas emissions from 2000 to 2011 in Shanghai (Data sources: Authors calculated the results based on the data from Shanghai Municipal Bureau of Statistics (http://www.stats-sh.gov.cn/) and Shanghai Municipal Human Resources and Social Security Bureau (http://www.12333sh.gov.cn))

(around 160 million US dollars) in 2012. This requires special attention as the remittance is a result of rural–urban migration instead of overseas emigration, and it is the latter that has been the subject of significant research hitherto. The family members of migrant workers in labor-outsourcing regions could benefit a lot from migrant remittance, and their use of remittance on consumption, investment in production, or saving is an influential component of economic development in the rural region or even in the whole country.

From the facts above, we know that migrant remittance has a great impact on the labor-outsourcing regions or countries, which attracts interest of both empirical and theoretical economists. Theoretical researches mainly considered the effects of migrant remittance on rural income distribution, agricultural production, development of rural economy, and some macroeconomic elements such as current exchange rate and so on. The typical studies that could be referred to are Stark et al. (1986), Taylor and Wyatt (1996), Quibria (1997), Rozelle et al. (1999), McCormick and Wahba (2000), Ball et al. (2013), and so forth. The current empirical studies focused mainly on the impact of migrant remittance on rural income smoothing, household poverty and inequality, household decisions, relative prices, and economic growth combined with the productive use of remittance on rural economy. The representative empirical works are Amuedo-Dorantes and Pozo (2011), Chiwuzulum Odozi et al. (2010), Grigorian and Melkonyan (2011), Nath and Vargas-Silva (2012), Pradhan et al. (2008), and Zarate-Hoyos (2004).

On the other hand, enormous theoretical and empirical studies showed the environmental effects of economic development from the perspective of labor transfer. For instance, Dean and Gangopadhyay (1997) used a three-sector model to analyze how limiting the export of intermediate goods would affect environmental pollution, rural–urban migration, and urban unemployment. Chaudhuri and Mukhopadhyay (2006) investigated the efficiency of imposing a pollution emission tax on the formal manufacturing sector in a three-sector general equilibrium model that included pollution effects that arose from the informal sector. Previous empirical research, such as Papola (1981) and Romatet (1983), suggested that the urban informal sector produced intermediate goods for the formal manufacturing sector, and the informal sector was, in fact, the main source of environmental pollution.

Li and Zhou (2013b) integrate intra-region labor migration and inter-region labor migration into forth sector model, analysis the regional economic and environmental effects of the central government's development policies on two regions.

However, the environmental impact exerted by an increase in remittance of rural–urban migrants in developing countries is largely ignored. Considering the example of China, the appearance of migrant remittance could be traced back to the middle of 1980s, the amount of which has been growing larger hitherto, and China is suffering from worsening environmental pollution. The city of Shanghai is not only a major receiver of transferred farm labors in China but also one of the major manufacturing bases. Figure 7.1 reflects the changes in the amount of migrant remittance and industrial waste gas emissions from 2000 to 2011 in Shanghai. The variation trend shows that changes in migrant remittance were nearly in line with industrial waste gas emissions.

This trend can be explained from a simple theoretical deduction: since migrant remittance is generated from the wage, rural–urban migrants motivated by altruism are striving to send more remittance home to improve the quality of lives for their families, and this will prompt them to increase revenue through hard work; on the other hand, the growth in remittance means the increase in their workload, which will lead to an enlargement in the scale of production in the urban sector, the result of which is an increase in pollution during the production process, so the amount of migrant remittance and of environmental pollution will grow at the same pace. Admittedly, there are many reasons which can cause pollution, such as an increase in exports of industrial products, urbanization, and so on.

However, if we do not seriously investigate the issue of remittance, which is taken to be one of the main reasons behind environmental pollution, it will be difficult for us to arrive at appropriate solutions for the environmental problems we face today. In order to clarify the relationship between remittance and environmental pollution and improve the environment, this chapter establishes a two-sector general equilibrium model and conducts a comparative static study to investigate the short-run and long-run impacts, respectively, of an increase in remittance of migrants on the environment. We find that an increase in the remittance of rural–urban migrants to labor-outsourcing regions will lead to environmental improvement in the short run but will deteriorate the environment in the long term.

The rest of this chapter is organized as follows: in Sect. 2, we set up the theoretical model; in Sect. 3, we conduct the theoretical analysis of the established model; and we draw conclusions in Sect. 4.

2 Theoretical Model

Consider a developing country with a closed economy, which consists of two sectors: the rural agricultural sector and the urban manufacturing sector. The urban manufacturing sector absorbs rural–urban migrants. There are three kinds of labor in this economy—the urban labor, the rural–urban migrants, and the rural labor. Because rural–urban migration control policies prevail in developing countries (Lall and Selod 2006; Zhang et al. 2005), we set the number of the rural workers who transfer to urban areas as given.

The urban sector utilizes urban labor, rural–urban migrants, and capital as factors of production. The wage rate of the manufacturing sector is downward rigid. The agricultural sector utilizes capital, remittance of migrants, and local labor as factors of production, and its wage is flexible. Furthermore, we assume that the production procedure of agricultural sector depends on environmental factors. That is to say, the environmental improvement will create correspondingly higher levels of output. Production in the manufacturing sector will generate pollution, which damages the environment through factors such as air and water. The production functions of the urban manufacturing sector and the rural agricultural sector are given separately by

$$Y_1 = F^1(L_1 + \bar{L}_{TR}, K_1) \tag{7.1}$$

$$Y_2 = g(E)F^2(L_2, a\bar{w}\bar{L}_{TR} + K_2) \tag{7.2}$$

where Y_1 and Y_2 are the outputs of the urban manufacturing sector and the rural agricultural sector, respectively. L_1 and L_2 are the urban labor employed by the urban manufacturing sector and the local rural labor employed by the rural agricultural sector, respectively. $\bar{L}_{TR}$ is the number of rural–urban migrants employed by urban manufacturing sector. K_1 and K_2 are the capital utilized by the urban manufacturing sector and the rural agricultural sector, respectively. w is the wage rate of the urban sector, which satisfies $\bar{w} > w_a$. If we assume that $0 < a < 1$, a represents the rural–urban migrants remittance rate, that is, the rural–urban migrants will send a proportion a of their income back to the labor-outsourcing region. F^1 and F^2 are the strictly quasi-concave and linearly homogeneous functions of the urban manufacturing sector and the rural agricultural sector, respectively. The quality of environment after pollution is denoted by E. Thus,

$$E = \bar{E} - \mu Y_1 \tag{7.3}$$

where $\bar{E}$ is the best quality of the environment, which is regarded as given. μ expresses the units of local pollution generated by one unit of production in the urban manufacturing sector. Taking the effect of environment on agricultural productivity into consideration, the denotation of Eq. (7.3) here is in accordance with Copeland and Taylor (1999) and Li and Zhou (2013a). $g(E)$, with the properties $g>0$, $g'>0$, and $g''>0$, represents the effect of environment on agricultural productivity.

Firstly, in the short run, capital is illiquid and the interest rate is regarded as given. Profit maximization yields

$$PF_L^1 = \bar{w} \tag{7.4}$$

$$gF_L^2 = w_a \tag{7.5}$$

where $F_L^i = \partial F^i/\partial L_i (i = 1, 2)$. Here, we normalize the price of output in the rural agricultural sector into unit. P is the relative price of output in the urban manufacturing sector in terms of the output in the rural agricultural sector. w_a is the wage rate of rural local labor employed by the rural agricultural sector; $\bar{w}$ is the wage rate of the urban sector, which satisfies $\bar{w} > w_a$.

The full employment condition of factor markets is shown as follows:

$$L_1 + L_2 + \bar{L}_{TR} = \bar{L} \tag{7.6}$$

where $\bar{L}$ is the labor endowment in the economy. We assume that all individuals in the economy have twice-differentiable, strictly quasi-concave, and homothetic utility functions. The utility-maximization problem of urban workers can be stated as follows:

$$\begin{aligned}&\textit{To choose}(c_1{}^1, c_2{}^1)\\&\textit{to maximize } u^1(c_1{}^1, c_2{}^1)\\&\textit{subject to } I^1 = Pc_1{}^1 + c_2{}^1\end{aligned}$$

where $c_1{}^1$ is the urban workers' utility-maximizing consumption of urban manufacturing products; $c_2{}^1$ is their utility-maximizing consumption of rural agricultural products; and $u^1(c_1{}^1, c_2{}^1)$ is the associated utility function. I^1 is their total budget.

The utility-maximization problem of rural local workers can be stated as follows:

$$\begin{aligned}&\textit{To choose}(c_1{}^2, c_2{}^2)\\&\textit{to maximize } u^2(c_1{}^2, c_2{}^2)\\&\textit{subject to } I^2 = Pc_1{}^2 + c_2{}^2\end{aligned}$$

where $c_1{}^2$ is the utility-maximizing consumption of urban manufacturing products; $c_2{}^2$ is the utility-maximizing consumption of rural agricultural products; and $u^2(c_1{}^2, c_2{}^2)$ is the associated utility function. I^2 is their total budget.

Because of the twice-differentiable, strictly quasi-concave, and homothetic utility functions and some other relevant relationships, the total budget of the urban worker and the rural local worker can be

$$I^1 = \bar{w}L_1 + (1-a)\bar{w}\bar{L}_{TR} + rK_1$$
$$I^2 = w_a L_2 + rK_2$$

Then, the utility-maximizing levels of consumption of urban manufacturing products are given by

$$c_1^1 = \frac{\beta_1}{P}[\bar{w}L_1 + (1-a)\bar{w}\bar{L}_{TR} + rK_1] \tag{7.7}$$

$$c_1^2 = \frac{\beta_2}{P}(w_a L_2 + rK_2) \tag{7.8}$$

where $\beta_1 = \frac{\partial u^1}{\partial c_1^1}\frac{c_1^1}{u^1}$ indicates the manufacturing product consumption elasticity of urban workers' utilities and $\beta_2 = \frac{\partial u^2}{\partial c_1^2}\frac{c_1^2}{u^2}$ for manufacturing product consumption elasticity of rural local workers' utilities, both of which are regarded as given. Considering real economic conditions, $\beta_1 < \beta_2$ and we furthermore assume that $\beta_1\bar{w} < \beta_2 w_a$.

The economy only produces two products. By virtue of Walras' law, it is evident that if one goods market clears, the other market will clear as well. The market-clearing condition can be demonstrated by

$$c_1^1 + c_1^2 = Y_1 \tag{7.9}$$

This is the short-term general equilibrium model. We have nine equations, from Eqs. (7.1), (7.2), (7.3), (7.4), (7.5), (7.6), (7.7), (7.8), and (7.9), which determine nine endogenous variables, Y_1, Y_2, L_1, L_2, E, w_a, P, ${c_1}^1$, and ${c_1}^2$.

In the long run, because of free flow of capital, K_1, K_2, and r are endogenous variables. Because of profit maximization and market clearing, we could obtain three more equations:

$$PF_K^1 = r \tag{7.10}$$

$$gF_K^2 = r \tag{7.11}$$

$$K_1 + K_2 = \bar{K} \tag{7.12}$$

where r is the interest rate for loans and $F_K^i = \partial F^i / K_i (i = 1, 2)$ and $\bar{K}$ are the capital endowment in the economy. The long-term model consists of the 12 equations, from Eqs. (7.1), (7.2), (7.3), (7.4), (7.5), (7.6), (7.7), (7.8), (7.9), (7.10), (7.11), and (7.12), which determine 12 endogenous variables: Y_1, Y_2, L_1, L_2, E, w_a, P, ${c_1}^1$, ${c_1}^2$, K_1, K_2, and r.

3 Comparative Static Analysis

Analyzing the established economy system, we know that given the value of P, we can solve for the equilibrium values of Y_1, Y_2, L_1, L_2, E, w_a, ${c_1}^1$, ${c_1}^2$, K_1, K_2, and r. Therefore, Y_1, Y_2, L_1, L_2, E, w_a, ${c_1}^1$, ${c_1}^2$, K_1, K_2, and r can be shown as functions of P. We substitute them into the 12 equations and then solve for the value of P.

First, we build a lemma to investigate the impact of an increase in the remittance of rural–urban migrants on the price of output produced by urban manufacturing sector.

Lemma In the economy assumed by us, an increase in the remittance of rural–urban migrants will decrease the price of output produced by urban manufacturing sector.

Proof Total differentiation of Eq. (7.9) yields

$$\frac{\partial c_1^1}{\partial P}dP - \bar{w}\bar{L}_{TR}da + \frac{\partial c_1^2}{\partial P}dP = \frac{dY_1}{dP}dP$$

$$\frac{dP}{da} = \frac{\bar{w}\bar{L}_{TR}}{\frac{\partial c_1^1}{\partial P} + \frac{\partial c_1^2}{\partial P} - \frac{dY_1}{dP}}$$

where $\partial c_1^1/\partial P < 0$ and $\partial c_1^2/\partial P < 0$. The Walrus price adjustment process can be established by the following excess demand function:

$$\dot{P} = c_1^1 + c_1^2 - Y_1$$

where $\dot{P} = dP/dt$.

It is necessary for us to get a stable solution of the established economic system when conducting the comparative static analysis. The above price adjustment process must satisfy the following condition to guarantee the existence of the equilibrium solutions:

$$\frac{\partial c_1^1}{\partial P} + \frac{\partial c_1^2}{\partial P} - \frac{dY_1}{dP} < 0.$$

Therefore, we can ge $(dP/da) < 0$

Q.E.D.

Now, on the basis of the lemma, the study of the economic and environmental effect of increasing remittance of rural–urban migrants will turn to analyzing how an increase in the price of output produced by urban manufacturing sector influences the other endogenous variables.

3.1 Short-Term Analysis

In the short-term analysis, the complete differentiation of Eqs. (7.3), (7.4), (7.5), (7.6), (7.7), (7.8), and (7.9) can be reorganized as

$$\begin{pmatrix} PF_{LL}^1 & 0 \\ (\beta_1\bar{w} - \beta_2 w_a - PF_L^1) & \beta_2 L_2 \end{pmatrix} \begin{pmatrix} dL_1 \\ dw_a \end{pmatrix} = \begin{pmatrix} -F_L^1 dP \\ Y_1 dP \end{pmatrix} \tag{7.13}$$

Define the determinant of square matrix in Eq. (7.13) as Δ, and calculate Δ to obtain $\Delta = PF_{LL}^1\beta_2 L_2 < 0.$

Solving Eq. (7.13) by using Cramer's rule, we can obtain

$$dL_1/dP = -\beta_2 L_2 F_L^1/\Delta > 0$$
$$dw_a/dP = \left[PY_1F_{LL}^1 + (\beta_1\bar{w} - \beta_2 w_a - PF_L^1)F_L^1\right]/\Delta > 0.$$

By the inequality $(dL_1/dP) > 0$ in Eq. (7.1), we will get $(dY_1/dL_1) > 0$, and this implies $(dY_1/dP) > 0$. From Eq. (7.3) we know that Y_1 and E move in the opposite direction, and so we achieve $(dE/dP) < 0$. Finally, on the basis of market-clearing condition, i.e., Eq. (7.6), when labor endowment is constant, L_2 moves in the opposite direction of L_1, which means $(dL_2/dP) > 0$.

Summarizing the results, we establish Proposition 7.1 and Table 7.1 as follows:

Proposition 7.1 In the short term, an increase in the remittance of rural–urban migrants will improve the quality of environment.

In accordance with Table 7.1, the proposition will lead to the following:

1. In the urban sector, the number of urban workers decreases and output decreases.
2. In the rural sector, the wages of rural labor decrease, and the number of local workers decreases.

Table 7.1 The results of the calculation of Eq. (7.13)

	L_1	w_a	Y_1	E	L_2
P	+	+	+	–	–
a	–	–	–	+	+

Note: "–" means that the ratio of the items in the horizontal column and the ones in the vertical column is "negative"; "0" implies that the ratio of the items in the horizontal column and the ones in the vertical column is 0; "+" means "positive", and "/" means "cannot be decided"

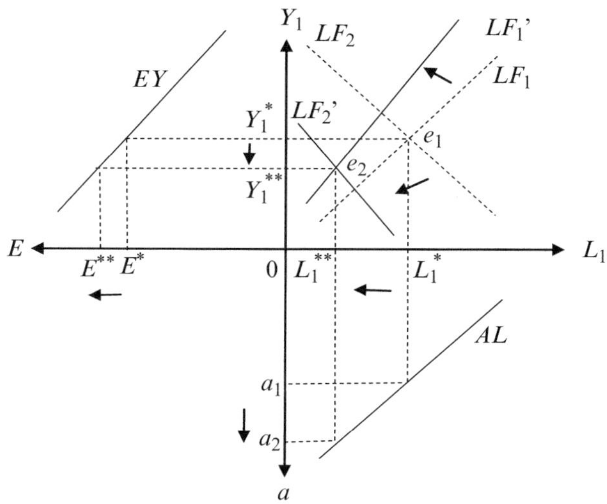

Fig. 7.2 Partial environmental effects of increasing remittance of the rural–urban migrants in the short term

Migrant remittance comes from the wage of rural–urban labor working in the urban manufacturing sector. When the rural–urban migrants increase the remittance rate, they will reduce their consumption in the labor-host region. Generally, the rural–urban migrants will reduce the consumption of products in both the rural agricultural sector and the urban manufacturing sector. In order to avoid a reduction in profits in the short run (when capital is illiquid), the urban manufacturing sector will respond with a reduction in output and labor employment. According to the analysis of Table 7.1, we can conclude that an increase in the remittance rate by rural–urban migrants will have the following economic effects on the labor-host region and labor-outsourcing region: in the labor-host region, the employment and output of urban manufacturing sector decrease, and hence there is an improvement in the quality of environment. In the labor-outsourcing region, the wage rate of rural agricultural sector decreases, and employment increases.

The following figure illustrates the partial effects of increasing remittance of rural–urban migrants on the environment. O is the origin. The left half of the horizontal axis is E, and the right half represents L_1. The upper half of the vertical axis is Y_1, and the lower half of the vertical axis is a.

In the first quadrant of Fig. 7.2, from the view of supply, we use line LF_1 to represent the relationship between L_1 and Y_1 depicted in Eq. (7.1), where its slope is $dY_1/dL_1 = \bar{w}/P$. It is easy to verify that L_1 and Y_1 move in the same direction from the supply perspective. From the perspective of demand, we use line LF_2 to represent the relationship between L_1 and Y_1; we substitute Eqs. (7.7) and (7.8) into Eq. (7.9), and by rearranging, it we achieve

$$PY_1 = \beta_1[\bar{w}_1 L_1 + (1-a)\bar{w}_1 \bar{L}_{TR} + rK_1] + \beta_2(w_a L_2 + rK_2) \tag{7.14}$$

where the slope of line LF_2 is $dY_1/dL_1 = [(\beta_1\bar{w} - \beta_2 w_a)/P]$. It is easy to confirm that L_1 and Y_1 move in the reverse direction from the aspect of demand. In the second quadrant of Fig. 7.2, line EY shows the relationship between E and Y_1 in Eq. (7.3). In the fourth quadrant, line AL describes the relation between a and L_1 given by the lemma and Eq. (7.13). We assume that the initial equilibrium values of L_1, Y_1, and E are L_1^*, Y_1^*, and E^*, respectively. After analyzing Eqs. (7.1) and (7.14), we can get the location of line LF_1 and line LF_2, which can be described by the first quadrant of Fig. 7.2. Line LF_1 intersects with line LF_2 at e_1. When the remittance of rural–urban migrants increases from a_1 to a_2, P will decrease by lemma. According to Eqs. (7.1) and (7.14), line LF_1 and line LF_2 will shift leftward to LF_1' and LF_2', respectively, the slopes of which are less steady than before, because, in the short run, as the price decreases, the absolute value of their slope increases. LF_1' meets line LF_2' at e_2. In this situation, it can be directly obtained from Fig. 7.2 that Y_1^* will decrease to Y_1^{**} and L_1^* will decrease to L_1^{**}. From line AL and line EY, we know that E^* will increase to E^{**}.

3.2 Long-Term Analysis

In the long-run analysis, the complete differentiation of Eqs. (7.3), (7.4), (7.5), (7.6), (7.7), (7.8), (7.9), (7.10), (7.11), and (7.12) can be reorganized as

$$\begin{pmatrix} PF_{LL}^1 & PF_{LK}^1 & 0 & 0 & 0 \\ gF_{LL}^2 & gF_{LK}^2 & 1 & -F_L^2 g' & 0 \\ (\beta_1\bar{w} - \beta_2 w_a) & r(\beta_1 - \beta_2) & \beta_2 L_2 & P/\mu & (\beta_1 K_1 + \beta_2 K_2) \\ PF_{KL}^1 & PF_{KK}^1 & 0 & 0 & -1 \\ gF_{KL}^2 & gF_{KK}^2 & 0 & -F_K^2 g' & 1 \end{pmatrix} \begin{pmatrix} dL_1 \\ dK_1 \\ dw_a \\ dE \\ dr \end{pmatrix} = \begin{pmatrix} -F_L^1 dP \\ 0 \\ Y_1 dP \\ -F_K^1 dP \\ 0 \end{pmatrix}. \tag{7.15}$$

Note that $k_1 = K_1/(L_1 + \bar{L}_{TR})$ and $k_2 = K_2/L_2$ represent the per capita amount of capital in the urban sector and the rural sector, respectively. Generally, the per capita amount of capital in the urban sector is greater than that in the rural sector, so that $k_1 > k_2$. The determinant of the coefficient matrix of the above equation system is denoted by Ω. Because F^1 and F^2 are linearly homogeneous, we know that

$$\Omega = Pg\beta_2 L_2 F_K^2 g'\left(F_{LK}^1 F_{LL}^2 - F_{LL}^1 F_{LK}^2\right) + \frac{P^2}{\mu} g\left(F_{LL}^1 F_{KK}^2 - F_{LK}^1 F_{KL}^2\right)$$
$$+ PF_{LL}^1(\beta_1 - \beta_2)F_K^2 g'$$
$$+ Pgg'\beta_2 L_2 F_L^2\left(F_{LL}^1 F_{KK}^2 - F_{LK}^1 F_{KL}^2\right) - Pg'F_K^2 F_{LK}^1(\beta_1 \bar{w} - \beta_2 w_a) > 0$$

We use the Cramer's rule to solve Eq. (7.15) and get $dr/dP>0$, but we cannot determine the signs of (dK_1/dP) and (dE/dP) (please refer to the Appendix A for details of the calculation procedure).

When we calculate the value of dE/dP, according to the preconditions, we can figure out the signs of the other items, which are positive, except the one of $Pg\left(F_{LL}^1 F_{KK}^2 - F_{LK}^1 F_{KL}^2\right) \cdot \left[Y_1 - (\beta_1 K_1 + \beta_2 K_2)\left(F_K^1 + \frac{L_1}{K_1} F_L^1\right)\right]$, which is unknown. In this expression, following the nature of the function and the economic realities, we know that $F_{LL}^1 F_{KK}^2 - F_{LK}^1 F_{KL}^2 > 0$. Then if we assume that $(K_1/K_2) > [\beta_2/(1-\beta_1)]$, we will have $(dE/dP)>0$. In terms of the inequality, if $\beta_1>1$, the assumption is inevitably tenable; even if $0<\beta_1<1$, there is an opportunity for the hypothesis to be established, because in many developing countries, the amount of capital employed in the urban sector, K_1, is much larger than that used in the rural sector, K_2.

When we calculate the value of dK_1/dP, we notice that the variation rate of g is $\hat{g} = (g'/g) > 0$, and let

$$A = r + \bar{w}(L_1/K_1), \quad B = \mu^{-1} + \hat{g}Y_1,$$
$$C = \beta_1 \bar{w} L_1 + \beta_2(1-a)\bar{w}\bar{L}_{TR}, \text{ and } D = \hat{g}(\bar{w}/P).$$

Then,

$$dK_1/dP = PrY_1\hat{g}F_{LL}^1 + AF_{LL}^1(\hat{g}C - PB)$$
$$+ gF_{KL}^2[\bar{w}B - D(C + \beta_1 rK_1)] + r(\beta_1\bar{w} - \beta_2 w_a)D.$$

Because $r(\beta_1\bar{w} - \beta_2 w_a)D < 0$, if inequality

$$F_{LL}^1[PrY_1\hat{g} + A(\hat{g}C - PB)] < gF_{KL}^2[D(C + \beta_1 rK_1) - \bar{w}B]$$

can be established, that is,

$$\frac{gF_{KL}^2}{F_{LL}^1} > \frac{\hat{g}(rPY_1 + AC) - PAB}{D(C + r\beta_1 K_1) - \bar{w}B} \tag{7.16}$$

we will have $(dK_1/dP) <0$.

To sum up, if $(K_1/K_2) > [\beta_2/(1-\beta_1)]$, we will achieve $(dE/dP) >0$; in addition, if Eq. (7.16) can be established, we will get $(dK_1/dP) <0$. In accordance with

Table 7.2 The results of the calculation of Eq. (7.14)

	L_1	E	r	Y_1	K_1	w_a
P	+	+	+	–	/	/
a	–	–	–	+	/	/

Note: the meanings of the signs are the same as those in Table 7.1

Eq. (7.3), we know that Y_1 and E move in the opposite direction so that we can obtain $(dY_1/dP) < 0$ (Please refer to Appendix A).

The summarized results can be found in Table 7.2, according to which we establish the following proposition.

Proposition 7.2 In the long term, an increase in the remittance of rural–urban migrants will deteriorate the quality of environment under the condition $(K_1/K_2) > [\beta_2/(1-\beta_1)]$.

It will produce some other economic impacts: (1) the rate of interest decreases, (2) the output produced in the urban sector increases, and (3) the amount of capital employed by urban sector increases based on Eq. (7.16).

We can figure out the explanation for Eq. (7.16) in the real economy: since the remittance of rural–urban migrants is taken as capital for the production process in the rural agricultural sector, the demand of capital, K_2, decreases. With a constant amount of capital endowment, the interest rate decreases; under the condition of free movement of capital, the urban firm who calls for the maximum of profit is bound to utilize more capital, K_1, in the long term, and thus we obtain $dK_1/dP < 0$.

Proposition 7.2 can also be illustrated by Fig. 7.3. O is the origin. The left half of the horizontal axis is E, and its right half represents K_1. The upper half of the vertical axis is Y_1, and the lower half of the vertical axis is a.

In the first quadrant of Fig. 7.3, from the supply perspective, we use line KF_1 to represent the relation between K_1 and Y_1 depicted in Eq. (7.1), where its slope is $(dY_1/dK_1) = (r/P)$. It is easy to verify that K_1 and Y_1 move in the same direction from the supply point of view. From the perspective of demand, we use line KF_2 to represent the relationship between K_1 and Y_1 described in Eq. (7.14), the slope of which is $(dY_1/dK_1) = [r(\beta_1 - \beta_2)/P]$. It is easy to confirm that K_1 and Y_1 move in the opposite directions from the view of demand.

In the second quadrant of Fig. 7.3, line EY shows the relation between E and Y_1 in Eq. (7.3). In the fourth quadrant, line AK describes the relation between a and K_1 given by the lemma and Eq. (7.13). After analyzing Eqs. (7.1) and (7.14), we can get the locations of lines KF_1 and KF_2, which can be described by the first quadrant of Fig. 7.3. Line KF_1 intersects with line KF_2 at e_1. Because r declines more sharply than P (for the detailed calculation of this result, please refer to Appendix B), as price decreases, the absolute value of their slopes increases. When the remittances of rural–urban migrants increase from a_1 to a_2, the decreasing P will make line KF_1 and line KF_2 shift leftward to KF_1' and KF_2', respectively, the slopes of which are less steady than before. Line KF_1' meets line KF_2' at e_2. Under these circumstances,

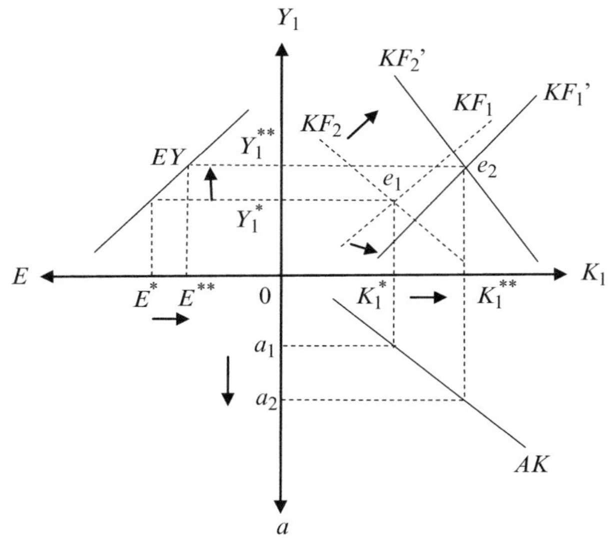

Fig. 7.3 Partial environmental effects of increasing remittance of the rural–urban migrants in the long term

it can be directly obtained from Fig. 7.3 that Y_1^* will increase to Y_1^{**} and K_1^* will increase to K_1^{**}. From line *AK* and line *EY*, we know that E^* will decrease to E^{**}.

Although the increasing remittance of rural–urban migrants in the short run will improve the environmental quality, it is worth noting that the increase in remittance will cause deterioration in the quality of environment in the long term. The main reason of this difference is that in the long run, along with the increasing remittance, the interest rate *r* declines more sharply than *P*, and the urban sector employs more capital. As a consequence, industrial production increases, which leads to environmental deterioration. However, the short-term interest rate is fixed and not influenced by remittance, so the urban sector will not increase capital investment according to the change of interest rate. These features have relatively clear policy implications, and it is important for countries to form reasonable strategies accordingly to ensure balanced development in their economies.

4 Conclusion

In this chapter, we investigate the effect of migrant remittance on the environment. We find that the rural–urban migrants' consumption is different from the urban citizens' because of their altruistic remittance. Because of this kind of disparity, firms have to adjust supply, which will affect the production scale. This exerts an impact on the environment as a result. In less developed countries, migrant remittance is a significant fund resource which benefits farmers and agricultural communities. It is important for the government to establish countermeasures which cannot only guarantee remittance but also protect the environment. It can be seen from the analysis above that an increase in the migrant remittance can improve the environment in the short term while worsen the environment in the long run. From the prospective of economic development, free capital flow between the urban and the rural sectors in the long term is an important symbol of improvement in social economy. But we are still at an initial stage when the capital is illiquid between these two sectors. As a result, the migrant remittance goes through a process from environmental enhancement to environmental degradation. We suggest in this chapter that policy-making authorities attach great importance to the environmental effects of migrant remittance. Proper measures should be taken to alleviate this problem so as to balance the development of both the urban and the rural economies and adjust the relationship between environmental protection and economic development.

Acknowledgment We would like to thank the reviewer(s) for the suggestive comments on improving this chapter. The present study is sponsored by the National Social Sciences Fund Project No.14JJD790016, for which the authors deeply appreciate. Any remaining errors are ours.

Appendices

Appendix A

We use the Cramer's rule to solve Eq. (7.15) and obtain

$$
\begin{aligned}
dL_1/dP = \{ & P\left(F_K^1 F_{LK}^1 - F_L^1 F_{KK}^1\right)\left[\frac{P}{\mu} + F_L^2 g'(\beta_1 K_1 + \beta_2 K_2)\right] \\
& - F_L^1\left[-g\beta_2 L_2 g' F_K^2 F_{LK}^2 + \frac{P}{\mu} g F_{KK}^2\right. \\
& \left. + g\beta_2 L_2 F_L^2 g' F_{KK}^2 + r(\beta_1 - \beta_2) F_K^2 g'\right] - PY_1 F_K^2 g' F_{LK}^1 \}/\Omega
\end{aligned}
$$

$$
\begin{aligned}
dK_1/dP = \{ & -P\left(\frac{L_1}{K_1}\bar{w} + r\right)\left(\frac{1}{\mu} + \dot{g}Y_1\right)F_{LL}^1 \\
& + \left(\frac{L_1}{K_1}\bar{w} + r\right)[\beta_1 \bar{w} L_1 + \beta_1 \bar{w}\bar{L}_{TR}(1-a)]\dot{g} F_{LL}^1 + PrY_1\dot{g} \cdot F_{LL}^1 \\
& + \bar{w}g\left(\frac{1}{\mu} + \dot{g}Y_1\right)F_{KL}^2 - \frac{\bar{w}}{P} g' F_{KL}^2 \left[\beta_1 \bar{w} L_1 + \beta_1 \bar{w}\bar{L}_{TR}(1-a)\right. \\
& \left. + \beta_1 r K_1\right] + \frac{\bar{w}}{P}\dot{g}\, r(\beta_1 \bar{w} - \beta_2 w_a) \}/\Omega
\end{aligned}
$$

$$
\begin{aligned}
dw_a/dP = \{ & Pg\left[F_K^1 F_K^2 g'(\beta_1 K_1 + \beta_2 K_2)\right. \\
& \left. + \frac{P}{\mu} F_K^1 - Y_1 F_K^2 g'\right]\left(F_{LL}^1 F_{LK}^2 - F_{LK}^1 F_{LL}^2\right) + rPF_L^1 F_K^1 g'(\beta_1 - \beta_2) F_{LL}^1 \\
& + PgF_L^1 g'\left[Y + F_K^1(\beta_1 K_1 + \beta_2 K_2)\right]\left(F_{LL}^1 F_{KK}^2 - F_{LK}^1 F_{KL}^2\right) \\
& - gF_L^1 g'(\beta_1 \bar{w} - \beta_2 w_a)\left[F_K^2 F_{LK}^2 + F_L^1\left(F_{KK}^1 + F_{KK}^2\right)\right] \\
& + rF_L^1 g'(\beta_1 - \beta_2)\left(gF_K^2 F_{LL}^2 + gF_L^1 F_{KL}^2 + PF_L^1 F_{KL}^1\right) \\
& + PgF_L^1(\beta_1 K_1 + \beta_2 K_2)\left(\frac{P}{\mu} + F_K^2 g'\right)\left(F_{KK}^1 F_{LL}^2 - F_{KL}^1 F_{LK}^2\right) \\
& + Pg\left(F_L^1\right)^2 g'(\beta_1 K_1 + \beta_2 K_2)\left(F_{KL}^1 F_{KK}^2 - F_{KK}^1 F_{KL}^2\right)\}/\Omega
\end{aligned}
$$

$$
\begin{aligned}
dE/dP = \{ & r(\beta_1 - \beta_2)\left[PF_K^1 F_{LL}^1 + F_L^1\left(gF_{KL}^2 + PF_{KL}^1\right)\right] \\
& + Pg\beta_2 L_2 F_K^1\left(F_{LK}^1 F_{LL}^2 - F_{LL}^1 F_{LK}^2\right) \\
& + Pg\left[Y_1 - (\beta_1 K_1 + \beta_2 K_2)\left(F_K^1 + \frac{L_1}{K_1} F_L^1\right)\right]\left(F_{LL}^1 F_{KK}^2 - F_{LK}^1 F_{KL}^2\right) \\
& + (\beta_1 \bar{w} - \beta_2 w_a)\left[F_L^1\left(PF_{KK}^1 + gF_{KK}^2\right) - PF_K^1 \cdot F_{LK}^1\right] \\
& + Pg\beta_2 L_2 F_L^1\left(F_{KL}^1 F_{LK}^2 - F_{KK}^1 F_{LL}^2\right)\}/\Omega
\end{aligned}
$$

$$
\begin{aligned}
dr/dP = \{ & \frac{g}{\mu} P^2 F_L^1\left(F_{KK}^1 F_{KL}^2 - F_{KL}^1 F_{KK}^2\right) \\
& + Pg\beta_2 L_2 g' F_L^1 F_L^2\left(F_{KK}^1 F_{KL}^2 - F_{KL}^1 F_{KK}^2\right) + Pg^2 \beta_2 L_2 g' \\
& \cdot \left(F_K^2\right)^2\left(F_{LK}^1 F_{LL}^2 - F_{LL}^1 F_{LK}^2\right) + F_K^2 g'\left[\Pr(\beta_1 - \beta_2)\left(F_K^1 F_{LL}^1 - F_L^1 F_{KL}^1\right)\right. \\
& \left. + P(\beta_1 \bar{w} - \beta_2 w_a)\left(F_L^1 F_{KK}^1 - F_K^1 F_{LK}^1\right)\right] \\
& + Pg\left(F_{LL}^1 F_{KK}^2 - F_{LK}^1 F_{KL}^2\right)\left[\frac{P}{\mu} F_K^1 + \beta_2 L_2 F_K^1 F_L^2 g' + \beta_2 L_2 F_K^2 F_L^2 (g')^2\right]\}/\Omega > 0.
\end{aligned}
$$

Appendix B

Completely differentiate Eqs. (7.4) and (7.10), and divided by dP on both sides of the equation, then we will have

$$
F_L^1 + PF_{LL}^1 \frac{dL_1}{dP} + PF_{LK}^1 \frac{dK_1}{dP} = 0 \tag{7.A1}
$$

$$
F_K^1 + PF_{KK}^1 \frac{dK_1}{dP} + PF_{KL}^1 \frac{dL_1}{dP} = \frac{dr}{dP} \tag{7.A2}
$$

From the linearly homogenous features of production functions, substitute Eq. (7.A2) into Eq. (7.A1), and rearranging it, we will achieve

$$\frac{\widehat{r}}{\widehat{P}} = \left[\left(F_K^1 + F_L^1\frac{L_1}{K_1}\right) + \left(K_1F_{KK}^1 + L_1F_{LK}^1\right)\frac{P\,dK_1}{K_1\,dP}\right]\frac{P}{r} = \frac{PY_1}{rK_1} > 1$$

where $\widehat{r}$ and $\widehat{P}$ are the change rates of interest rate and price, i.e., $\widehat{r} > \widehat{P}$.

References

Amuedo-Dorantes, C., & Pozo, S. (2011). Remittances and income smoothing. *American Economic Review, 101*, 582.

Ball, C. P., Lopez, C., & Reyes, J. (2013). Remittances, inflation and exchange rate regimes in small open economies. *The World Economy, 36*(4), 487–507.

Bhagwati, J. N., & Srinivasan, T. N. (1977). Education in a 'job ladder' model and the fairness-in-hiring rule. *Journal of Public Economics, 7*(1), 1–22.

Chaudhuri, S., & Mukhopadhyay, U. (2006). Pollution and informal sector: A theoretical analysis. *Journal of Economic Integration, 21*(2), 363–378.

Chiwuzulum Odozi, J., Awoyemi, T. T., & Omonona, B. T. (2010). Household poverty and inequality: The implication of migrants' remittances in Nigeria. *Journal of Economic Policy Reform, 13*(2), 191–199.

Copeland, B. R., & Taylor, M. S. (1999). Trade, spatial separation, and the environment. *Journal of International Economics, 47*(1), 137–168.

Dean, J. M., & Gangopadhyay, S. (1997). Export bans, environmental protection, and unemployment. *Review of Development Economics, 1*(3), 324–336.

Djajić, S. (1985). Human capital, minimum wage and unemployment: A Harris-Todaro Model of a developed open economy. *Economica, 52*, 491–508.

Grigorian, D. A., & Melkonyan, T. A. (2011). Destined to receive: The impact of remittances on household decisions in Armenia. *Review of Development Economics, 15*(1), 139–153.

Hoyos, G. A. Z. (2008). International labor migration as a strategy of economic stabilization at the household level in Mexico and Central America. *Papeles de Población, 14*(56), 19–36.

Lall, S. V., & Selod, H. (2006). *Rural-urban migration in developing countries: A survey of theoretical predictions and empirical findings* (Vol. 3915). Washington, DC: World Bank Publications.

Li, X., & Zhou, Y. (2013a). An economic analysis of remittance of unskilled migration on skilled–unskilled wage inequality in labor host region. *Economic Modelling, 33*, 428–432.

Li, X., & Zhou, Y. (2013b). Development policies, transfer of pollution abatement technology and trans-boundary pollution. *Economic Modelling, 31*, 183–188.

McCormick, B., & Wahba, J. (2000). Overseas employment and remittances to a dual economy. *The Economic Journal, 110*(463), 509–534.

Nath, H. K., & Vargas-Silva, C. (2012). Remittances and relative prices. *Review of Development Economics, 16*(1), 45–61.

Papola, T. S. (1981). Dissecting the informal sector. *Economic and Political Weekly, 16*, 1272–1274.

Pradhan, G., Upadhyay, M., & Upadhyaya, K. (2008). Remittances and economic growth in developing countries. *The European Journal of Development Research., 20*(3), 497–506.

Quibria, M. G. (1997). International migration, remittances and income distribution in the source country: A synthesis. *Bulletin of Economic Research, 49*(1), 29–46.

Romatet, E. (1983). Calcutta's informal sector: Theory and reality. *Economic and Political Weekly, 16*, 2115–2128.
Rozelle, S., Edward Taylor, J., & DeBrauw, A. (1999). Migration, remittances, and agricultural productivity in China. *American Economic Review, 89*(2), 287–291.
Stalker, P. (2002). Migration trends and migration policy in Europe. *International Migration, 40* (5), 151–179.
Stark, O., Edward Taylor, J., & Yitzhaki, S. (1986). Remittances and inequality. *The Economic Journal, 96*, 722–740.
Taylor, J. E., & Wyatt, T. J. (1996). The shadow value of migrant remittances, income and inequality in a household-farm economy. *The Journal of Development Studies, 32*(6), 899–912.
Zarate-Hoyos, G. A. (2004). Consumption and remittances in migrant households: Toward a productive use of remittances. *Contemporary Economic Policy, 22*(4), 555–565.
Zhang, J., et al. (2005). Economic returns to schooling in urban China, 1988 to 2001. *Journal of Comparative Economics, 33*(4), 730–752.

Chapter 8
Environment and Labor Movement of Skilled Labor and Unskilled Labor Between Sectors

Xiaochun Li, Yuanting Xu, and Dianshuang Wang

Abstract In this chapter, we divide the labor into skilled and unskilled labor to investigate the impact that the heterogeneous labor transfer between sectors has on the environment under the international skilled and unskilled labor movements and the price change of the agricultural products. The main conclusions are: under certain conditions, skilled labor inflow deteriorates the environment, while its outflow improves the environment; unskilled labor inflow improves the environment, while its outflow deteriorates the environment; and the increasing price of the agricultural products improves the environment, while the decreasing price deteriorates the environment.

Keywords Environment • Heterogeneous labor movement • Agriculture product price

1 Introduction

The transfer of heterogeneous labor force between different sectors is often considered in studies of income disparity and employment. Marjit and Kar (2005) divided labor force in an economy into skilled and unskilled labor and established a general equilibrium model of a two-sector economy. They studied the income disparity with the assumption that there is no unemployment or flow of capital between sectors. Yabuuchi and Chaudhuri (2007) took skilled labor as a specific factor, whereas unskilled labor could move freely between sectors. Based on the assumption of nonexistence of unemployment in either sector, they analyzed the impact of international factors on changes of income. Beladi et al. (2008) analyzed the impact of inflow of international factors on the wage disparity between the skilled labor and unskilled labor through a two-sector general equilibrium model. This chapter is based on the assumptions of full employment and free movement of

X. Li (✉)
Business School, Nanjing University, Nanjing, China
e-mail: xiaochun@nju.edu.cn

Y. Xu • D. Wang
School of Economics, Nanjing University, 22 Hankou Road, Nanjing, Jiangsu 210093, China

X. Li (ed.), *Labor Transfer in Emerging Economies*, New Frontiers in Regional Science: Asian Perspectives 12, DOI 10.1007/978-981-10-3569-2_8

skilled labor between sectors and existence of unemployment of the unskilled labor. Gupta and Dutta (2010) made an assumption that skilled labor moves between trade and non-trade sectors, while unskilled labor does not, upon which they established a general equilibrium model and studied the impact of changes in factor endowments and in price of tradable goods on unemployment and the relative wages of skilled and unskilled labor. Chaudhuri and Banerjee (2010) divided the rural sector into the advanced and the backward subsectors and established a general four-sector equilibrium model. They studied the income effect of capital inflow under the premise of existence of unemployment of skilled labor and immobility between sectors, as well as full employment and full mobility of the unskilled labor between the two rural sectors and immobility of unskilled labor between the rural and urban sectors. However, with regard to the real-world economic activities in the developing countries, the impact of the transfer of heterogeneous labor is not limited to income disparity and employment.

On the other hand, since the 1990s, there have been many studies in the academia on the impact of inter-sector labor transfer in developing countries on the environment from different perspectives, particularly the impact of labor transfer on pollution based on the Harris-Todaro model, such as Beladi and Rapp (1993), Beladi and Frasca (1999), Daitoh (2003, 2008), Tawada and Sun (2010), Daitoh and Omote (2011), and Kondoh (2012), which involve taxation, environmental policy, and improvement of labor market. However, we note that all the aforesaid studies on the labor transfer and environment are based on a common premise, namely, labor is homogeneous, which is different from the reality where labor is actually heterogeneous. As a result, the impact of labor quality on environment is a focus of academic studies in developing countries. Some Chinese scholars pointed out that increasing skilled labor endowment would have an impact of improving the environment.[1] Therefore, we would like to study the impact of the transfer of heterogeneous labor between sectors on the environment.

In this chapter, we will divide the entire labor force into the skilled and unskilled sectors and studied the impact of heterogeneous labor transfer between sectors on the environment under the conditions of free flow of international labor factors and change of agricultural products prices. The main conclusion of this chapter is that, under certain circumstances, inflow of skilled labor could deteriorate the environment; on the other hand, the outflow of labor could improve the environment. The inflow of unskilled labor would, however, improve the environment, and the outflow would deteriorate the environment. In the following, we will establish an analytical model in the second part, made a theoretical analysis in the third part, and draw a conclusion thereupon the last part.

2 The Model

We consider a small open developing economy with two sectors, namely, the urban sector and the agricultural sector. The economy uses four production factors, which are skilled labor L_S, unskilled labor L_U, capital K, and land N. The urban sector uses skilled labor, unskilled labor, and capital to produce the import-competing goods. The agricultural sector uses skilled labor, unskilled labor, and land to produce exportable goods. The urban sector is skilled labor-intensive, and the agricultural sector is unskilled labor-intensive. The production functions of the urban and agricultural sectors are given by:

$$X_1 = F^1(L_{S1}, L_{U1}, K) \tag{8.1}$$

$$X_2 = eF^2(L_{S2}, L_{U2}, N) \tag{8.2}$$

F^1 and F^2 are production functions increasing corresponding to each factor and satisfying linear homogenous and strictly quasi-concave properties.

In the production function of the agricultural sector,

$$\frac{e = \bar{E} - \mu X_1}{\bar{E}} \tag{8.3}$$

where e represents the environment of the economy. When $e = 1$, the environment is in the best condition. It becomes worse when e decreases. $\bar{E}$ represents the environment endowment when there is no pollution in the economy. μ is the pollution that the urban sector discharges for producing one unit of good. We assume that only the production of the urban sector causes pollution emission to make the environment worse. The harmful substance emitted, such as waste gas, waste residue, and wastewater, pollutes water and soil for agricultural use through atmosphere, rivers, and other media. Hence, the product efficiency of the agricultural sector decreases.

Under the condition that the markets are perfectly competitive, we could obtain that:

$$p_1 = a_{S1}w_{S1} + a_{U1}\overline{w_U} + a_{K1}r \tag{8.4}$$

$$p_2 = a_{S2}w_{S2} + a_{U2}w_{U2} + a_{N2}R \tag{8.5}$$

where $a_{ij}(i = S, U, K, N; j = 1, 2)$ is the amount of the ith factor used in the jth sector in order to produce one unit of output. w_{S1} is the wage rate of skilled labor in the urban sector. w_{S2} is the wage rate of skilled labor in the agricultural sector. $\overline{w_U}$ is the wage rate of unskilled labor in the urban sector. w_{U2} is the wage rate of unskilled labor in the agricultural sector. r is the interest rate of capital in the urban sector. R is the rent of land used in the agricultural sector. p_j represent the product prices of the urban sector and the agricultural sector, respectively. In this chapter, we assume that all the products are tradable and hence the product prices are given internationally.

Generally, developing countries lack skilled labor. Therefore, we assume that skilled labor is fully employed with no unemployment, and they move freely between the urban and agricultural sectors. This chapter assumes that the wage rate of unskilled labor in the urban sector is given exogenously, which means that it is downward rigid. However, in the agricultural sector, the wage rate of unskilled labor w is fully elastic. We use L_{UU} to denote the number of unemployed unskilled labor in the urban sector and λ to denote the unemployment rate of unskilled labor in this sector. Hence, $\lambda = L_{UU}/L_{U1} = L_{UU}/a_{U1}X_1$. Therefore, in the unskilled labor market equilibrium, the wage rate in the agricultural sector equals the expected wage income in the urban sector, which equals to the downward rigid wage rate $\overline{w_U}$ multiplied by the probability of obtaining a job in this sector $L_{U1}/(L_{U1} + L_{UU})$. Thus, the allocation mechanism of the skilled labor and unskilled labor are shown as:

$$w_{S1} = w_{S2} \tag{8.6}$$

$$w_{U2} = \frac{L_{U1}}{L_{U1} + L_{UU}} \overline{w_U} \tag{8.7}$$

or:

$$(1 + \lambda) w_{U2} = \overline{w_U} \tag{8.7'}$$

The market-clearing conditions of the four production factors, skilled labor, unskilled labor, capital, and land, could be shown as follows:

$$a_{S1}X_1 + a_{S2}X_2 = L_S \tag{8.8}$$

$$a_{U1}X_1 + a_{U2}X_2 + \lambda a_{U1}X_1 = L_U \tag{8.9}$$

$$a_{K1}X_1 = K \tag{8.10}$$

$$a_{N2}X_2 = N \tag{8.11}$$

where L_S, L_U, K, and N represent the endowment of skilled labor, unskilled labor, capital, and land, respectively.

The basic theoretical model has been built, which consists of nine equations, (8.3), (8.4), (8.5), (8.6), (8.7′), (8.8), (8.9), (8.10), and (8.11). Nine endogenous variables are determined, and they are w_{S1}, w_{S2}, w_{U2}, r, R, λ, e, X_1, and X_2.

3 Environment and Labor Transfer Between Sectors

Differentiating Eqs. (8.3), (8.4), (8.5), (8.6), (8.7′), (8.8), (8.9), (8.10), and (8.11) and writing in a matrix notation, we can obtain the following equation:

$$\begin{pmatrix} \theta_{S1} & 0 & \theta_{K1} & 0 & 0 & 0 \\ \theta_{S2} & \theta_{U2} & 0 & \theta_{N2} & 0 & 0 \\ A & \lambda_{S2}S_{SU}^2 & \lambda_{S1}S_{SK}^1 & \lambda_{S2}S_{SN}^2 & \lambda_{S1} & \lambda_{S2} \\ B & C & D & \lambda_{U2}S_{UN}^2 & (1+\lambda)\lambda_{U1} & \lambda_{U2} \\ S_{KS}^1 & 0 & S_{KK}^1 & 0 & 1 & 0 \\ S_{NS}^2 & S_{NU}^2 & 0 & S_{NN}^2 & 0 & 1 \end{pmatrix} \begin{pmatrix} \widehat{w}_{S1} \\ \widehat{w}_{U2} \\ \widehat{r} \\ \widehat{R} \\ \widehat{X}_1 \\ \widehat{X}_2 \end{pmatrix} = \begin{pmatrix} \widehat{p}_1 \\ \widehat{p}_2 \\ \widehat{L}_S \\ \widehat{L}_U \\ \widehat{K} \\ \widehat{N} \end{pmatrix} \tag{8.12}$$

and

$$e\widehat{e} + (1-e)\widehat{X}_1 = 0 \tag{8.13}$$

where "$\widehat{\ }$" represents the rate of change, $\theta_{ij}(i=S,U,K,N;j=1,2)$ is the distributive share of factor i in the jth sector (e.g., $\theta_{S1}=a_{S1}w_{S1}/p_1$), λ_{ij} is the allocated share of factor i in the jth sector (e.g., $\lambda_{S1}=a_{S1}X_1/L_S$), and S_{ij}^h is the partial elasticity of substitution between factors i and j in the hth sector (e.g., $S_{SU}^2=\frac{\partial a_{S2}}{\partial w_{U2}}\frac{w_{U2}}{a_{S2}}$), $S_{ij}^h>0$ $(i\neq j)$ and $S_{ij}^h<0(i=j)$. We also have:

$$A=\lambda_{S1}S_{SS}^1+\lambda_{S2}S_{SS}^2<0,\quad B=(1+\lambda)\lambda_{U1}S_{US}^1+\lambda_{U2}S_{US}^2>0,$$
$$C=\lambda_{U2}S_{UU}^2-(1+\lambda)\lambda_{U1}<0,\quad D=(1+\lambda)\lambda_{U1}S_{UK}^1>0.$$

The partial elasticity of substitution between factors plays an important role in the following discussion. Therefore, in this chapter, we make the following assumptions:

Assumption 8.1

$$\frac{S_{UK}^1}{\theta_{K1}}>\frac{S_{US}^1}{\theta_{S1}}$$

Assumption 8.1 implies that unskilled labor is more substitutable with capital than with skilled labor in the urban sector.

Assumption 8.2

$$\frac{S_{SN}^2}{\theta_{N2}}>\frac{S_{SU}^2}{\theta_{U2}}$$

Assumption 8.2 implies that skilled labor is more substitutable with land than with unskilled labor in the agricultural sector.

3.1 Labor Transfer Between Sectors Under the International Skilled Labor Movement

Skilled labor in developing countries will sometimes leave because of low wages. In reality, there are also some situations in which skilled labor moves to developing countries from outside. Recently, high unemployment rate in some developed countries results in unemployed and retired skilled labor moving to the developing countries to find job opportunities. Therefore, in this chapter, we not only consider skilled labor outflow but also their inflow.

We can obtain the following by solving Eq. (8.12):

$$\widehat{x}_1/\widehat{L}_S = \left(\theta_{K1}S^1_{KS} - \theta_{S1}S^1_{KK}\right)\left[\theta_{U2}\lambda_{U2}\left(S^2_{UN} - S^2_{NN}\right) - \theta_{N2}\left(C - \lambda_{U2}S^2_{NU}\right)\right]/\Delta > 0 \tag{8.14}$$

$$\widehat{w}_{S1}/\widehat{L}_S = -\theta_{K1}\left[\theta_{U2}\lambda_{U2}\left(S^2_{UN} - S^2_{NN}\right) - \theta_{N2}\left(C - \lambda_{U2}S^2_{NU}\right)\right]/\Delta < 0 \tag{8.15}$$

$$\widehat{r}/\widehat{L}_S = \theta_{S1}\left[\theta_{U2}\lambda_{U2}\left(S^2_{UN} - S^2_{NN}\right) - \theta_{N2}\left(C - \lambda_{U2}S^2_{NU}\right)\right]/\Delta > 0 \tag{8.16}$$

where Δ is the determinant of the matrix in Eq. (8.12) and $\Delta > 0$ (see Appendix).

Differentiating the equation $a_{S1}X_1 = L_{S1}$, we could obtain the following from Eqs. (8.14), (8.15), and (8.16):

$$\frac{\widehat{L}_{S1}}{\widehat{L}_S} = \frac{\widehat{X}_1}{\widehat{L}_S} + S^1_{SS}\frac{\widehat{w}_{S1}}{\widehat{L}_S} + S^1_{SK}\frac{\widehat{r}}{\widehat{L}_S} > 0 \tag{8.17}$$

According to Eq. (8.17) and $\frac{\widehat{X}_1}{\widehat{L}_S} = \frac{\widehat{X}_1}{\widehat{L}_{S1}}\frac{\widehat{L}_{S1}}{\widehat{L}_S}$, we could get that:

$$\widehat{X}_1/\widehat{L}_{S1} > 0 \tag{8.18}$$

$$\widehat{e}/\widehat{L}_{S1} < 0 \tag{8.19}$$

Differentiating equation $a_{U1}X_1 = L_{U1}$, we could obtain the following equation from Eqs. (8.14), (8.15), and (8.16) and Assumption 8.1:

$$\frac{\widehat{L}_{U1}}{\widehat{L}_S} = \frac{\widehat{X}_1}{\widehat{L}_S} + S^1_{US}\frac{\widehat{w}_{S1}}{\widehat{L}_S} + S^1_{UK}\frac{\widehat{r}}{\widehat{L}_S} > 0 \tag{8.20}$$

According to Eq. (8.20) and $\frac{\widehat{X}_1}{\widehat{L}_S} = \frac{\widehat{X}_1}{\widehat{L}_{U1}}\frac{\widehat{L}_{U1}}{\widehat{L}_S}$, we could get that:

$$\widehat{X}_1/\widehat{L}_{U1} > 0 \tag{8.21}$$

$$\widehat{e}/\widehat{L}_{U1} < 0 \tag{8.22}$$

With the six equations (8.17), (8.18), (8.19), (8.20), (8.21), and (8.22) and Assumption 8.1, we can obtain the following proposition:

Proposition 8.1 Under Assumption 8.1, the skilled labor inflow increases employment of skilled labor of the urban sector and causes the unskilled labor from the agricultural sector to migrate to the urban sector, which deteriorates the environment. Conversely, the skilled labor outflow decreases the employment of skilled labor of the urban sector and causes the urban unskilled labor to move to the agricultural sector, which improves the environment.

The urban sector is more skilled labor-intensive than the agricultural sector. Therefore, the skilled labor inflow increases the skilled labor endowment in the economy. According to the Rybczynski theorem, skilled labor inflow leads to an expansion of the urban sector and a contraction of the agricultural sector following the Rybczynski effect. With the unchanged capital endowment, the urban sector should employ more skilled and unskilled labor to increase the output. The increasing output of the urban sector increases pollution and deterioration of the environment. Conversely, using the same method, we could also analyze the impacts of the skilled labor outflow.

3.2 *Labor Transfer Between Sectors Under the International Unskilled Labor Movement*

We consider the impacts of both the outflow and inflow of international unskilled labor on the wage disparity and unemployment rate in the developing countries. Although the former situation (outflow) is common in the developing countries, the latter (inflow) also exists in the real developing economies.[2]

Under Assumption 8.2, we could obtain the following by solving Eq. (8.12):

$$\widehat{X}_1/\widehat{L}_U = \lambda_{S2}\left(\theta_{S1}S^1_{KK} - \theta_{K1}S^1_{KS}\right)\left(\theta_{U2}S^2_{SN} - \theta_{N2}S^2_{SU} - \theta_{U2}S^2_{NN} + \theta_{N2}S^2_{NU}\right)/\Delta < 0 \tag{8.23}$$

$$\widehat{w}_{S1}/\widehat{L}_U = \theta_{K1}\lambda_{S2}\left(\theta_{U2}S^2_{SN} - \theta_{N2}S^2_{SU} - \theta_{U2}S^2_{NN} + \theta_{N2}S^2_{NU}\right)/\Delta > 0 \tag{8.24}$$

$$\widehat{r}/\widehat{L}_U = -\theta_{S1}\lambda_{S2}\left(\theta_{U2}S^2_{SN} - \theta_{N2}S^2_{SU} - \theta_{U2}S^2_{NN} + \theta_{N2}S^2_{NU}\right)/\Delta < 0 \tag{8.25}$$

Differentiating equation $a_{S1}X_1 = L_{S1}$, we could obtain the following from Eqs. (8.23), (8.24), and (8.25):

$$\frac{\widehat{L_{S1}}}{\widehat{L_U}} = \frac{\widehat{X_1}}{\widehat{L_U}} + S_{SS}^1 \frac{\widehat{w_{S1}}}{\widehat{L_U}} + S_{SK}^1 \frac{\widehat{r}}{\widehat{L_U}} < 0 \tag{8.26}$$

According to Eq. (8.26) and $\frac{\widehat{X_1}}{\widehat{L_U}} = \frac{\widehat{X_1}}{\widehat{L_{S1}}} \frac{\widehat{L_{S1}}}{\widehat{L_U}}$, we could get that

$$\widehat{X}_1/\widehat{L}_{S1} > 0 \tag{8.27}$$

$$\widehat{e}/\widehat{L}_{S1} < 0 \tag{8.28}$$

Differentiating the equation $a_{U1}X_1 = L_{U1}$, we could obtain the following equation from Eqs. (8.23), (8.24), and (8.25) and Assumption 8.1:

$$\frac{\widehat{L_{U1}}}{\widehat{L_U}} = \frac{\widehat{X_1}}{\widehat{L_U}} + S_{US}^1 \frac{\widehat{w_{S1}}}{\widehat{L_U}} + S_{UK}^1 \frac{\widehat{r}}{\widehat{L_U}} < 0 \tag{8.29}$$

According to Eq. (8.29) and $\frac{\widehat{X_1}}{\widehat{L_U}} = \frac{\widehat{X_1}}{\widehat{L_{U1}}} \frac{\widehat{L_{U1}}}{\widehat{L_U}}$, we could get that:

$$\widehat{X}_1/\widehat{L}_{U1} > 0 \tag{8.30}$$

$$\widehat{e}/\widehat{L}_{U1} < 0 \tag{8.31}$$

With the six Equations (8.26), (8.27), (8.28), (8.29), (8.30), and (8.31) and Assumption 8.1 and Assumption 8.2, we can obtain the following proposition:

Proposition 8.2 Under Assumptions 8.1 and 8.2, the inflow of unskilled labor causes the urban unskilled as well as skilled labor to migrate to the agricultural sector, which improves the environment. Conversely, the outflow of unskilled labor increases the employment of unskilled labor of the urban sector and causes the agricultural skilled labor and unskilled labor to migrate to the urban sector, which deteriorates the environment.

The agricultural sector is more unskilled labor-intensive than the urban sector. Therefore, the unskilled labor inflow increases the unskilled labor endowment in the economy. According to the Rybczynski theorem, unskilled labor inflow leads to an expansion of the agricultural sector and a contraction of the urban sector following the Rybczynski effect. With the unchanged land endowment, the agricultural sector should employ more skilled and unskilled labor to increase the output. Hence, demand for both production factors increases, and both the urban skilled and unskilled labor migrate to the agricultural sector. The decreasing output of the urban sector decreases the pollution and improves the environment. Conversely, using the same method, we could also analyze the situation of decreased unskilled labor endowment.

3.3 Labor Transfer Between Sectors Under the Price Change of Agricultural Products

We consider the impacts that the labor transfer between sectors has on the environment under the condition of change of price of agricultural products. We can obtain the following by solving Eq. (8.12):

$$\widehat{X}_1/\widehat{p}_2 = \lambda_{S2}\left(\theta_{S1}S^1_{KK} - \theta_{K1}S^1_{KS}\right)V/\Delta < 0 \tag{8.32}$$

$$\widehat{w}_{S1}/\widehat{p}_2 = \lambda_{S2}\theta_{K1}V/\Delta > 0 \tag{8.33}$$

$$\widehat{r}/\widehat{p}_2 = -\lambda_{S2}\theta_{S1}V/\Delta < 0 \tag{8.34}$$

where $V = \lambda_{U2}\left[S^2_{NU}\left(S^2_{US} + S^2_{SN}\right) + S^2_{SU}\left(S^2_{UN} - S^2_{NN}\right) - S^2_{UU}S^2_{NS}\right] - CS^2_{SN} - (1+\lambda)\lambda_{U1}S^2_{NN} > 0$.

Differentiating equation $a_{S1}X_1 = L_{S1}$, we could obtain the following from Eqs. (8.32), (8.33), and (8.34):

$$\frac{\widehat{L}_{S1}}{\widehat{p}_2} = \frac{\widehat{X}_1}{\widehat{p}_2} + S^1_{SS}\frac{\widehat{w}_{S1}}{\widehat{p}_2} + S^1_{SK}\frac{\widehat{r}}{\widehat{p}_2} < 0 \tag{8.35}$$

According to Eq. (8.35) and $\frac{\widehat{X}_1}{\widehat{p}_2} = \frac{\widehat{X}_1}{\widehat{L}_{S1}}\frac{\widehat{L}_{S1}}{\widehat{p}_2}$, we could get that

$$\widehat{X}_1/\widehat{L}_{S1} > 0 \tag{8.36}$$

$$\widehat{e}/\widehat{L}_{S1} < 0 \tag{8.37}$$

Differentiating equation $a_{U1}X_1 = L_{U1}$, we could obtain the following equation from Eqs. (8.32), (8.33), and (8.34) and Assumption 8.1:

$$\frac{\widehat{L}_{U1}}{\widehat{p}_2} = \frac{\widehat{X}_1}{\widehat{p}_2} + S^1_{US}\frac{\widehat{w}_{S1}}{\widehat{p}_2} + S^1_{UK}\frac{\widehat{r}}{\widehat{p}_2} < 0 \tag{8.38}$$

According to Eq. (8.38) and $\frac{\widehat{X}_1}{\widehat{p}_2} = \frac{\widehat{X}_1}{\widehat{L}_{U1}}\frac{\widehat{L}_{U1}}{\widehat{p}_2}$, we could get that

$$\widehat{X}_1/\widehat{L}_{U1} > 0 \tag{8.39}$$

$$\widehat{e}/\widehat{L}_{U1} < 0 \tag{8.40}$$

With the six equations (8.35), (8.36), (8.37), (8.38), (8.39), and (8.40) and Assumption 8.1, we can obtain the following proposition:

Proposition 8.3 Under Assumptions 8.1, increase of agricultural product price causes the urban skilled and unskilled labor to migrate to the agricultural sector, which improves the environment; conversely, decrease of agricultural product price causes the agricultural skilled and unskilled labor to migrate to the urban sector, which deteriorates the environment.

The agricultural sector is more unskilled labor-intensive than the urban sector. Therefore, according to the Stolper-Samuelson effects, increase of agricultural product price raises wage rate of unskilled labor in the agricultural sector, which attracts unskilled labor in the urban sector to migrate to the agricultural sector. Increase of unskilled labor employment of the agricultural sector increases the output and the demand for skilled labor in this sector. This also attracts the skilled labor in the urban sector to migrate to the agricultural sector. The decrease of employment of both skilled and unskilled labor in the urban sector decreases the output of the urban sector as well as pollution. Hence, the environment of the economy improves. Conversely, using the same method, we could analyze the impacts of decreasing agricultural product price.

4 Conclusion

This article analyzed the impact of labor transfer between the skilled and unskilled sectors on the environment, considering free flow of international labor factor and price change of agricultural products. Our study expands the practicality of theoretical studies of the impact of labor transfer on the environment. Nonetheless, it is just a beginning, and we shall proceed to the other related topics, such as taxation, environmental policies, and labor market reform in our future studies.

It also should be pointed out that labor transfer of skilled and unskilled labor among departments is normal. In the meantime, environmental problems are not negligible in many Asian developing countries including China. Therefore, our conclusion is quite consultative for properly dealing with the relationship between economic activity and the environment, as well as relevant policy-making.

Appendix

Under the present model, the dynamic adjustment process for the supply side is as follows:

$$\dot{X}_1 = d_1(p_1 - a_{S1}w_{S1} - a_{U1}\bar{w}_U - a_{K1}r) \tag{8.A1}$$

$$\dot{X}_2 = d_2(p_2 - a_{S2}w_{S1} - a_{U2}w_{U2} - a_{N2}R) \tag{8.A2}$$

$$\dot{w}_{S1} = d_3(a_{S1}X_1 + a_{S2}X_2 - L_S) \tag{8.A3}$$

$$\dot{w}_{U2} = d_4\left(a_{U1}X_1 + a_{U2}X_2 + \frac{\overline{w_U} - w_{U2}}{w_{U2}}a_{U1}X_1 - L_U\right) \quad (8.A4)$$

$$\dot{r} = d_5(a_{K1}X_1 - K) \quad (8.A5)$$

$$\dot{R} = d_6(a_{N2}X_2 - N) \quad (8.A6)$$

where "." represents differentiation with respect to time and $d_j(j = 1, 2, 3, 4, 5, 6, 7, 8)$ is the positive coefficient measuring the speed of adjustment and $d_j > 0$.

Marshallian adjustment process is assumed for quantities when the demand price differs from the supply price in the goods markets. A Walrasian adjustment mechanism is assumed for the factor prices with the fixed endowment in the factor markets. The determinant of the Jacobian matrix of equations (8.A1), (8.A2), (8.A3), (8.A4), (8.A5), and (8.A6) is:

$$|J| = d_1 d_2 \ldots d_6 p_1 p_2 KNL_S L_U \begin{vmatrix} 0 & 0 & -\theta_{S1} & 0 & -\theta_{K1} & 0 \\ 0 & 0 & -\theta_{S2} & -\theta_{U2} & 0 & -\theta_{N2} \\ \lambda_{S1} & \lambda_{S2} & A & \lambda_{S2}S^2_{SU} & \lambda_{S1}S^1_{SK} & \lambda_{S2}S^2_{SN} \\ (1+\lambda)\lambda_{U1} & \lambda_{U2} & B & C & D & \lambda_{U2}S^2_{UN} \\ 1 & 0 & S^1_{KS} & 0 & S^1_{KK} & 0 \\ 0 & 1 & S^2_{NS} & S^2_{NU} & 0 & S^2_{NN} \end{vmatrix}$$

It can also be written as follows:

$$|J| = d_1 d_2 \cdots d_6 p_1 p_2 KNL_S L_U \Delta$$

Therefore, according to the Routh-Hurwitz theorem, a necessary condition for the local stability of the system is that the determinant of the Jacobian matrix is positive. Hence, it is assumed that the equilibrium in this chapter is stable under the condition that $|J| > 0$. We could obtain that $\Delta > 0$.

References

Beladi, H., & Frasca, R. (1999). Pollution control under an urban binding minimum wage. *The Annals of Regional Science, 33*, 523–533.

Beladi, H., & Rapp, J. (1993). Urban unemployment and the backward incidence of pollution control. *The Annals of Regional Science, 27*, 153–163.

Beladi, H., Chaudhuri, S., & Yabuuchi, S. (2008). Can international factor mobility reduce wage inequality in a dual economy. *Review of International Economics, 16*, 893–903.

Chaudhuri, S., & Banerjee, D. (2010). Foreign capital inflow, skilled-unskilled wage inequality and unemployment of unskilled labour in a fair wage model. *Economic Modelling, 27*, 477–486.

Daitoh, I. (2003). Environmental protection and urban unemployment: Environmental policy reform in a polluted dualistic economy. *Review of Development Economics, 7*, 496–509.

Daitoh, I. (2008). Environmental protection and trade liberalization in a small open dual economy. *Review of Development Economics, 12*, 728–736.

Daitoh, I., & Omote, M. (2011). The optimal environmental tax and urban unemployment in an open economy. *Review of Development Economics, 15*, 168–179.

Gupta, M. R., & Dutta, P. B. (2010). Skilled-unskilled wage inequality, nontraded good and endogenous supply of skilled labour: A theoretical analysis. *Economic Modelling, 27*, 923–934.

Kondoh, K. (2012). Unemployment, environmental policy, and international migration. *The Journal of International Trade & Economic Development, 21*(5), 677–690.

Marjit, S., & Kar, S. (2005). Emigration and wage inequality. *Economics Letters, 88*(1), 141–145.

Tawada, M., & Sun, S. (2010). Urban pollution, unemployment and national welfare in a dualistic economy. *Review of Development Economics, 14*(2), 311–322.

Yabuuchi, S., & Chaudhuri, S. (2007). International migration of labour and skilled–unskilled wage inequality in a developing economy. *Economic Modelling, 24*(1), 128–137.

Chapter 9
Development Policies, Transfer of Pollution Abatement Technology, and Trans-boundary Pollution

Xiaochun Li and Yu Zhou

Abstract In this chapter, we integrate intra-region labor migration and inter-region labor migration into the Harris-Todaro model in the presence of unidirectional trans-boundary pollution. We conduct a simple comparative static analysis of regional economic and environmental effects of the central government's development policies on two regions, reducing the transfer cost of inter-region labor migration and increasing the capital subsidy to the less developed region. In addition, we compare the environmental and regional economic effects of the transfer of pollution abatement technology in two regions.

Keywords Harris-Todaro • Unidirectional trans-boundary pollution • Labor transfer cost • Capital subsidy • Pollution abatement technology

1 Introduction

Current theoretical research on trans-boundary pollution are focusing on the following two aspects: first, trans-boundary pollution's impact on international trades between nations, specifically, comparative advantage, trade terms, and gains from trade and trade policy, and second, trans-boundary pollution's impact on inter-regional environmental policy and factor flow, of which the representative researches are Hoel and Shapiro (2003), Haavio (2005), and Candel-Sanchez (2006). Hoel and Shapiro (2003) studied how environmental policy-making of each region is influenced by inter-regional households' perfect mobility in the presence of trans-boundary pollution. On the basis of their work, Haavio(2005) investigated the inter-regional households' imperfect mobility influence on the environmental policy-making of each region; Sigman (2004) studied regional

X. Li (✉)
Business School, Nanjing University, Nanjing, China
e-mail: xiaochun@nju.edu.cn

Y. Zhou
School of Economics, Nanjing University, 22 Hankou Road, Nanjing, Jiangsu 210093, China

X. Li (ed.), *Labor Transfer in Emerging Economies*, New Frontiers in Regional Science: Asian Perspectives 12, DOI 10.1007/978-981-10-3569-2_9

intergovernmental free-riding's effect on environmental policy-making and sewage discharge level in the presence of trans-boundary pollution; and Candel-Sanchez (2006) adapted the compensation principles proposed by Varian(1994) and studied the optimal allocation of trans-boundary pollution between regions.

Yet the above researches are mostly set in background of developed countries, that is, the integrated economy thus limits their application to the identical analysis in a dual economy. For example, despite the strong economic growth, China is suffering from worsening environmental pollution among which trans-boundary pollution is an important part. Due to China's eastern and western geographical differences, the direction of river flow and atmospheric circulation is generally from west to east, presenting a trans-boundary pollution trend from west to east. Trend from west to east is also shown in the intra-region migration flow, a result of the western backward economy and eastern coastal rapid economic development. On the other hand, in order to achieve the goal of coordinated inter-regional development, the Chinese government put forward in 2000 the "scale development of the western region," which accelerated western economic growth but also exacerbated the west-to-east trans-boundary pollution issue. Therefore, current research results under existing framework are not applicable to China's trans-boundary pollution problems.

This chapter is based on a dual economy, integrating both intra-region and inter-region labor immigration into the Harris-Todaro model in the presence of unidirectional trans-boundary pollution. This chapter will focus on governmental impletion of transportation systems and communication facilities, an effort to reduce transfer cost of intra-region labor migration (time cost, mental cost, and economic cost) so as to promote labor migration, as well as the influence of governmental capital subsidy and development policy, aimed at the less developed region, on the natural environment and economy. It further compares regional and economic effects brought by the pollution abatement technology improvement in different regions. We come to the conclusion that infrastructure construction to reduce transfer cost of intra-region labor migration has no impact on trans-boundary pollution; the capital subsidy to the less developed region will worsen the local natural environment and increase the trans-boundary pollution. The transfer of the pollution abatement technology is favorable to the improvement of the whole environment.

The rest of this chapter is organized as follows: In Sect. 2, we set up the theoretical model in an extended Harris-Todaro framework; in Sect. 3, we conducted a simple comparative static analysis of the established model; and in Sect. 4, we provide the concluding remarks.

2 The Theoretical Model

Consider a small, closed economy consisting of two regions: region 1 and region 2. Region 1 is the less developed region, which has two sectors, rural agricultural sector 1 and urban industrial sector 1; agricultural sector 1 utilizes the local rural labor and sector-specific capital as factors of production. The output of agricultural

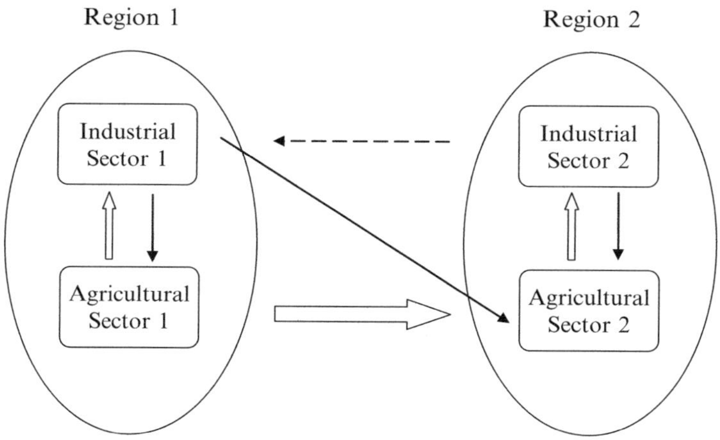

Fig. 9.1 Factors' mobility and pollution dissemination
Note (1) "⟶": direction of dissemination of pollution
(2) "⇨": direction of labor migration
(3) "– →": direction of capital inflow

sector 1 also depends on the surrounding environment, that is, the better the rural environment, the more output will be produced. The local rural labors not only transfer from rural areas to urban areas in region 1 but also migrate to region 2; the wage rate of agricultural sector 1 is flexible; industrial sector 1 utilizes local rural migrants, urban labor, and capital as factors of production. The wage rate is downward rigid; industrial production will generate pollution, which imposes damages upon not only the local rural environment but also the rural environment in region 2, through agents like air or water. Region 2 is the well-developed region, also with two sectors, rural agricultural sector 2 and urban industrial sector 2; agricultural sector 2 utilizes the local rural labor, rural migrants from region 1, and sector-specific capital as factors of production. The output of agricultural sector 2 depends on the surrounding environment as well. The rural labors of region 2 only transfer from rural areas to urban areas in region 2; the wage rate of agricultural sector 2 is flexible; industrial sector 2 utilizes local rural migrants, inter-region rural migrants, urban labor, and capital as factors of production. The wage rate is downward rigid; industrial production will also generate pollution, which just imposes damages upon the local rural environment without any trans-boundary pollution; here we further assume that the capital could perfectly mobile between two industrial sectors.

For the sake of promoting coordinated development of the two regions, the central government makes efforts to develop the infrastructure, such as transportation systems and communication facilities. At the same time, the central government also put up capital to provide support for the industrial sector in the less developed region. In addition, the central government's energy saving and emission reduction policy will promote the pollution abatement technology level in different regions.

The directions of factors' mobility and pollution dissemination can be illustrated in Fig. 9.1.

2.1 Region 1

2.1.1 Industrial Sector 1

The production of industrial sector 1 is

$$M_1 = F^{M_1}(L_{M_1}, K_{M_1}) \tag{9.1}$$

where M_1 is the level of output; L_{M_1} and K_{M_1} are labor and capital inputs, respectively. The function F^{M_1} is assumed to be strictly quasi-concave and linearly homogeneous.[1] Profit maximization yields

$$p_{M_1} F_L^{M_1} = \bar{w}_1 \tag{9.2}$$

where p_{M_1} is the relative price of the industrial product in terms of the agricultural product of region 1; $\bar{w}_1$ is the institutionally fixed wage rate.

2.1.2 Agricultural Sector 1

The production function of agricultural sector 1 is

$$A_1 = g_1(E_1) F^{A_1}(L_{A_1}, \bar{K}_{A_1}) \tag{9.3}$$

where A_1 is the level of output; L_{A_1} and $\bar{K}_{A_1}$ are labor and capital inputs, respectively. Denote that E_1 is the quality of rural environment after pollution. $g_1(E_1)$, with the properties, $g_1 > 0$, $g_1' > 0$, and $g_1'' < 0$, represents the effect of rural environment on agricultural productivity. Thus:

$$E_1 = \bar{E}_1 - \alpha \lambda_1 M_1 \tag{9.4}$$

where $\bar{E}_1$ is the best quality of the rural environment, which is regarded as given; λ_1 expresses the units of local pollution generated by one unit production of industrial sector 1; α,which satisfies $\alpha \in (0, 1)$, is propositional of the pollution generated by

---

[1]In the present paper, we assume that all the production functions share the same properties with that of the industrial sector 1. Moreover, we have $F_J^i = \partial F^i / \partial J$ and $F_{\mathrm{Jk}}^i = \partial (F^i)^2 / \partial J \partial k$, for example, $F_L^{M_1} = \partial F^{M_1} / \partial L$ and $F_{\mathrm{LK}}^{M_1} = \partial^2 F^{M_1} / \partial L \partial K$.

industrial sector 1 in region 1; and $1-\alpha$ is the rest propositional of the pollution disseminating to region 2. Profit maximization yields

$$g_1(E_1)F_L^{A_1} = w_{A_1} \tag{9.5}$$

where w_{A_1} is the flexible wage rate.

2.1.3 Regional Endowments and Factor Mobility

The full-employment condition in the factor markets can be written as

$$L_{M_1} + L_{U_1} + L_{A_1} = \bar{L}_1 - L_{tr} \tag{9.6}$$

$$K_{M_1} - \bar{K}_{tr} = \bar{K}_1 \tag{9.7}$$

The intra-region migration equilibrium yields

$$w_{A_1} = \frac{L_{M_1}}{L_{M_1} + L_{U_1}}\bar{w}_1 \tag{9.8}$$

where L_{U_1} is the amount of the urban unemployment; $\bar{K}_{\mathrm{tr}}$ is the amount of the capital subsidy.

2.2 *Region 2*

2.2.1 Industrial Sector 2

The production of the industrial sector 2 is

$$M_2 = F^{M_2}(L_{M_2}, K_{M_2}) \tag{9.9}$$

where M_2 is the level of output; L_{M_2} and K_{M_2} are labor and capital inputs, respectively. Profit maximization yields

$$p_{M_2}F_L^{M_2} = \bar{w}_2 \tag{9.10}$$

where p_{M_2} is the relative price of the industrial product in terms of the agricultural product of region 1; $\bar{w}_2$ is the institutionally fixed wage.

2.2.2 Agricultural Sector 2

The production function of agricultural sector 2 is

$$A_2 = g_2(E_2)F^{A_2}(L_{A_2}, \bar{K}_{A_2}) \tag{9.11}$$

where A_2 is the level of output; L_{A_2} and $\bar{K}_{A_2}$ are labor and capital inputs, respectively. Denote that E_2 is the current quality of rural environment after pollution. $g_2(E_2)$, with the properties, $g_2 > 0$, $g_2' > 0$, and $g_2'' < 0$, represents the effect of rural environment on agricultural productivity. Thus:

$$E_2 = \bar{E}_2 - \lambda_2 M_2 - (1 - \alpha)\lambda_1 M_1 \tag{9.12}$$

where $\bar{E}_2$ is the best quality of the rural environment; λ_2 expresses the units of local pollution generated by one unit production of industrial sector 2. Profit maximization yields

$$g_2(E_2)p_A F_L^{A_2} = w_{A_2} \tag{9.13}$$

where p_A is the relative price of the industrial product in terms of the agricultural product of region 1; w_{A_2} is the flexible wage rate.

2.2.3 Regional Endowments and Factor Mobility

The full-employment condition can be written as

$$L_{M_2} + L_{U_2} + L_{A_2} = \bar{L}_2 + L_{tr} \tag{9.14}$$

$$K_{M_2} + \bar{K}_{tr} = \bar{K}_2 \tag{9.15}$$

The intra-region migration equilibrium yields

$$w_{A_2} = \frac{L_{M_2}}{L_{M_2} + L_{U_2}} \bar{w}_2 \tag{9.16}$$

where L_{U_2} is the amount of the urban unemployment.

The inter-region migration equilibrium yields

$$w_{A_1} + C = \frac{L_{M_2}}{L_{M_2} + L_{U_2} + L_{A_2}} \bar{w}_2 + \frac{L_{A_2}}{L_{M_2} + L_{U_2} + L_{A_2}} w_{A_2}$$

Replace (9.16) into the above equation and we have

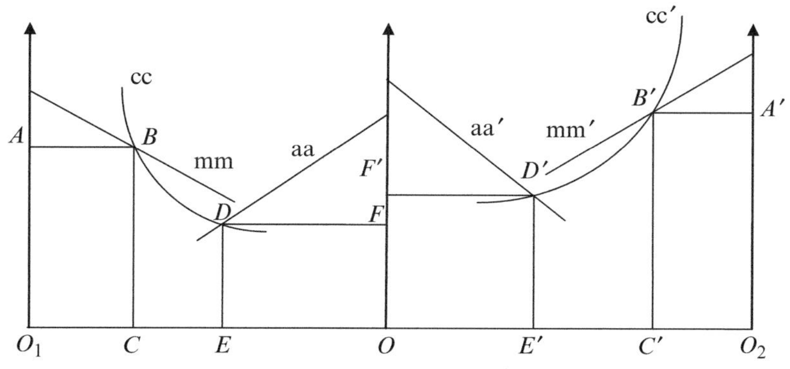

Fig. 9.2 Labor allocation mechanisms of two regions in equilibrium

$$w_{A_1} + C = w_{A_2} \tag{9.17}$$

where C is the transfer cost. The central government could reduce inter-regional labor transfer costs, such as the time cost, mental cost, and economic cost, by developing the infrastructure, to encourage region 1's rural labor to transfer to region 2. That is the reason why we treat C as the policy variable here.

The basic model has been established. The endogenous variables are M_1, L_{M_1}, K_{M_1}, A_1, L_{A_1}, E_1, w_{A_1}, L_{U_1}, L_{tr}, M_2, L_{M_2}, K_{M_2}, A_2, L_{A_2}, E_2, w_{A_2}, and L_{U_2}. The policy variables are C, $\bar{K}_{tr}$, λ_1, and λ_2. The following figure illustrates the labor allocation mechanisms of the two regions in equilibrium.

In Fig. 9.2, O_1O and O_2O on the horizontal axis represent the equilibrium amount of labors in region 1and region 2, respectively, that is, $O_1O = \bar{L}_1 - L_{tr}$ and $O_2O = \bar{L}_2 + L_{tr}$. Draw the vertical axes passing O_1, O, and O_2, respectively, which represent the marginal value of production of industrial sector 1, agricultural sector 1(agricultural sector 2), and industrial sector 2, respectively. mm, aa, aa$'$, and mm$'$ refer to the marginal production curves of industrial sector 1, agricultural sector 1, agricultural sector 1, and industrial sector 2, respectively. Since the wage rate of industrial 1, $\bar{w}_1(O_1A)$, is given, we draw a line parallel to the horizontal axis and passing through A, which meets mm at B.We draw another line perpendicular to O_1O and passing through B, which meets the horizontal axis at C. Thus, we have $O_1C = L_{M_1}$. cc is a rectangular hyperbola through point B, which meets aa at point D. We draw a line parallel to the horizontal axis and passing through D, which meets the vertical axis (O is the original point) at F; we can get $OF = w_{A_1}$. Draw another line perpendicular to the horizontal axis and passing through D, which meets the horizontal axis at E; we know that $OE = L_{A_1}$. Then, we can easily get $CE = L_{U_1}$. Since the wage rate of industrial 2, $\bar{w}_2(O_2A')$, is given, we employ the same approach to get $O_2C' = L_{M_2}$, $OE' = L_{A_2}$, $OF' = w_{A_2}$, and $C'E' = L_{U_2}$. The inter-region labor migration equilibrium in (9.17),which means $w_{A_2} - w_{A_1} = C$, can be illustrated by the difference between $OF$and OF', that is, $FF' = C$.

Table 9.1 Results of comparative static analysis of development policies

	dK_{M_1}	dL_{M_1}	dM_1	dE_1	dK_{M_2}	dL_{M_2}	dM_2	dE_2	dw_{A_1}
dC	/	/	/	/	/	/	/	/	−
$d\bar{K}_{tr}$	+	+	+	−	−	−	−	*	*
	dL_{A_1}	dL_{U_1}	dw_{A_2}	dL_{A_2}	dL_{U_2}	dL_{tr}	dA_1	dA_2	
dC	+	+	+	−	−	−	+	−	
$d\bar{K}_{tr}$	*	*	*	*	*	*	*	*	

Note: "−" and "+" mean that the changes of the exogenous variables will make the endogenous variables change in the opposed and same directions, respectively; "/" means that the changes of exogenous variables have no impacts on endogenous variables; and "*" means that the changes of exogenous variables have ambiguous impacts on endogenous variables

3 The General Equilibrium

The whole model can be solved as follows. Equations (9.7), (9.2), (9.1), and (9.4) could solve for the equilibrium values of K_{M_1}, L_{M_1}, M_1, and E_1. Then Eqs. (9.15), (9.10), (9.9), and (9.12) can determine the equilibrium values of K_{M_2}, L_{M_2}, M_2, and E_2, which are conditional on the equilibrium value of M_1. Given the equilibrium values of E_1 andE_2, the equilibrium values of w_{A_1}, L_{U_1}, L_{A_1}, L_{tr}, w_{A_2}, L_{U_2}, and L_{A_2} could be determined by (9.5), (9.6), (9.8), (9.13), (9.14), (9.16), and (9.17). Substituting E_1 and L_{A_1} into (9.3) and E_2 and L_{A_2} into (9.11), we can easily get the equilibrium values of A_1 and A_2. Now, let us focus our attention on the comparative static properties of the model, the regional economic and environmental effects of the development policies, and the transfer of the pollution abatement technology in two different regions.

3.1 Regional Economic and Environmental Effects of Development Policies

Total differentiation of Eqs. (9.5), (9.6), (9.8), (9.13), (9.14), (9.16), and (9.17) yields the following equation systems:

$$\begin{pmatrix} 1 & -g_1F_{LL}^{A_1} & 0 & 0 & 0 & 0 & 0 \\ 0 & 0 & 1 & -g_2p_AF_{LL}^{A_2} & 0 & 0 & 0 \\ 0 & 1 & 0 & 0 & 1 & 0 & 1 \\ 0 & 0 & 0 & 1 & 0 & 1 & -1 \\ 1 & 0 & -1 & 0 & 0 & 0 & 0 \\ L_{M_1}+L_{U_1} & 0 & 0 & 0 & w_{A_1} & 0 & 0 \\ 0 & 0 & L_{M_2}+L_{U_2} & 0 & 0 & w_{A_2} & 0 \end{pmatrix} \bullet \begin{pmatrix} dw_{A_1} \\ dL_{A_1} \\ dw_{A_2} \\ dL_{A_2} \\ dL_{U_1} \\ dL_{U_2} \\ dL_{tr} \end{pmatrix}$$

$$= \begin{pmatrix} 0 \\ 0 \\ 0 \\ 0 \\ -1 \\ 0 \\ 0 \end{pmatrix} dC + \begin{pmatrix} -F_L^{A_1}g_1'\lambda_1\left(\dfrac{F_{LK}^{M_1}}{F_{LL}^{M_1}} - F_K^{M_1}\right) \\ p_AF_L^{A_2}g_2'\left[\lambda_2\left(-\dfrac{F_{LK}^{M_2}}{F_{LL}^{M_2}} + F_K^{M_2}\right) - (1-\alpha)\lambda_1\left(-\dfrac{F_{LK}^{M_1}}{F_{LL}^{M_1}} + F_K^{M_1}\right)\right] \\ \dfrac{F_{LK}^{M_1}}{F_{LL}^{M_1}} \\ -\dfrac{F_{LK}^{M_2}}{F_{LL}^{M_2}} \\ 0 \\ -(\bar{w}_1 - w_{A_1})\dfrac{F_{LK}^{M_1}}{F_{LL}^{M_1}} \\ (\bar{w}_2 - w_{A_2})\dfrac{F_{LK}^{M_2}}{F_{LL}^{M_2}} \end{pmatrix} d\bar{K}_{tr} \tag{9.18}$$

Define the determinant of square matrix in (9.18) as Δ and calculate Δ to obtain:

$$\begin{aligned} \Delta = {} & g_1F_{LL}^{A_1}w_{A_1}\left[w_{A_2} - g_2p_AF_{LL}^{A_2}(L_{M_2}+L_{U_2})\right] \\ & + w_{A_2}g_2p_AF_{LL}^{A_2}\left[w_{A_1} - g_1F_{LL}^{A_1}(L_{M_1}+L_{U_1})\right] \\ & < 0 \end{aligned}$$

Solving (9.18) by using Cramer's rule, we can obtain Table 9.1:

Summarizing the results in Table 9.1, we establish the results as follows:

Proposition 9.1 The central government reducing the transfer cost will have no impacts on the qualities of the environment in region 1 and region 2.

From Proposition 9.1, we know that the infrastructure development would not do any damage to the qualities of the environment in both regions, as well as giving rise to the trans-boundary pollution. From Table 9.1, we can also know that the central government reducing the transfer cost will have the following economic effects on region 1 and region 2. In region 1, the wage rate, the employment, and the output of the agricultural sector increase. Unemployment in the urban areas decreases; the number of migrant labors from region 1 to region 2 increases. In region 2, the wage rate of the agricultural sector decreases, but the employment and

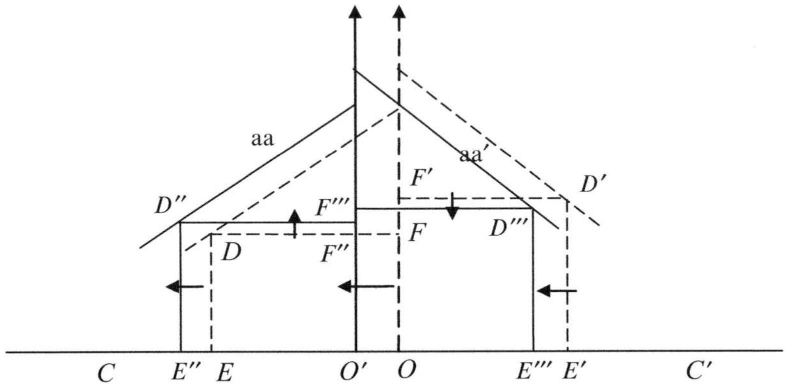

Fig. 9.3 Partial regional economic effects of reducing the transfer cost

the output of the agricultural sector increase. Unemployment in the urban areas increases. The above regional economic effects show us that the reason why the central government reducing the transfer cost will have no impacts on the qualities of the environment in region 1 and region 2 is that the output level of the industrial sector in region 1 remains unchanged.

The partial economic effects of Proposition 9.1 could be illustrated by the following figure on the basis of Fig. 9.2.

We know that reducing the transfer cost will increase the amount of inter-region migrants from (9.17), which means that the vertical axis passing through O will shift rightward. Without generality, we assume that the vertical axis moves along the horizontal axis to the point O'. Reducing the transfer cost has no impact on the natural environment of both regions. Both agricultural marginal production curves move with the vertical axis passing through O. Denote that the rectangular hyperbola *cc* and *cc*' interact with *aa* and *aa*' at D'' and D'''. We draw a line parallel to the horizontal axis and passing through D'', which meets the vertical axis passing through O' at E''. Draw another line perpendicular to the horizontal axis and passing through D'', which meets the horizontal axis at F''. Thus, we get the wage rate of agricultural sector 1, $O'F''$, and the amount of labor employment, $O'E''$, in the new equilibrium. Furthermore, we can know that the amount of urban unemployment in region 1 is CE''. Do the same thing and we can get the wage rate of agricultural sector 2 $O'F'''$, the amount of labor employment $O'E''$, and the amount of urban unemployment in region 2 $C'E'''$. From Fig. 9.3, we know that in the new equilibrium, the wage rate and the employment of the agricultural sector 1 increase. The amount of the urban unemployment in region 1 decreases. In region 2, the wage rate of the agricultural sector decreases, but the employment of the agricultural sector increases. Unemployment in the urban areas increases.

Proposition 9.2 The central government giving the capital subsidy to region 1 will deteriorate the quality of natural environment of region 1, which is also accompanied by the increase of trans-boundary pollution to region 2.

When region 1's industrial sector gets the capital subsidy, the capital employed for the production increases; the consequence of which is region 1's industrial sector enlarges the production scale. Thus, the increase of the output level leads to the deterioration of the local natural environment. What we can learn from Proposition 9.2 is that when the government wants to put up capital to provide support for certain projects in the less developed region, the projects should be identified beforehand, in order to abate the pollution generated by these projects. From Table 9.1, we can also know that the central government giving the capital subsidy to region 1 will have the following economic effects in both regions. In region 1, labor and capital inputs expand. Thus, the output of the industrial sector increases. In region 2, labor and capital inputs contract. Thus, the output of the industrial sector decreases.

The demand side of region 1 is represented by the expenditure function, which is defined as $e^1(p_{M_1}, U_1)$, where U_1 is region 1's utility level. We assume that the fraction of the inter-region migrant incomes, β, is remitted back home. Hence, region 1's budget constraint can be stated as

$$e^1(p_{M_1}, U_1) = w_{A_1}(\bar{L}_1 - L_{tr}) + \beta w_{A_2} L_{tr} \tag{9.19}$$

Denote that $e^2(p_A, p_{M_2}, U_2)$ is the expenditure function of region 2, where U_2 is region 2's utility level. Thus we have

$$e^2(p_A, p_{M_2}, U_2) = w_{A_2}\bar{L}_2 + (1-\beta) w_{A_2} L_{tr} \tag{9.20}$$

The welfare effect of reducing the transfer cost can be obtained by totally differentiating Eqs. (9.18) and (9.19), respectively, to yield[2]

$$e_U^1 \frac{dU_1}{dC} = (\bar{L}_1 - L_{tr})\frac{dw_{A_1}}{dC} - w_{A_1}\frac{dL_{tr}}{dC} + \beta \frac{dw_{A_2} L_{tr}}{dC} \tag{9.19'}$$

$$e_U^2 \frac{dU_2}{dC} = [\bar{L}_2 + (1-\beta)L_{tr}]\frac{dw_{A_2}}{dC} + (1-\beta) w_{A_2}\frac{dL_{tr}}{dC} \tag{9.20'}$$

Proposition 9.3 The central government reducing the transfer cost will have the following welfare effects:

1. In region 1, if $(\bar{L}_1 - L_{tr})\frac{dw_{A_1}}{dC} < w_{A_1}\frac{dL_{tr}}{dC} - \beta\frac{dw_{A_2}L_{tr}}{dC}$, reducing the transfer cost decreases the regional utility level; if $(\bar{L}_1 - L_{tr})\frac{dw_{A_1}}{dC} > w_{A_1}\frac{dL_{tr}}{dC} - \beta\frac{dw_{A_2}L_{tr}}{dC}$, the opposite occurs, and the regional utility level will increase.

[2]The increase of the capital subsidy, $\bar{K}_{tr}$, has ambiguous impacts on both regional utility levels.

Table 9.2 Results of comparative static analysis of transfer of pollution abatement technology

	dK_{M_1}	dL_{M_1}	dM_1	dE_1	dK_{M_2}	dL_{M_2}	dM_2	dE_2	dw_{A_1}
$d\lambda_1$	/	/	/	–	/	/	/	–	–
$d\lambda_2$	/	/	/	/	/	/	/	–	–
	dL_{A_1}	dL_{U_1}	dw_{A_2}	dL_{A_2}	dL_{U_2}	dL_{tr}	dA_1	dA_2	
$d\lambda_1$	*	+	–	*	+	*	*	*	
$d\lambda_2$	+	+	–	–	+	–	+	–	

Note: "–" and "+" mean that the changes of the exogenous variables will make the endogenous variables change in the opposed and same directions, respectively; "/" means that the changes of exogenous variables have no impacts on endogenous variables; and "*" means that the changes of exogenous variables have ambiguous impacts on endogenous variables

2. In region 1, if $[\bar{L}_2 + (1-\beta)L_{tr}]\frac{dw_{A_2}}{dC} > -(1-\beta)w_{A_2}\frac{dL_{tr}}{dC}$, reducing the transfer cost decreases the regional utility level; if $[\bar{L}_2 + (1-\beta)L_{tr}]\frac{dw_{A_2}}{dC} < -(1-\beta)w_{A_2}\frac{dL_{tr}}{dC}$, the opposite occurs, and the regional utility level will increase.

3.2 *Regional Economic and Environmental Effects of Transfer of Pollution Abatement Technology*

Total differentiation of Eqs. (9.5), (9.6), (9.8), (9.13), (9.14), (9.16), and (9.17) yields the following equation systems:

$$\begin{pmatrix} 1 & -g_1F_{LL}^{A_1} & 0 & 0 & 0 & 0 & 0 \\ 0 & 0 & 1 & -g_2p_AF_{LL}^{A_2} & 0 & 0 & 0 \\ 0 & 1 & 0 & 0 & 1 & 0 & 1 \\ 0 & 0 & 0 & 1 & 0 & 1 & -1 \\ 1 & 0 & -1 & 0 & 0 & 0 & 0 \\ L_{M_1}+L_{U_1} & 0 & 0 & 0 & w_{A_1} & 0 & 0 \\ 0 & 0 & L_{M_2}+L_{U_2} & 0 & 0 & w_{A_2} & 0 \end{pmatrix} \bullet \begin{pmatrix} dw_{A_1} \\ dL_{A_1} \\ dw_{A_2} \\ dL_{A_2} \\ dL_{U_1} \\ dL_{U_2} \\ dL_{tr} \end{pmatrix}$$
$$= \begin{pmatrix} -\alpha M_1F_L^{A_1}g_1' \\ -(1-\alpha)M_1p_AF_L^{A_2}g_2' \\ 0 \\ 0 \\ 0 \\ 0 \\ 0 \end{pmatrix} d\lambda_1 + \begin{pmatrix} 0 \\ -M_2p_AF_L^{A_2}g_2' \\ 0 \\ 0 \\ 0 \\ 0 \\ 0 \end{pmatrix} d\lambda_2 \tag{9.21}$$

Solving (9.21) by using Cramer's rule, we can get Table 9.2.

In view of the results in Table 9.2, we can establish the following results:

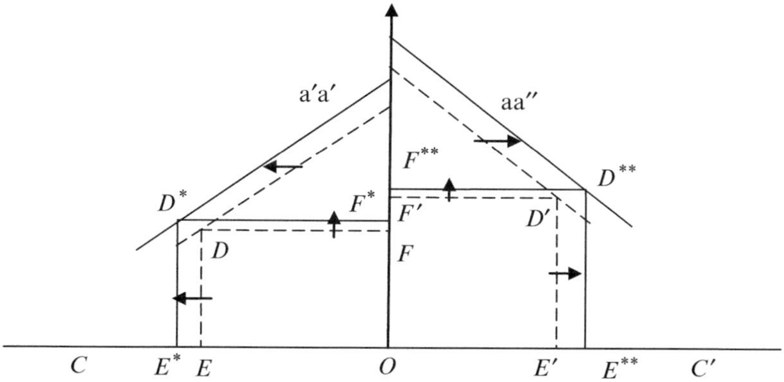

Fig. 9.4 Partial regional economic effects of transfer of pollution abatement technology in region 1

Proposition 9.4 The transfer of the pollution abatement technology in region 1 will improve the quality of natural environment in region 1, accompanied by the decrease of trans-boundary pollution. In addition, the quality of natural environment of region 2 also improves. The transfer of the pollution abatement technology in region 2 will improve the quality of natural environment of region 2 with the quantity of trans-boundary pollution unchanged.

The economic insight of Proposition 9.4 is straightforward, but it clearly shows that improving the technology level of pollution abatement of the less developed region is more pressing, because it could increase the quality of the natural environment in both regions.

Some parts of Proposition 9.4 can be also illustrated in Fig. 9.4. For the sake of simplicity, we assume that the transfer of the pollution abatement technology in region 1 has no impact on the amount of the inter-region migrants. The transfer of the pollution abatement technology improves the natural environment of both regions. Thus, the marginal production curves of agricultural sector 1 and agricultural sector 2 will move leftward to $a'a'$ and rightward to aa'', respectively. Denote that the rectangular hyperbola cc and cc' interact with $a'a'$ and aa'' at D^* and D^{**}. We draw a line parallel to the horizontal axis and passing through D^*, which meets the vertical axis passing through O at E^*. Draw another line perpendicular to the horizontal axis and passing through D^*, which meets the horizontal axis at F^*. Thus, we get the wage rate of agricultural sector 1, OF^*, and the amount of labor employment, OE^*, in the new equilibrium. Furthermore, we can know that the amount of urban unemployment in region 1 is CE^*. Do the same thing, and we can get the wage rate of agricultural sector 2, OF^{**}, the amount of labor employment, OE^{**}, and the amount of urban unemployment in region 2, $C'E^{**}$. In the new equilibrium, the wage rate of the agricultural sector 1 increases. Unemployment in the urban areas of region 1 decreases. The wage rate of the agricultural sector 2 increases. Unemployment in the urban areas of region 2 increases.

From Table 9.2, we can also know that the transfer of the pollution abatement technology in region 1 will have the following regional economic effects: In region 1, the wage rate of the agricultural sector increases; unemployment in the urban areas decreases. In region 2, the wage rate of the agricultural sector increases; unemployment in the urban areas increases. However, the transfer of the pollution abatement technology in region 2 will have the following regional economic effects: In region 1, the wage rate of the agricultural sector increases, but the employment and the output of the agricultural sector decrease; unemployment in the urban areas decreases; the number of migrant labors from region 1 to region 2 increases. In region 2, the wage rate, the employment, and the output of the agricultural sector increase; unemployment in the urban areas decreases.

According to (9.19) and (9.20), we have[3]:

$$e_U^1 \frac{dU_1}{d\lambda_2} = [\bar{L}_1 - (1-\beta)L_{tr}]\frac{dw_{A_1}}{d\lambda_2} + (\beta w_{A_2} - w_{A_1})\frac{dL_{tr}}{d\lambda_2} \tag{9.19''}$$

$$e_U^2 \frac{dU_2}{d\lambda_2} = [\bar{L}_2 + (1-\beta)L_{tr}]\frac{dw_{A_2}}{d\lambda_2} + (1-\beta)w_{A_2}\frac{dL_{tr}}{d\lambda_2} \tag{9.20''}$$

Proposition 9.5 The transfer of the pollution abatement technology in region 2 will have the following welfare effects:

1. In region 1, if $\beta w_{A_2} - w_{A_1} > 0$ or $\beta w_{A_2} - w_{A_1} < 0$ and $[\bar{L}_1 - (1-\beta)L_{tr}]\frac{dw_{A_1}}{d\lambda_2} < -(\beta w_{A_2} - w_{A_1})\frac{dL_{tr}}{d\lambda_2}$, the transfer of the pollution abatement technology decreases the regional utility level. If $\beta w_{A_2} - w_{A_1} < 0$ and $[\bar{L}_1 - (1-\beta)L_{tr}]\frac{dw_{A_1}}{d\lambda_2} > -(\beta w_{A_2} - w_{A_1})\frac{dL_{tr}}{d\lambda_2}$, the opposite occurs, and the regional utility level will increase.
2. In region 2, the transfer of the pollution abatement technology increases the regional utility level.

4 Concluding Remarks

In this chapter, we integrate intra-region labor migration and inter-region labor migration into the Harris-Todaro model in the presence of unidirectional trans-boundary pollution. We conduct a simple comparative static analysis of regional economic and environmental effects of the central government's development policies on two regions, reducing the transfer cost of inter-region labor migration

[3]The transfer of the pollution abatement technology in region 1 has ambiguous impacts on both regional utility levels.

and increasing the capital subsidy to the less developed region. In addition, we compare the environmental and regional economic effects of the transfer of pollution abatement technology in two regions.

The main contributions of the present paper are: First, we consider an economy consisting of two regions, in the presence of unidirectional trans-boundary pollution in the framework of the Harris-Todaro model. The unidirectional trans-boundary pollution results from the different locations of the two regions.[4] Second, we analyze the regional economic and environmental effects of two development policies, reducing the transfer cost of inter-region labor migration by the development of the infrastructure, and increasing the capital subsidy to the less developed region, which are seldom discussed by the existing researches but important in practice. Third, we integrate intra-region labor migration and inter-region labor migration into the Harris-Todaro model.

It is clear that further analysis should take capital mobility into consideration as well as relaxing the unidirectional trans-boundary pollution assumption. All in all, the present paper is an attempt to provide the foundation for future research.

Trans-boundary pollution can be both national and international. Asian countries are no exception. Although this paper only analyzes the situation of national trans-boundary pollution, due to the similarity of analytical method, the conclusion can be easily generalized to international situation, providing positive reference value for all kinds of trans-boundary pollution.

References

Candel-Sanchez, F. (2006). The externalities problem of transboundary and persistent pollution. *Journal of Environmental Economics and Management, 52*, 517–526.

Haavio, M. (2005). Transboundary pollution and household mobility: Are they equivalent? *Journal of Environmental Economics and Management, 50*, 252–275.

Hoel, M., & Shapiro, P. (2003). Population mobility and transboundary environmental problems. *Journal of Public Economics, 87*, 113–124.

Sigman, H. (2004). Transboundary spillovers and decentralization of environmental policies. *Journal of Environmental Economics and Management, 50*(1), 82–101.

Varian, H. (1994). A solution to the problem of externalities when agents are well-informed. *American Economic Review, 85*, 1278–1293.

[4]With the rapid economic development of the eastern coastal areas of China, the tightly regulations of industrial pollution emissions force the heaving polluting industries to move to the west regions. However, the pollution generated by these heavy polluting industries disseminated to the east regions again, through the agents like air and rivers. This is the unidirectional trans-boundary pollution in this chapter.

Part IV
Modern Agriculture

This part consists of four papers. This part of the book theoretical analysis of the modern agriculture, we divide rural agriculture into dualistic structure, which is relatively rare in Harris-Todaro studies. Chapter 10 studies the economic effect of government policies promoting the development of modern agriculture in theoretical. Developing modern agriculture is one of the main directions of industry nurturing agriculture when industrial process reaches somehow moment. This chapter analyzes the effect of policies to promote advanced agricultural development with the existence of the urban private sector capital investment in modern agriculture. Chapter 11 is the continuation of Chap. 10, prior to the development of advanced agricultural; transfer labor coming from traditional agriculture only goes to urban for new work, but when there is advanced agriculture, rural labor has more chance to transfer advanced agriculture. The transfer form must be changed after the development of advanced agriculture. Under the assumption that wages in the advanced agricultural sector are higher than in the traditional agricultural sector, this chapter analyzes the effect of policies to promote the development of the advanced agriculture. Chapter 12 investigates the effect of international flow of factors on unemployment and the wage gap with the existence of modern agriculture. Chapter 13 is our recently completed paper, which is a content supplement for Chaps. 10 and 11. There has a theoretical breakthrough in Harris-Todaro theory research, which mainly solves the problem of setting labor wage of the modern agricultural sector; the so-called modern agriculture sector is between industry sector and traditional agriculture sector. This chapter provides a theoretical framework for future researching emerging economies having dual agricultural economic structure.

Chapter 10
A Study on Urban Private Capital and the Transfer of Labor in the Modern Agricultural Sector

Xiaochun Li and Qin Shen

Abstract As urban private capital enters the modern agriculture industry, it divides the agricultural sector into the modern sector and the traditional sector. This chapter establishes a general equilibrium model to study the economic impact of governmental policies aimed at promoting modern agriculture. The main conclusions of this chapter are that interest subsidies implemented by the government to promote modern agriculture can reduce the transfer of labor from the rural areas to the cities, but encourage the movement of rural labor to the modern agricultural sector. Conversely, wage rate subsidies for the modern agricultural sector will lead to rises in the urban unemployment rate and a decrease in the quantity of labor in the traditional agricultural sector.

Keywords Private capital • Modern agriculture • Transfer of labor

1 Introduction

Throughout history, agricultural production in developing countries was generally family based. Its small scale made unlikely the involvement of urban private capital, which is usually large in sum (except in the field of informal finance). Meanwhile, owners of urban private capital were often reluctant to spend time and human capital on small loans, resulting in the stagnation of capital flows between the urban and rural sectors. However, this situation is changing in some developing countries. For instance, China abolished agricultural tax in 2006 to facilitate the agricultural development Zhong et al. (2011). In addition, certain local governments in China have promoted the "modern agriculture" business, leading urban private capital to flow to these rural areas. "Modern agriculture" generally refers to

X. Li (✉)
Business School, Nanjing University, Nanjing, China
e-mail: xiaochun@nju.edu.cn

Q. Shen
School of Economics, Nanjing University, 22 Hankou Road, Nanjing, Jiangsu 210093, China

X. Li (ed.), *Labor Transfer in Emerging Economies*, New Frontiers in Regional Science: Asian Perspectives 12, DOI 10.1007/978-981-10-3569-2_10

the newly emerged agricultural sector, which is guided by market demand and adopts modern facilities and technologies to achieve higher yields than traditional agriculture (Wang and Han 2010). There are many ways to implement modern agriculture, but they all need more capital investment than traditional agriculture. In order to obtain sufficient capital, several Chinese local governments have established special funds to provide help to rural households (Wang 2011). The local governmental organizations or the collectives of several "modern agricultural households," which have knowledge of marketing and operations, arrange their lands and other farmers' lands and work together and manage the process from producing to selling in a collective way. In China, although modern agriculture is deemed a good means of lifting peasants from poverty, governmental funding alone is insufficient. Therefore, urban private capital (hereafter referred to as "urban capital") is used in some regions to develop modern agriculture (Ju 2011). However, due to a lack of profound theoretical research and inexperience in the operation of this sector, modern agriculture is still not very well understood, and during its development, many problems, ranging from industrialization and production efficiency to environmental protection, have emerged (Wang and Han 2010).

In addition, most studies on economic development and labor migration employ the general equilibrium to analyze the policy effects in labor migration. For example, Tiwari et al. (2002) analyzed the reform of Chinese labor market in the general equilibrium framework, concluding that an open labor market would promote economic development. At the same time, a number of existing literatures divide the urban sector into the formal sector and the informal sector, when they employ the Harris–Todaro model to analyze economic development and labor migration – typical studies include Gupta (1993), Grinols (1991), Chandra and Khan (1993), and Din (1996). Nonetheless, the use of a segmented rural labor market is still rare at present. Gupta (1997a) separated the modern agricultural sector from the traditional agricultural sector and employed a four-sector model to analyze the impact of changes in commodity price in a small, open developing economy. It was found that increases in the prices of the modern agricultural products could raise the wages of the two rural sectors and the urban informal sector and lower the interest rate of the informal sector, while increasing urban unemployment at the same time. Gupta (1997b) also considered a small open economy consisting of four sectors. He elaborated upon the invalidity of the Brecher–Alejandro (1977) proposition when incorporating the costs of migration and skill acquisition. Chaudhuri (2006) and Chaudhuri (2007) also divided the rural sector into the modern and the traditional agricultural sector. The former studied the fit and importance of labor market reform in developing countries with a three-sector general equilibrium model. The research showed that liberalization of the labor market could lead to increases in rural wages and social welfare, but would lower the return to land capital and the urban wage rate. Chaudhuri (2007) addressed the issue of why developing countries demand foreign capital despite the detrimental effects predicted by conventional literature regarding a three-sector Harris–Todaro model. He found that an inflow of foreign capital with full repatriation of its earnings may still improve social welfare and lower urban unemployment.

However, all of the above literature presumes that the modern agricultural sector and the traditional agricultural sector share the same wage rate, which contradicts the objective of developing the modern agriculture and is unable to explain the theoretical motivation for labor in the traditional agricultural sector to transfer to the modern agricultural sector. In addition, this assumption doesn't precisely describe the growing modern agricultural sector in developing countries. For example, the wage rate of the modern agricultural sector is significantly higher than that of the traditional agricultural sector in China. Furthermore, none of the existing literature focuses on the economic impact of public policies on developing modern agriculture in the context of urban capital flows to the rural sector.

In order to analyze the economic impact of public policies aimed at promoting the development of modern agriculture with the inflow of capital from the urban sector, this chapter further divides the agricultural sector into the modern subsector and the traditional one and adopts the Harris–Todaro model to analyze the labor migration. The difference is that the wage rate of the modern subsector in our paper is higher than that of the traditional one. Under the premise that the government encourages development of modern agriculture, this chapter adopts a comparative static method to analyze the economic effects of the following policies:

1. The government provides special funds or information about private lending and subsidizes the interests of such lending.[1]
2. The government implements wage rate subsidies in the modern agricultural sector.
3. Increases in the factor endowment create measurable economic differences.

This chapter is an extension of current theoretical research and geometrically demonstrates the transfer mechanism of labor among three sectors: the urban sector, the rural modern agricultural sector, and traditional agricultural sector. We find that interest subsidies to promote modern agriculture could bring more beneficial effects than wage rate subsidies to the same sector.

In the following, the second part of this chapter is devoted to the establishment of a general equilibrium model, the third part is a theoretical analysis based on the established model, and the fourth part is a summary and conclusion.

2 Model Establishment

This chapter models a three-sector closed economy. The three sectors are the urban sector, the modern agricultural sector, and the traditional agricultural sector. The model studied by this chapter is under the assumption that the modern sector was recently established and is still developing. The urban and the modern agricultural sectors both use two factors of production: labor and capital, whereas the traditional agricultural sector only uses the labor factor. In order to establish the model, we further have the following premises about the economy.

[1]There are precedents in China; see Zheng et al. (2009) and Wang (2011).

1. This chapter considers partial unskilled-labor mobility from the traditional agricultural sector to the urban sector and modern agricultural sector. Capital flows freely between the urban sector and the modern agricultural sector.
2. The wage rate of the urban sector is exogenous, while the wages of the two agricultural sectors float freely. Further, the wage rate of the urban sector exceeds that of the rural sector, while the wage rate of the modern agricultural sector exceeds that of the traditional sector.
3. The market is fully competitive, and the factor endowment is exogenous.

Assume the production function of the respective sectors as follows:

$$M = F^1(L_1, K_1) \tag{10.1}$$

$$A = g(K_2)F^2(L_2) \tag{10.2}$$

$$B = F^3(L_3) \tag{10.3}$$

Here, M, A, and B refer to the production of the urban sector, the modern agricultural sector, and the traditional agricultural sector, respectively; L_1, L_2, and L_3 refer to their respective quantity of labor; K_1 and K_2 are the capital of the urban industrial and the modern agricultural sector, respectively; and K_2 is the loan from the urban private sector. In addition, F^1 is linearly homogeneous and a strictly concave function; $F^i(i=2,3)$ is concave. Define $g=g(K_2)$ as the scale-effect function of the modern agricultural sector's use of capital, and g is a concave function with the properties $g=g(K_2)>1$, $K_2 > 0$, and $g'=g'(K_2)>0$, $g''=g''(K_2)<0$, When $K_2 = 0$, we assume $g(0)=1$, which means without capital investment, the modern agricultural sector deteriorates to the traditional agricultural sector.

Let L be the total endowment of labor in the entire economy, and L_{uu} be the urban unemployment; there is

$$L_1 + L_2 + L_3 + L_{uu} = L \tag{10.4}$$

Let $\lambda = \frac{L_{uu}}{L_1}$ be the unemployment rate of the urban sector; thus Eq. (10.4) becomes

$$(1+\lambda)L_1 + L_2 + L_3 = L \tag{10.4'}$$

In addition, we assume that labor in the traditional agricultural sector cannot be fully transferred to the modern agricultural sector, and the absorption of labor by the modern agricultural sector is constrained by capital in this sector. Thus, the relationship between the employment of labor and the capital is as follows:

$$L_2 = \begin{cases} f(K_2), f'(K_2) > 0, & f''(K_2) < 0, K_2 < K_2^* \\ f(K_2^*), f'(K_2^*) = 0, & K_2 = K_2^* \\ f(K_2), f'(K_2) \leq 0, f''(K_2) > 0, & K_2 > K_2^* \end{cases} \quad (10.5)$$

The first half of Eq. (10.5) is set as the basis for the development of the modern agriculture, and this chapter researches this situation in particular.

Let K be the total endowment of capital in the entire economy. Capital in the economy is fully used by the urban and the modern agricultural sector:

$$K_1 + K_2 = K \quad (10.6)$$

We use $\bar{w}_1$, w_2, and w_3 to represent the wage rate of the urban sector, the modern agricultural sector, and the traditional agricultural sector, respectively. From the profit maximization condition, we could obtain the following three equations:

$$p_1 F_L^1 = \bar{w}_1 \quad (10.7)$$

$$p_2 g(K_2) F_L^2 = w_2 \quad (10.8)$$

$$F_L^3 = w_3 \quad (10.9)$$

In the above equations, $F_L^i = \partial F^i / \partial L_i (i = 1, 2, 3)$. $\bar{w}_1$ is an exogenous variable. p_1 and p_2 refer to the product price of the urban sector and the modern agricultural sector in terms of the product price of the traditional agricultural sector.

If r is the interest rate for loans, we could obtain the following equations based on profit maximization and the free flow of capital between the urban industrial sector and the modern agricultural sector:

$$p_1 F_K^1 = r \quad (10.10)$$

$$p_2 g'(K_2) F^2 = r \quad (10.11)$$

In the above equations, $F_K^1 = \partial F^1 / \partial K_1, \quad g'(K_2) = \partial g / \partial K_2$.

With regard to the labor allocation mechanism Harris and Todaro (1970), this chapter adopts the three-sector Harris-Todaro-type migration equilibrium condition. In this chapter, unemployment exists in the urban sector; hence, labor transferred from the traditional agricultural sector has the risk of being unemployed. However, labor in the traditional agricultural sector will compare the actual wage in their sector with the expected wage of the urban sector and the modern sector and will move to the other two sectors if the expected wage of these two sectors is higher. At the equilibrium point, we have

$$\frac{L_1}{(1+\lambda)L_1 + L_2} \bar{w}_1 + \frac{L_2}{(1+\lambda)L_1 + L_2} w_2 = w_3 \quad (10.12)$$

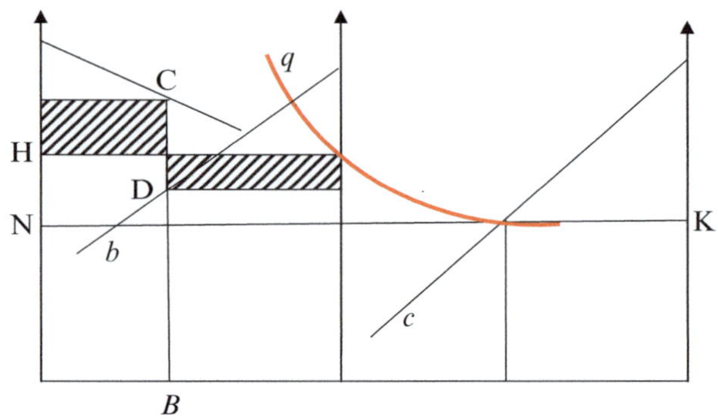

Fig. 10.1 The labor transfer mechanism

In Eqs. (10.1), (10.2), (10.3), (10.4), (10.5), (10.6), (10.7), (10.8), (10.9), (10.10), (10.11), and (10.12), there are altogether nine endogenous variables, namely, $L_1, L_2, L_3, K_1, K_2, \lambda, w_2, w_3$, and r. $L, K, \bar{w}_1, p_1$, and p_2 are exogenous variables. The nine equations (10.4′), (10.5), (10.6), (10.7), (10.8), (10.9), (10.10), (10.11), and (10.12) could decide the values of the nine endogenous variables. Thus, we have completed the establishment of the general equilibrium model.

According to Eq. (10.12), we could describe the labor transfer mechanism in the economy as follows by reorganizing this equation:

$$L_1\bar{w}_1 + L_2w_2 = w_3[(1+\lambda)L_1 + L_2] = w_3(L - L_3) \qquad (10.12')$$

In Fig. 10.1, the horizontal axis means labor endowment L in the economy. The left part of the vertical axis starting from the original point O_1 refers to the wage rate level of the urban sector; the right part starting from the original point O_3 refers to the wage rate level of the traditional agricultural sector. Since $\bar{w}_1$ is exogenous, we let $O_1A = \bar{w}_1$ and make a line parallel to the horizontal axis passing the point A, which also crosses the marginal production of labor in the urban sector aa at C. Make another line perpendicular to the horizontal axis O_1O_3, which passes C and crosses O_1O_3 at B. Then, we get $O_1B = L_1$. Combine Eqs. (10.5), (10.6), (10.7), (10.10), and (10.11), then we get K_2 and L_2. Let $O_2B = L_2$; we will decide the position of O_2. Then, a vertical line from the original point of O_2 would show the wage rate level of the modern agricultural sector. Assume that the line BC and the marginal production of labor in the modern agricultural sector bb intersect at D. Draw a line parallel to the horizontal axis O_1O_3 which crosses D and intersects with the middle vertical axis at E. From Eq. (10.8), we know that $O_2E = w_2$. Find one point H on the left vertical axis, so that $O_1H = \frac{L_1\bar{w}_1+L_2w_2}{L_1+L_2}$. Draw a parallel line to the horizontal axis O_1O_3 passing the point H and intersecting the middle vertical axis at G. Now, we have $S_{\text{AHFC}} = S_{\text{FDEG}}$. (The two shaded areas in Fig. 10.2 are equal in size.) Finally, make a right hyperbola qq passing G and intersecting the marginal production of labor cc at J. Then, draw a line passing J, which is perpendicular to the horizontal axis O_1O_3 and intersects O_1O_3 at M. Then, draw another line passing J and parallel to the horizontal axis O_1O_3, which intersects with the left and right

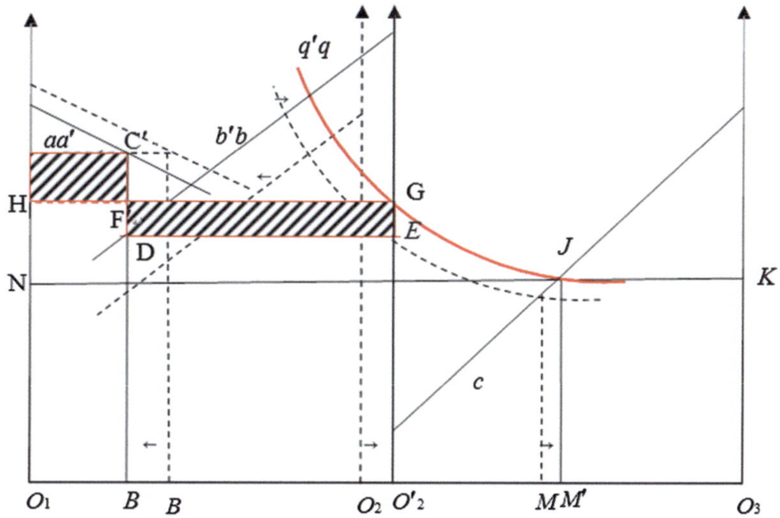

Fig. 10.2 The economic impact of subsidizing loan interest for the modern agricultural sector

vertical axis at N and K, respectively. It can be derived that $O_3M = L_3$, $O_2M = L_{uu}$, $JM = KO_3 = NO_1 = w_3$.

Therefore, the hyperbola qq illustrates the labor transfer mechanism as shown by Eq. (10.12′).

3 Theoretical Analysis

The above model can be divided into two subsystems. Eq. (10.5), (10.6), (10.7), (10.10), and (10.11) determining the endogenous variables L_1, L_2, K_1, K_2, and r can be defined as the "capital system." Eqs. (10.4), (10.8), (10.9), and (10.12) determining the endogenous variables L_3, λ, w_2, andw_3 could be defined as the "labor system."

3.1 The Economic Impact of Subsidizing Interest from Loans by the Modern Agricultural Sector

If the government implements policy to subsidize the loans of the modern agricultural sector and the rate of subsidy is s_1, then, Eq. (10.11) becomes

$$p_2 g'(K_2)F^2 = r(1 - s_1) \tag{10.11'}$$

We have the complete differential of the capital system Eqs. (10.5), (10.6), (10.7), (10.10), and (10.11′) and make $s_1 = 0$ at the initiation of the subsidy policy. Then, we could get the following linear equation set (complete differential):

$$\begin{bmatrix} 0 & 1 & 1 & 0 \\ F^1_{LL} & F^1_{LK} & 0 & 0 \\ p_1 F^1_{KL} & p_1 F^1_{KK} & 0 & -1 \\ 0 & 0 & -p_2\left(g'' F^2 + g' F^2_L f'\right) & 1 \end{bmatrix} \begin{bmatrix} dL_1 \\ dK_1 \\ dK_2 \\ dr \end{bmatrix} = \begin{bmatrix} 0 \\ 0 \\ 0 \\ rds_1 \end{bmatrix} \tag{10.13}$$

Let Δ be the determinant of the coefficient matrix, and we have the following:

$$\Delta = p_1\left(F^1_{LL}F^1_{KK} - F^1_{KL}F^1_{LK}\right) + p_2 F^1_{LL}\left(g'' F^2 + g' f' F^2_L\right)$$

The function F^1 is linearly homogeneous; therefore, $F^1_{LL}F^1_{KK} - F^1_{KL}F^1_{LK} = 0$. Based on the condition of systematic stability in our assumed economy, there must be $p_2\left(g'' F^2 + g' f' F^2_L\right) < 0$, which could be demonstrated by Lemma 10.1.

Lemma 10.1 In the economy, $p_2\left(g'' F^2 + g' f' F^2_L\right) < 0$ *iff* $f' > 0$.

Proof Totally differentiating Eq. (10.11), we have

$$p_2 g''(K_2)F^2(L_2)dK_2 + p_2 g'(K_2)F^2_L(L_2)f' dK_2 = dr$$

Therefore,

$$p_2\left[g''(K_2)F^2(L_2) + g'(K_2)F^2_L(L_2)\right]f' = dr/dK_2$$

As capital flows into the modern agricultural sector, the interest rate should fall. Therefore, $dr = dK2 < 0$. Note that $f' > 0$, which means $p_2\left(g'' F^2 + g' f' F^2_L\right) < 0$.

Using Crammer's rule to solve Eq. (10.13), we can decide the impact of change of s_1 on the endogenous variables L_1, K_1, K_2, and r, as shown in Table 10.1. Furthermore, we could analyze the influence of s_1 on other endogenous variables.

Table 10.1 The results of the calculation of Eqs. (10.13) and (10.15) (for the calculation process in detail, please refer to Appendix A)

	dL_1	dL_2	dL_3	$d\lambda$	dK_1	dK_2	dr	dw_2	dw_3
$ds1$	–	+	–	/	–	+	0	+	+

Notice: "–" means the ratio of the items in the horizontal column and ds_1 is "negative" and"0" refers to the ratio of the items in the horizontal columns and ds_1 is 0; "+" means "positive," and "/" means "cannot decide"

The complete differential of Eqs. (10.4), (10.8), (10.9), and (10.12) in the labor system could be reorganized as

$$\begin{bmatrix} L_1 & 1 & 0 \\ 0 & 0 & 1 \\ L_1 w_3 & [(1+\lambda)L_1 + L_2]F^3_{LL} & -L_2 \end{bmatrix} \begin{bmatrix} d\lambda \\ dL_3 \\ dw_2 \end{bmatrix} = \begin{bmatrix} -(1+\lambda)dL_1 - f' dK_2 \\ p_2\left(g'' F^2 + g' f' F^2_L\right) dK_2 \\ [\bar{w}_1 - (1+\lambda)w_3]dL_1 + (w_2 - w_3)dL_2 \end{bmatrix} \tag{10.14}$$

Let Ω be the determinant of the coefficient matrix of Eq. (10.14); we have

$$\Omega = -L_1\left\{[(1+\lambda)L_1 + L_2]F^3_{LL} - w_3\right\} > 0$$

Before the next step analysis, we should establish Lemma 10.2, which consists of the following two inequalities in our assumed economy:

Lemma 10.2 In our assumed economy, we have the following two inequalities:

1. $g'F^2_L + gf'F^2_{LL} > 0$ *iff '>0.*
2. $\bar{w}_1 dL_1/ds_1 + w_2 dL_2/ds_1 > 0$.

Proof 1. The total differential of Eq. (10.8) is the following:

$$p_2\left(g'F^2_L + gf'F^2_{LL}\right)dK_2 = dw_2$$

Therefore,

$$p_2\left(g'F^2_L + gf'F^2_{LL}\right) = dw_2/dK_2$$

As $dw_2/dK_2 > 0$ (this is because urban capital flows into the modern agricultural sector, the concentration of rural labor increases, and the rise of wage rate is the main force driving the concentration of labor), we could get $g'F^2_L + gf'F^2_{LL} > 0$ if f'>0.

2. With the emergence of the modern agricultural sector, rural labor moves to the modern agricultural sector. Thus, the absolute value of the loss in wage rate of the traditional agricultural sector due to reduction of labor must be less than the wage rate increase in the modern agricultural sector due to the increase of labor; otherwise the migration of labor could not be explained. Therefore, $\bar{w}_1 dL_1/ds_1 + w_2 dL_2/ds_1 > 0$.

Using Cramer's Rule to solve Eq. (10.14), we could directly determine the impact of change in s_1 on the endogenous variables L_3, λ, and w_2. Further, the inequality$g'F_L^2 + gf'F_{LL}^2 > 0$ could be used to decide the sign of dw_2/ds_1, and the inequality $\bar{w}_1 dL_1/ds_1 + w_2 dL_2/ds_1 > 0$ to decide the sign of dL_3/ds_1, as shown in Table 10.1.

To sum up, we arrive at the following Proposition 10.1.

Proposition 10.1 Subsidizing the interest of loans for the modern agricultural sector would have the following economic impact:

1. The labor employment in the urban sector decreases, and urban capital flows to the modern agricultural sector.
2. The interest rate of loans for the modern agricultural sector, the sector's labor employment, and wage rate all rise.
3. The labor employment in the traditional agricultural sector falls, but the wage rate level rises.

After subsidizing the modern agricultural sector's capital interests, those losing their jobs in the urban sector become the urban unemployed, and at the same time, the traditional agricultural laborers prior to belonging to the urban unemployment would migrate to the modern sector. Thus, we cannot accurately determine the change of the urban unemployment rate. The reason why subsidizing the modern agricultural sector would cause decreases of labor employment in the urban sector is not because of the decrease of rural migration of labor, but because rural labor has a better destination, with higher wages and decreased transportation costs, i.e., the modern agricultural sector. Therefore, rural labor is less likely to migrate to the urban sector. This situation is in accordance with Propositions 1(2) and 1(3). This is a positive finding, which corresponds to the general policy direction of the government to solve the "three problems" of agriculture. This policy allows the modern agricultural sector to absorb capital at a lower interest rate, hence leading to higher wages and more labor employed in this sector. Undoubtedly, such policy benefits the modern agricultural sector in its development. However, when implementing this policy, the shortage of labor in the urban sector should be taken into consideration. Proper measures should be taken to alleviate the problem and balance the development of both the urban and the rural economy.

The economic impact of subsidizing capital for the modern agricultural sector is shown in Fig. 10.2. From Table 10.1, we know that subsidizing the modern agricultural sector decreases K_1 and moves the marginal production of labor curve for the urban industrial sector *aa* and the marginal production of labor curve for the modern agricultural sector *bb* leftward to $a'a'$ and $b'b'$, respectively. With reference to the establishment in Fig. 10.1, we could know that subsidizing capital in the modern agricultural sector would make the middle vertical axis move rightward (from O_2 to O'_2) and the labor distribution mechanism curve *qq* right upward to $q'q'$. Therefore, the points B', D', E', F', G', H', K', M', N', *and* J' in Fig. 10.2 represent the points *B*, *D*, *E*, *F*, *G*, *H*, *K*, *M*, *N*, and *J* in Fig. 10.1 after the move. The new hires in the urban sector, the modern agricultural sector, and the traditional agricultural sector L_1, L_1, and L_3 shrink to O_1B', O_1B', and O_3M',

Table 10.2 The results of calculation for Eq. (10.15) (for the calculation process in detail, please refer to Appendix B)

	dL_1	dL_2	dL_3	$d\lambda$	$dKdK_1$	dK_2	dr	dw_2	dw_3
$ds2$	0	0	–	+	0	0	0	+	+

Notice: the meanings of the signs are the same as those in Table 10.1

respectively. Moreover, the quantity of unemployment in the urban department is O'_2M'. The wage rate w_2 in the modern agricultural sector rises to O'_2E'.

3.2 The Economic Impact of Subsidizing Wages for the Modern Agricultural Sector

If wages in the modern agricultural sector are subsidized, and the subsidy rate is s_2, then Eq. (10.8) becomes

$$p_2 g(K_2)F_L^2 = w_2(1 - s_2) \tag{10.8'}$$

Let $s_2 = 0$ at the initiation of the subsidy policy, then the complete differential of Eqs. (10.4′), (10.5), (10.6), (10.7), (10.8′), (10.9), (10.10), (10.11), and (10.12) could be reorganized into the following linear equation set:

$$\begin{bmatrix} 0 & 0 & 0 & 1 & 1 & 0 \\ F_{LL}^1 & 0 & 0 & F_{LK}^1 & 0 & 0 \\ -p_1 F_{KL}^1 & 0 & 0 & -p_1 F_{KK}^1 & p_2\left[g'(K_2)F_L^2 f' + g''(K_2)F^2\right] & 0 \\ 0 & 0 & 0 & 0 & p_2\left[g(K_2)F_{LL}^2 f' + g'(K_2)F_L^2\right] & -1 \\ 1+\lambda & 1 & L_1 & 0 & f' & 0 \\ \bar{w}_1 & w_3 - (L-L_3)F_{LL}^3 & 0 & 0 & w_2 f' & L_2 \end{bmatrix} \times \begin{bmatrix} dL_1 \\ dL_3 \\ d\lambda \\ dK_1 \\ dK_2 \\ dw_2 \end{bmatrix} = \begin{bmatrix} 0 \\ 0 \\ 0 \\ -w_2 \\ 0 \\ 0 \end{bmatrix} ds_2 \tag{10.15}$$

Let Δ_2 be the determinant of the coefficient matrix, and we have

$$\Delta_2 = L_1\left[w_3 - (L - L_3)F_{LL}^3\right]\Delta > 0$$

To solve Eq. (10.15) based on Cramer's Rule, we could get that in Table 10.2. According to Table 10.2, we arrive at the following proposition.

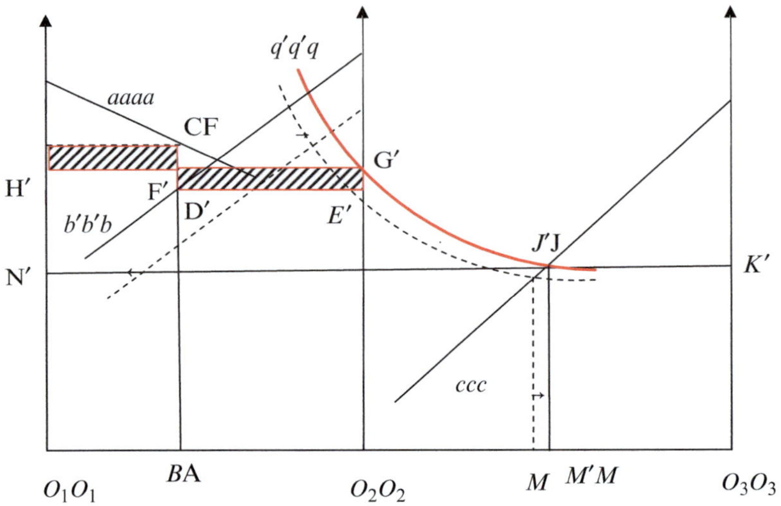

Fig. 10.3 The economic impact of wage rate subsidies in the modern agricultural sector

Proposition 10.2 Subsidizing the wage rate of the modern agricultural sector has the following economic impact:

1. It raises the urban unemployment rate, but does not affect the quantity of labor, wage rate, or capital level of the urban sector.
2. It does not affect the quantity of labor and the capital level in the modern agricultural sector, but the wage rate will rise.
3. The quantity of labor in the traditional agricultural sector will fall, but the wage rate level will rise.

Special attention should be paid to the economic effect of the wage subsidy to the modern agricultural sector. On one hand, it does not affect employment in the urban sector or in the modern agricultural sector. On the other, it promotes labor migration out of the traditional rural sector. From Proposition 2(1), we find that all of the transferred labor becomes the unemployed in the urban sector, as wage rate subsidies to the modern agricultural sector will definitely promote this sector development, which encourages rural labor to seek to maximize their wealth as soon as possible. Nevertheless, as the policy will not influence capital flows in the economy and employment in the modern agricultural sector is determined by its capital, this policy cannot change employment in the modern agricultural sector;

thus, rural labor could only transfer to the urban sector, which contributes to the blind nature to this migration and the probability of being unemployed for the migrants. When implementing such policy to influence macroeconomic demand, the government should pay special attention to its negative impact on the urban sector, where it can raise urban unemployment. For this reason, as the policy is carried out, the government should positively explore new job markets, broaden the employment field, and encourage industry to increase employment to reduce the unemployment rate.

The economic impact of subsidizing wages for the modern agricultural sector can be described in Fig. 10.3. To subsidize wages in the modern agricultural sector, from $p_2 g(K_2)F_L^2 = w_2(1 - s_2)$, we could know that the marginal production of the labor curve of the modern agricultural sector moves right upward. It is not difficult for us to prove that the wage rate level of the modern agricultural sector moves from O_2E to O_2E' and the labor distribution mechanism curve qq moves right upward to $q'q'$. Therefore, the points D', E', F', G', H', K', M', N', and J' in Fig. 10.3 represent the points $B, D, E, F, G, H, K, M, N$, and J in Fig. 10.1 after the move. At this time, the unemployment in the urban sector is O_2M'.

Compared with the general situation in which the production is the function of both capital and labor, the production of the modern agricultural sector is decided by capital only, so the interest rate subsidy to the modern agricultural sector will raise the output more directly and obtain better economic effect. This point can also be shown by the comparison of Propositions 10.1 and 10.2.

Comparing Propositions 10.1 and 10.2, we find that the interest rate subsidy to the modern agricultural sector is superior to the wage subsidy to this sector because the former generates more positive effects than the latter. This is because the modern agricultural sector's labor is determined by its capital. Therefore, the interest rate subsidy to the modern agricultural sector should be the first choice for the relevant departments when making decisions.

3.3 *The Economic Impact of the Change in Factor Endowments*

Having completely differentiated the capital system Eqs. (10.4′), (10.5), (10.6), (10.7), (10.8), (10.9), (10.10), (10.11), and (10.12), we have the following linear equation set:

Table 10.3 The results of the calculation for Eq. (10.16) (for the detailed calculation of the results, please refer to the Appendix C)

	$dL1$	$dL2$	$dL3$	$d\lambda$	$dK1$	$dK2$	dr	$dw2$	$dw3$
dK	+	0	–	–	+	0	0	0	+
dL	0	0	+	+	0	0	0	0	–

Notice: the signs have the same meaning as those in Table 10.1

$$\begin{bmatrix} 0 & 0 & 0 & 1 & 1 & 0 \\ F^1_{LL} & 0 & 0 & F^1_{LK} & 0 & 0 \\ -p_1F^1_{KL} & 0 & 0 & -p_1F^1_{KK} & p_2\left[g'(K_2)F^2_Lf' + g''(K_2)F^2\right] & 0 \\ 0 & 0 & 0 & 0 & p_2\left[g(K_2)F^2_{LL}f' + g'(K_2)F^2_L\right] & -1 \\ 1+\lambda & 1 & L_1 & 0 & f' & 0 \\ \bar{w}_1 & w_3 - (L-L_3)F^3_{LL} & 0 & 0 & w_2f' & L_2 \end{bmatrix}$$

$$\times \begin{bmatrix} dL_1 \\ dL_3 \\ d\lambda \\ dK_1 \\ dK_2 \\ dw_2 \end{bmatrix} = \begin{bmatrix} dK \\ 0 \\ 0 \\ 0 \\ 0 \\ 0 \end{bmatrix} + \begin{bmatrix} 0 \\ 0 \\ 0 \\ 0 \\ dL \\ w_3dL \end{bmatrix} \tag{10.16}$$

Denote Δ_3 as the determinant of the coefficient matrix, and we have

$$\Delta_3 = \Delta_2 = L_1\left[w_3 - (L - L_3)F^3_{LL}\right]\Delta > 0$$

Solving Eq. (10.16) based on Cramer's Rule, we could get that represented in Table 10.3.

According to Table 10.3, we could have the following proposition.

Proposition 10.3 The increase in the labor endowment is fully absorbed by urban unemployment. In addition, the increase in the capital endowment has the following economic impact:

1. It increases the urban labor employment and lowers the urban unemployment rate, and all the increased capital endowment is absorbed by the urban sector.
2. It has no effect on the capital, labor, and the wage rate of the modern agricultural sector.
3. It decreases the labor employment of the traditional agricultural sector and raises its wage rate.

From Proposition 10.3, we know that the economic impact of the increase in capital endowment is better than that of the growth of labor endowment because the former brings significant benefits to the urban sector and the traditional agricultural sector, while neither of them generates any impact on the modern agricultural sector. Therefore, the policy makers should consider taking advantage of the increase in capital to develop the modern agricultural sector and pay attention to the negative impact of labor growth at the same time.

3.4 The Social Welfare Impact of Wage Rate Subsidy Policy to the Modern Agricultural Sector

We assume a closed economy. If $G = G(p_1, p_2, \bar{L})$ is the total output, then

$$G(p_1, p_2, \bar{L}) = p_1 M + p_2 A + B \tag{10.17}$$

If the function of the minimum expenditure in the economy is $e = e(p_1, p_2, U)$, and U is the social utility level, therefore, we get the following equation:

$$e = e(p_1, p_2, U) = G(p_1, p_2, \bar{L}) \tag{10.18}$$

Putting Eq. (10.16) into Eq. (10.17) and obtaining the complete differential of both sides of Eq. (10.17), we get

$$\begin{aligned} e_U dU &= dG = p_1 dM + p_2 dA + dB \\ &= p_1 F_L^1 dL_1 + p_1 F_K^1 dK_1 + p_2 \left[g(K_2) F_{LJ}^2 f' + g'(K_2) F^2 \right] dK_2 + F_L^3 dL_3 \end{aligned}$$

According to Table 10.2, we know

$$\begin{aligned} e_U \frac{dU}{ds_2} &= p_1 F_L^1 \frac{dL_1}{ds_2} + p_1 F_K^1 \frac{dK_1}{ds_2} + p_2 \left[g(K_2) F_{LJ}^2 f' + g'(K_2) F^2 \right] \frac{dK_2}{ds_2} + F_L^3 \frac{dL_3}{ds_2} \\ &= \frac{-w_2 L_2 F_L^3}{w_3 - (L - L_3) F_{LL}^3} \end{aligned}$$

The above equation means that the wage rate subsidy for the modern agricultural sector will decrease the social welfare level, which is contrary to the goals of policy makers. Although the wage rate subsidy for the modern agricultural sector aims at promoting development of this sector, according to Proposition 10.2, it will lead to an increase of the unemployment rate in the urban sector, which is the main reason for the fall of the social welfare level. Therefore, in real economic conditions, if it is necessary to subsidize wage rate for the modern agricultural sector, counter-unemployment measures in the urban sector must be adopted to ensure that the social welfare level would not be decreased.

4 Conclusion

This chapter studies the economic impact of public policies aimed at promoting the development of modern agriculture under the premise of free capital flows between the urban sector and the modern agricultural sector. Based on economic circumstances in developing countries, we divided the rural sector into the modern agricultural sector and the traditional agricultural sector in our general equilibrium model. We established that the wage of the modern agricultural sector is higher than that of the traditional agricultural sector, which differs from existing related literature, therefore expanding the field of current research in methods. We considered the impacts of two major policies, subsidizing loan interest to the modern agricultural sector and subsidizing the wage rate of labor in this sector, and investigated the economic impact of factor endowment changes. According to our research, the interest rate subsidy to the modern agricultural sector is superior to the wage rate subsidy to this sector, and the economic impact of the increase in capital endowment is better than that of labor endowment growth. The three propositions and the social welfare effect of wage rate subsidies can be used as a reference for the policy makers in their promotion of modern agricultural development.

Due to the constraint on the discussion scope, the paper has the following directions for further studies.

1. The impact of the policies on the urban sector would be more accurate if the urban sector is divided into the formal subsector and informal subsector.
2. In some developing countries with a relatively high level of agricultural development, rural capital may also be involved in the modern agricultural business and studies on this situation might be more valuable for those countries.

Finally, it is worth noting that besides China and India, many developing countries in Asia are dedicated to develop modern agriculture. The conclusion of this paper provides a meaningful reference for the government to formulate the policy of developing advanced agriculture, particularly under the background that the city private sector participates actively in the investment of modern agriculture. The following Chaps. 10, 11, and 12 study the economic problems related to modern agriculture from different perspectives, and there is significant reference for Asian countries.

Appendix A

By total differentiation of the capital system Eqs. (10.5), (10.6), (10.7), (10.10), and (10.11′) and making $s_1 = 0$ at the initiation of the subsidy policy, we get the following linear equation system (total differentiation):

$$\begin{bmatrix} 0 & 1 & 1 & 0 \\ F^1_{LL} & F^1_{LK} & 0 & 0 \\ p_1 F^1_{KL} & p_1 F^1_{KK} & 0 & -1 \\ 0 & 0 & -p_2\left(g'' F^2 + g' F^2_L f'\right) & 1 \end{bmatrix} \begin{bmatrix} dL_1 \\ dK_1 \\ dK_2 \\ dr \end{bmatrix} = \begin{bmatrix} 0 \\ 0 \\ 0 \\ rds_1 \end{bmatrix} \tag{10.A1}$$

Let Δ be the determinant of the coefficient matrix, and we have

$$\Delta = p_1\left(F^1_{LL}F^1_{KK} - F^1_{KL}F^1_{LK}\right) + p_2 F^1_{LL}\left(g'' F^2 + g' f' F^2_L\right).$$

The total differentiation of Eqs. (10.4), (10.8), (10.9), and (10.12) in the labor system can be reorganized as

$$\begin{bmatrix} L_1 & 1 & 0 \\ 0 & 0 & 1 \\ L_1 w_3 & [(1+\lambda)L_1 + L_2]F^3_{LL} & -L_2 \end{bmatrix} \begin{bmatrix} d\lambda \\ dL_3 \\ dw_2 \end{bmatrix} = \begin{bmatrix} -(1+\lambda)dL_1 - f' dK_2 \\ p_2\left(g'' F^2 + g' f' F^2_L\right) dK_2 \\ [\bar{w}_1 - (1+\lambda)w_3]dL_1 + (w_2 - w_3)dL_2 \end{bmatrix} \tag{10.A2}$$

Let Ω be the determinant of the coefficient matrix of Eq. (10.A2), and we have

$$\Omega = -L_1\left\{[(1+\lambda)L_1 + L_2]F^3_{LL} - w_3\right\} > 0$$

Solving Eq. (10.A1) by Cramer's Rule, we get

$$dK_1/ds_1 = rF^1_{LL}/\Delta < 0,\ dL_1/ds_1 = -rF^1_{LK}/\Delta < 0,\ dK_2/ds_1 = -rF^1_{LL}/\Delta > 0$$
$$dL_2/ds_1 = f' dK_2/ds_1 > 0,\ \ dr/ds_1 = rp_1\left(F^1_{LL}F^1_{KK} - F^1_{KL}F^1_{LK}\right)/\Delta = 0$$

Solving Eq. (10.A2) by Crammer's Rule, we get

$$dw_2/ds_1 = p_2\left(g' F^2_L + gf' F^2_{LL}\right) dK_2/ds_1 > 0$$

$$dL_3/ds_1 = \frac{p_2 L_1 L_2\left(g' F^2_L + gf' F^2_{LL}\right) dK_2/ds_1 + L_1(\bar{w}_1 dL_1/ds_1 + w_2 dL_2/ds_1)}{\Omega}$$

$$dw_3/ds_1 = F^3_{LL} dL_3/ds_1 > 0$$

$$d\lambda/ds_1 = \frac{-\left\{\left[[\bar{w}_1 - (1+\lambda)w_3]dL_1/ds_1 + F^3_{LL}[(1+\lambda)L_1 + L_2]\right[(1+\lambda)dL_1/ds_1}{+dL_2/ds_1\left]p_2\left(g' F^2_L + gF^2_{LL} f'\right) dK_2/ds_1 - (w_2 - w_3)dL_2/ds_1\right\}}/\Omega$$

Appendix B

Let $s_2 = 0$ at the initiation of the subsidizing policy, and then the total differentiation of Eqs. (10.4′), (10.5), (10.6), (10.7), (10.8′), (10.9), (10.10), (10.11), and (10.12) could be reorganized into the following linear equation system:

$$\begin{bmatrix} 0 & 0 & 0 & 1 & 1 & 0 \\ F_{LL}^1 & 0 & 0 & F_{LK}^1 & 0 & 0 \\ -p_1 F_{KL}^1 & 0 & 0 & -p_1 F_{KK}^1 & p_2\left[g'(K_2)F_L^2 f' + g''(K_2)F^2\right] & 0 \\ 0 & 0 & 0 & 0 & p_2\left[g(K_2)F_{LL}^2 f' + g'(K_2)F_L^2\right] & -1 \\ 1+\lambda & 1 & L_1 & 0 & f' & 0 \\ \bar{w}_1 & w_3 - (L-L_3)F_{LL}^3 & 0 & 0 & w_2 f' & L_2 \end{bmatrix} \times \begin{bmatrix} dL_1 \\ dL_3 \\ d\lambda \\ dK_1 \\ dK_2 \\ dw_2 \end{bmatrix} = \begin{bmatrix} 0 \\ 0 \\ 0 \\ -w_2 \\ 0 \\ 0 \end{bmatrix} ds_2 \tag{10.B1}$$

Let Δ_2 be the determinant of coefficient matrix, and we have

$$\Delta_2 = L_1\left[w_3 - (L - L_3)F_{LL}^3\right]\Delta > 0$$

From Eq. (10.B1), we have

$$dK_1/ds_2 = dL_1/ds_2 = dK_2/ds_2 = dL_2/ds_2 = f' dK_2/ds_2 = dr/ds_2 = 0$$

$$dw_2/ds_2 = w_2 > 0,\ d\lambda/ds_2 = \frac{w_2 L_2}{L_1\left[w_3 - (L - L_3)F_{LL}^3\right]} > 0,$$

$$dw_3/ds_2 = F_{LL}^3 dL_3/ds_2 > 0$$

Appendix C

By total differentiation of the capital system Eqs. (10.4′), (10.5), (10.6), (10.7), (10.8), (10.9), (10.10), (10.11), and (10.12), we get the following linear equation set:

$$\begin{bmatrix} 0 & 0 & 0 & 1 & 1 & 0 \\ F_{LL}^1 & 0 & 0 & F_{LK}^1 & 0 & 0 \\ -p_1F_{KL}^1 & 0 & 0 & -p_1F_{KK}^1 & p_2\left[g'(K_2)F_L^2f' + g''(K_2)F^2\right] & 0 \\ 0 & 0 & 0 & 0 & p_2\left[g(K_2)F_{LL}^2f' + g'(K_2)F_L^2\right] & -1 \\ 1+\lambda & 1 & L_1 & 0 & f' & 0 \\ \bar{w}_1 & w_3-(L-L_3)F_{LL}^3 & 0 & 0 & w_2f' & L_2 \end{bmatrix}$$
$$\times \begin{bmatrix} dL_1 \\ dL_3 \\ d\lambda \\ dK_1 \\ dK_2 \\ dw_2 \end{bmatrix} = \begin{bmatrix} dK \\ 0 \\ 0 \\ 0 \\ 0 \\ 0 \end{bmatrix} + \begin{bmatrix} 0 \\ 0 \\ 0 \\ 0 \\ dL \\ w_3dL \end{bmatrix}$$

Let $\Delta_3$be the determinant of the coefficient matrix, and we have

$$\Delta_3 = \Delta_2 = L_1\left[w_3 - (L - L_3)F_{LL}^3\right]\Delta > 0$$

By calculating, we get

$$dK_1/dK = 1,\ dL_1/dK = -\frac{F_{LK}^1}{F_{LL}^1} > 0,\ dw_3/dK = F_{LL}^3 dL_3/dK > 0,$$
$$dK_1/dL = 1,\ dw_3/dL = F_{LL}^3 dL_3/dL < 0$$

References

Brecher, R. A., & Diaz Alejandro, C. F. (1977). Tariffs, foreign capital and immiserizing growth. *Journal of International Economics, 7*(4), 317–322.

Chandra, V., & Ali Khan, M. (1993). Foreign investment in the presence of an informal sector. *Economica, 60*(237), 79–103.

Chaudhuri, S. (2006). Labour market reform, welfare and unemployment in a small open economy. *Keio Economics Studies, 43*(2), 1–17.

Chaudhuri, S. (2007). Foreign capital, welfare and urban unemployment in the presence of agricultural dualism. *Japan and the World Economy, 19*, 149–165.

Din, M. (1996). International capital mobility and development policy in a dual economy. *Review of International Economics, 6*, 185–201.

Grinols, E. L. (1991). Unemployment and foreign capital: the relative opportunity costs of domestic labor and welfare. *Economica, 58*(229), 107–121.

Gupta, M. (1993). Rural-urban migration, informal sector and development policies: A theoretical analysis. *Journal of Development Economics, 41*, 137–151.

Gupta, M. (1997a). Informal sector and informal capital market in a small open less-developed economy. *Journal of Development Economics, 52*(2), 409–428.

Gupta, M. (1997b). Foreign capital and the informal sector: comments on Chandra and Khan. *Economica, 64*(254), 353–363.

Harris, J., & Todaro, M. (1970). Migration, unemployment and development: A two-sector analysis. *American Economic Review, 60*, 126–142.
Ju, J. M. (2011). The problems and solutions in the development of modern agriculture. *Modern Agricultural Technology, 7*, 377–380.
Tiwari, P., Kawakami, T., & Doi, M. (2002). Dual labor markets and trade reform in China. *The Journal of Policy Reform, 5*(2), 101–113.
Wang, J. H. (2011). Analysis on the impact of capital subsidies on the large-scale assignment of rural land. *Jiangsu Rural Economics, 3*, 51–52.
Wang, Z., & Han, X. F. (2010). A selective study on the development of modern agriculture in China. *Rural Economy, 12*, 63–64.
Zheng, J. C., Liu, H. Z., Zhou, J. T., Zhen, R. H., & Li, N. (2009). Study on the goals and models of modern agricultural development in Jiangsu province. *Jiangsu Agricultural Academic Journal, 25*(1), 1–5.
Zhong, C. P., Turvey, C., Zhang, J., & Xu, C. S. (2011). Does taxation have real effects on agricultural output? Theory and empirical evidence from China. *Journal of Economic Policy Reform, 14*(3), 227–242.

Chapter 11
Analyzing the Effect of Advanced Agriculture Development Policy

Xiaochun Li, Qin Shen, Chunlei Gu, and Meng Ni

Abstract This chapter broadens the scope of current theoretical studies, divides rural agriculture into two sectors—advanced and traditional—and takes into consideration the land factor and the urban informal sector. Under the assumption that wages in the advanced agricultural sector are higher than in the traditional agricultural sector, this chapter analyzes the effect of policies to promote advanced agricultural development with the comparative static method. The main conclusions of this chapter are wage subsidization of the advanced agricultural sector, in addition to having the same economic impact as interest subsidies on the advanced agricultural sector, could also increase the land employment in the advanced agricultural sector, and reduce that in the traditional agricultural sector. Therefore, the effect of wage subsidizing policies is stronger than that of interest subsidies, while land rent subsidies for the advanced agricultural sector have the same economic effect as wage subsidies.

Keywords Advanced agriculture • Traditional agriculture • Transfer of labor

JEL Code J60 • I30 • R10

1 Introduction

When studying economic development and transfer of labor, the urban economy is often divided into two sectors, namely, the formal and the informal ones. Since the 1990s, using the Harris-Todaro model (Harris and Todaro 1970) to study the transfer of rural labor to the urban formal and informal sectors has been a hot topic, on which Grinols (1991), Gupta (1993), Chandra and Khan (1993), Din (1996), and Yabuuchi and Beladi (2001) all have published papers.

In recent years, there have been studies that further divide the rural labor market into the advanced and the traditional agricultural sectors. This is because many

X. Li (✉)
Business School, Nanjing University, Nanjing, China
e-mail: xiaochun@nju.edu.cn

Q. Shen • C. Gu • M. Ni
School of Economics, Nanjing University, 22 Hankou Road, Nanjing, Jiangsu 210093, China

X. Li (ed.), *Labor Transfer in Emerging Economies*, New Frontiers in Regional Science: Asian Perspectives 12, DOI 10.1007/978-981-10-3569-2_11

emerging economies like India, China, and Brazil are making great effort under the market principle to introduce advanced agricultural equipment and technology to develop their agricultural industry, resulting in higher yields compared to traditional agricultural methods.

The existing literature considering advanced agriculture and the transfer of labor adopts two main research methods: one divides the economy into three sectors, namely, the urban sector, the advanced agricultural sector, and the traditional agricultural sector, and studies the economic effect of policies on promoting the development of the advanced agricultural sector assuming the transfer of rural labor. The other divides the economy into four sectors. The urban sector is divided into formal and informal, while the rural sector is divided into advanced agricultural and traditional agricultural, and studies the economic effects of government policies that promote the development of the advanced agricultural sector.

The literature using the three-sector model includes Chaudhuri (2006, 2007), Li and Shen (2012), and so on. Chaudhuri (2006) analyzes the rationality and importance of reforming the labor market in developing countries with the three-sector general equilibrium model. His research shows that, under certain circumstances, liberalization of the labor market can lead to an increase in the rural wage ratio, a decrease in the ratio of return on the land capital, a decrease in the urban wage, and an increase in social welfare. Chaudhuri (2007) analyzes the reasons developing countries attract external capital and the rise of unemployment during the reform process. He discovers that increased foreign capital can improve social welfare and reduce the urban unemployment rate.

Li and Shen (2012), on the other hand, study the economic effect of government development policies to introduce urban private capital to the advanced agricultural sector. Their main conclusion is that interest subsidizing policies could reduce the transfer of rural labor to urban areas, but such policies could also promote the transfer of rural labor to the advanced agricultural sector. Wage subsidizing policies could lead to an increase of the urban unemployment rate and a decrease of the laborers in the traditional agricultural sector.

The four-sector research examines past divisions in the urban economy to study the relationship between the employment situation of rural laborers upon entering cities and the development of advanced agriculture. Among the literature using the four-sector model, Gupta (1997a) analyzes the impact of the changes of product price markets in a less-developed, small, but open economy on formal and informal capital. His study finds that subsidizing the product prices in the advanced agricultural sector could be conducive to economic development. Gupta (1997b) uses the four-sector general equilibrium model to prove the invalidity of the Brecher-Alejandro (1977) proposition under the premise of introducing external capital and the existence of the costs of transfer and human resources training.

Though the above research, whether adopting the three-sector or four-sector model, show different advantages, they also have limitations. First, the research does not explicitly count the land factor as part of the production function, whereas land is an important factor in both the advanced and traditional agricultural sectors. Second, Gupta (1997a, b) and Chaudhuri (2006, 2007) made the same assumption that the wages in the advanced and traditional agricultural sectors are the same, which defies the purpose of advancement in agricultural production and fails to account for the theoretical motivation of the transfer of labor from the traditional agricultural sector to the advanced one. Generally, the main incentive for labor transfer is wage level—homogenous labor in the lower wage sector will transfer to the higher one. If the wage in the advanced agricultural sector equals that of the traditional one, it is difficult to guarantee sufficient labor force for the advanced sector. This assumption is also out of synch with the reality of the development of the advanced agricultural sector in developing countries. For example, in China, wages in the advanced agricultural sector are obviously higher than in the traditional one.[1] On the other hand, though Li and Shen's (2012) study took into consideration the wage difference between the two agricultural sectors, their model neglects the employment situation of rural laborers after entering the cities and the rural land factor, which cannot be disregarded in the real economy.

Under more general conditions, in order to clarify the policy effect of promoting advanced agricultural development, this chapter assumes different wage levels in the advanced and traditional agricultural sectors, takes into consideration the land factor of the urban informal sector, and analyzes the effect of policies to promote advanced agricultural development with the comparative static method:

1. Subsidizing capital interest for the advanced agricultural sector
2. Subsidizing wages for the advanced agricultural sector
3. Subsidizing land rent for the advanced agricultural sector
4. Change of labor and capital endowment in the economy

This chapter broadens the scope of current theoretical studies and finds that wage subsidization for the advanced agricultural sector, in addition to the same economic impact as the interest subsidies on the advanced agricultural sector, could also increase land employment in the advanced agricultural sector and reduce that in the traditional agricultural sector. Therefore, the effect of wage subsidizing policies is better than that of interest subsidies, but land rent subsidies for the advanced agricultural sector will have the same economic effect as wage subsidies. In the second part of this chapter, we establish a general equilibrium model, in the third part we present a theoretical analysis based on the established model, and in the fourth part we offer a conclusion.

2 Model

In this chapter, we assume a four-sector closed economy. The four sectors are the urban formal sector, the urban informal sector, the advanced agricultural sector, and the traditional agricultural sector. Among them, the advanced agricultural sector is

[1]Please refer to Zheng et al. (2009), analysis on the target and model of modern high-efficiency agricultural development.

a newly established one. The urban formal sector uses two factors of production: labor and capital. The urban informal sector only uses one factor: labor. The advanced agricultural sector uses three factors: labor, capital, and land. And the traditional agricultural sector uses labor and land. The labor of the traditional agricultural sector moves to the urban formal sector, the urban informal sector, and the advanced agricultural sector. Capital flows freely between the urban formal and advanced agricultural sectors. Land flows freely between the traditional and advanced agricultural sectors. The production functions of each of the said sectors are:

$$Y_1 = F^1(L_1, K_1) \tag{11.1}$$

$$Y_2 = F^2(L_2) \tag{11.2}$$

$$Y_3 = g(K_3)F^3(L_3, T_3) \tag{11.3}$$

$$Y_4 = F^4(L_4, T_4) \tag{11.4}$$

$Y_i(i = 1, 2, 3, 4)$ indicates the output of the urban formal sector, the urban informal sector, the advanced agricultural sector, and the traditional agricultural sector, respectively. $L_i, (i = 1, 2, 3, 4)$ indicates the quantity of labor of each sector. K_1 and K_3 indicate the capital investment in the urban formal sector and the advanced agricultural sector, respectively. T_3 and T_4 indicate the land investment in the modern and traditional agricultural sectors, respectively. $g = g(K_3)$ can be deemed as the scale effect function of the investment in the advanced agricultural sector. We assume that when $K_3 = 0$, $g(0) = 1$, which means, when lacking capital investment, the advanced agricultural sector will retrograde to the traditional agricultural sector. In addition, we also assume that $g(K_3) > 1$, $g^{'}(K_3) > 0$, $g^{''}(K_3) < 0$, and $\forall K_3 > 0$. The production functions Y_1, Y_2, Y_3, and Y_4 are strictly quasi concave, among which Y_1, Y_2, and Y_4 are first-order homogeneous and Y_3 satisfies the feature of increasing return to scale.

We also assume that the transfer of labor from the traditional to the advanced agricultural sector is not limitless. In the early establishment of the advanced agricultural sector, the quantity of labor transferred from the traditional agricultural sector is bound by the capital of the advanced agricultural sector. The relationship between its employed labor and capital is as follows:

$$L_3 = \begin{cases} f(K_3), f'(K_3) > 0, f^{''}(K_3) < 0, K_3 < K_3^* \\ f(K_3^*), \quad f'(K_3^*) = 0, K_3 = K_3^* \\ f(K_3), f'(K_3) \leq 0, f^{''}(K_3) > 0, K_3 > K_3^* \end{cases} \tag{11.5}$$

It should be noted that the first half of Eq. (11.5) describes the development period of advanced agriculture, on which this chapter is focusing.

Using L, K, and T to indicate the endowment of labor, capital, and land in the entire economy, which are all exogenous, we have the following equations under the condition of full employment:

$$L_1 + L_2 + L_3 + L_4 = L. \tag{11.6}$$

$$K_1 + K_3 = K \tag{11.7}$$

$$T_3 + T_4 = T \tag{11.8}$$

$\bar{w}_1$, w_2, w_3, and w_4 indicate the wages in the urban formal sector, the urban informal sector, the advanced agricultural sector, and the traditional agricultural sector, respectively. r and τ indicate the return of capital and land, respectively. To maximize the profit of each sector, we have the following equations:

$$p_1 F_L^1 = \overline{w_1} \tag{11.9}$$

$$p_2 F_L^2 = w_2 \tag{11.10}$$

$$p_3 g F_L^3 = w_3 \tag{11.11}$$

$$F_L^4 = w_4 \tag{11.12}$$

$$p_1 F_K^1 = r \tag{11.13}$$

$$p_3 g' F^3 = r \tag{11.14}$$

$$p_3 g F_T^3 = \tau \tag{11.15}$$

$$F_T^4 = \tau \tag{11.16}$$

In the above, $F_L^i = \partial F^i / \partial L_i$ $(i = 1, 2, 3, 4)$; $F_K^i = \partial F^i / \partial K_i$ $(i = 1, 3)$; $F_T^i = \partial F^i / \partial T_i (i = 3, 4)$; because of labor unions and ubiquitous local protectionism, the wage in the urban formal sector shows a downward rigidity, so $\bar{w}_1$ is an exogenous variable; p_1, p_2, and p_3 refer to the product price in the urban formal sector, the urban informal sector, and the advanced agricultural sector, in terms of the product price in the traditional agricultural sector.

We assume that labor moves from the traditional agricultural sector to the advanced agricultural sector, the urban formal and informal sectors. Thus, according to Harris-Todaro model, when the transfer of labor reaches equilibrium, the labor wage of the rural traditional agricultural sector should be equal to the expected wage of the other three sectors:

$$\frac{L_1\overline{w_1} + L_2w_2 + L_3w_3}{L_1 + L_2 + L_3} = w_4 \quad (11.17)$$

To transform Eq. (11.17), we get

$$L_1\overline{w_1} + L_2w_2 + L_3w_3 = w_4(L - L_4) \quad (11.17')$$

The presumption of the above equation is the wage in the urban formal sector and the advanced agricultural sector is higher than the wage in the traditional one, so labor in the traditional sector would transfer to the advanced agricultural sector and the urban formal sector. However, it is easy to observe that $w_4 > w_2$, and one possible explanation for the transfer of traditional sector labor to the urban informal sector with lower wages is that migrant workers "temporarily" transfer to the urban informal sector to wait for job opportunities and higher wages in the urban formal sector. Up to now we have established the model. From Eqs. (11.1), (11.2), (11.3), (11.4), (11.5), (11.6), (11.7), (11.8), (11.9), (11.10), (11.11), (11.12), (11.13), (11.14), (11.15), (11.16), and (11.17), there are altogether 17 endogenous variables, which are $Y_1, Y_2, Y_3, Y_4, L_1, L_2, L_3, L_4, K_1, K_3, T_3, T_4, w_2, w_3, w_4, r$, and τ, and seven exogenous variables, L, K, T, $\bar{w}_1$, p_1, p_2, and p_3.

3 Economic Analysis

This section focuses on the economic effect of interest, wage, and land subsidies on the advanced agricultural economy. We will also discuss the effect of increasing the endowment of factors on the economy.

3.1 *The Economic Effect of Interest Subsidies on the Advanced Agricultural Sector*

If the government subsidizes the interest of loans for the advanced agricultural sector with the rate of s_1, Eq. (11.14) can be rewritten as:

$$p_2g'(K_2)F^2 = r(1 - s_1) \quad (11.14')$$

Then, the total differential of (11.5), (11.6), (11.7), (11.8), (11.9), (11.10), (11.11), (11.12), (11.13), (11.14′), (11.15), (11.16), and (11.17′) is:

$$\begin{bmatrix} F^1_{LL} & 0 & 0 & -F^1_{LK} & 0 & 0 & 0 \\ 0 & 0 & 0 & p_3\left(g'F^3_L + gF^3_{LL}f'\right) & p_3gF^3_{LT} & -1 & 0 \\ 0 & 0 & F^4_{LL} & 0 & -F^4_{LT} & 0 & -1 \\ p_1F^1_{KL} & 0 & 0 & -\left[p_1F^1_{KK} + p_3\left(g''F^3 + g'F^3_Lf'\right)\right] & -p_3g'F^3_T & 0 & 0 \\ 0 & 0 & -F^4_{TL} & p_3\left(g'F^3_T + gF^3_{TL}f'\right) & p_3gF^3_{TT} + F^4_{TT} & 0 & 0 \\ 1 & 1 & 1 & f' & 0 & 0 & 0 \\ \overline{w_1} & w_2 + L_2p_2F^2_{LL} & w_4 & w_3f' & 0 & L_3 & -(L - L_4) \end{bmatrix}$$

$$\times \begin{bmatrix} dL_1 \\ dL_2 \\ dL_4 \\ dK_3 \\ dT_3 \\ dw_3 \\ dw_4 \end{bmatrix} = \begin{bmatrix} 0 \\ 0 \\ 0 \\ rds_1 \\ 0 \\ 0 \\ 0 \end{bmatrix}$$

The coefficient matrix (11.18) is:

$$\begin{aligned} \Delta_1 = \; & p_3F^1_{LL}\left(g''F^3 + g'F^3_Lf'\right)\left[w_2 + L_2p_2F^2_{LL} - w_4 + F^4_{LL}(L - L_4)\right]\left(p_3gF^3_{TT} + F^4_{TT}\right) \\ & -p_1F^4_{TL}F^1_{KL}F^1_{LK}p_3gF^3_{LT}(L - L_4) - p_3g'F^3_TF^4_{TL}F^1_{LK}\left(w_2 + L_2p_2F^2_{LL} - \overline{w_1}\right) \\ & -p_3^2g'F^1_{LL}F^3_T\left(g'F^3_T + gF^3_{TL}f'\right)\left[w_2 + L_2p_2F^2_{LL} - w_4 + F^4_{LL}(L - L_4)\right] \\ & +p_3g'F^3_TF^1_{LL}F^4_{LT}\left[w_3f' - \left(w_2 + L_2p_2F^2_{LL}\right)f' + p_3L_3\left(g'F^3_L + gF^3_{LL}f'\right)\right] \\ & -F^4_{TL}F^4_{LT}(L - L_4)p_3F^1_{LL}\left(g''F^3 + g'F^3_Lf'\right) \end{aligned}$$

Since the sign of Δ_1 cannot be directly determined, we will use dynamic adjustment to decide its sign. The process detail is explained in Appendix A. After the dynamic adjustment, we get $\Delta_1 > 0$.

Before solving Eq. (11.18), we will prove the following two lemmas.

Lemma 11.1 When $f' > 0$, the assumed economy in this chapter satisfies the inequality $p_3\left(g''F^3 + g'f'F^3_L\right) < 0$.

Proof The total differential of Eq. (11.14) is:

$$p_3g''F^3(L_3)dK_3 + p_3g'F^3_L(L_3)f'dK_3 = dr.$$

Therefore,

$$p_3g''F^3(L_3) + p_3g'F^3_L(L_3)f' = dr/dK_3.$$

With increasing inflow of capital to the advanced agricultural sector, its interest rate should fall. So we have $dr/dK_3 < 0$, and $f' > 0$, which means $p_3\left(g''F^3 + g'f'F^3_L\right) < 0$. End of proof.

Lemma 11.2 In the assumed economy in this chapter, when $f' > 0$, $g'F^3_L + gF^3_{LL}f' > 0$.

Table 11.1 The calculation result of Eq. (11.18) (please refer to Appendix B for details of the calculation procedure)

	dL_1	dL_2	dL_3	dL_4	dK_1	dK_3	dT_3	dT_4	dr	dw_2	dw_3	dw_4	$d\tau$
ds_1	–	/	+	/	–	+	/	/	0	/	/	/	/

Note: "–" means that the ratio of the items in the above horizontal column to ds_1 is negative, "+" means the ratio is positive, and "/" means the sign cannot be decided

Proof The total differential of Eq. (11.11) can be written as the following equation:

$$p_3\left(g'F_L^3 + gF_{LL}^3 f'\right)dK_3 = dw_3.$$

It should be noted that $dw_3/dK_3 > 0$ (this is because, with the increase of urban capital flowing to the advanced agricultural sector, rural labor will become more condensed, and rising wage is the main force increasing labor condensation), it could be inferred that $g'F_L^3 + gF_{LL}^3 f' > 0$. End of proof.

Using the Cramer rule to solve Eq. (11.18) and Lemma 11.2, we can get Table 11.1 as follows:

Proposition 11.1 The interest subsidies for the advanced agricultural sector will not affect the interest rate but will have the following economic impacts:

1. Reducing the labor and capital employment in the urban formal sector
2. Increasing the labor and capital employment in the advanced agricultural sector

The essence of subsidizing capital interest for the advanced agricultural sector is to make the capital using interest of advanced sector smaller than urban formal sector and then reduce the capital using cost of advanced sector. Using a two-sector (urban sector and rural sector) Harris-Todaro framework, Khan and Naqvi (1983) and Chao and Yu (1992) analyze the economic impacts of reduction in the capital differential, respectively; their main researches are the impacts of change in the capital differential on social welfare, but Proposition 11.1 in this chapter considers more impacts.

Subsidizing capital interest for the advanced agricultural sector will cause more capital from the urban formal sector to flow to the advanced agricultural sector, and thus the capital utilization environment of the advanced agricultural sector will improve, as will the working environment. In the early period of establishing the advanced agricultural sector, the improvement of the working environment will attract more rural labor to transfer to the advanced agricultural sector and less to the urban formal environment, which is indicated by Proposition 11.1. It is worth noting that Proposition 11.1 in this chapter is different from the three-sector model which considers unemployment in Li and Shen (2012). Proposition 11.1 cannot determine whether interest subsidies for the advanced agricultural sector will reduce labor employment in the traditional sector or not, but Li and Shen (2012) unambiguously conclude that they will. This difference can be explained by

Table 11.2 The calculation result of Eq. (11.19) (please refer to Appendix B for the details of the calculation process)

	dL_1	dL_2	dL_3	dL_4	dK_1	dK_3	dT_3	dT_4	dr	dw_2	dw_3	dw_4	$d\tau$
ds_2	−	/	+	/	−	+	+	−	0	/	/	/	/

Note: The meaning of above signs is the same as in Table 11.1

this four-sector model: the interest subsidies for the advanced agricultural sector will reduce employment in the urban formal sector, which lowers the expectation of transferring to the urban formal sector for the labors in the urban informal sector. As a result, labor transferring to the urban sector declines. Therefore, if the increased labor transfer to the advanced agricultural sector is smaller than the decrease in those to the urban sector, employment in the traditional agricultural sector will rise.

3.2 *The Economic Effect of Wage Subsidies for the Advanced Agricultural Sector*

If the government subsidizes the wages of the advanced agricultural sector at the rate of s_2, then Eq. (11.11) becomes:

$$p_3 g F_L^3 = w_3(1 - s_2) \tag{11.11$'$}$$

The total differential of (11.5), (11.6), (11.7), (11.8), (11.9), (11.10), (11.11′), (11.12), (11.13), (11.14), (11.15), (11.16), and (11.17′) is:

$$\begin{bmatrix} F_{LL}^1 & 0 & 0 & -F_{LK}^1 & 0 & 0 & 0 \\ 0 & 0 & 0 & p_3\left(g'F_L^3 + gF_{LL}^3 f'\right) & p_3 g F_{LT}^3 & -1 & 0 \\ 0 & 0 & F_{LL}^4 & 0 & -F_{LT}^4 & 0 & -1 \\ p_1 F_{KL}^1 & 0 & 0 & -\left[p_1 F_{KK}^1 + p_3\left(g'' F^3 + g' F_L^3 f'\right)\right] & -p_3 g' F_T^3 & 0 & 0 \\ 0 & 0 & -F_{TL}^4 & p_3\left(g'F_T^3 + gF_{TL}^3 f'\right) & p_3 g F_{TT}^3 + F_{TT}^4 & 0 & 0 \\ 1 & 1 & 1 & f' & 0 & 0 & 0 \\ \overline{w_1} & w_2 + L_2 p_2 F_{LL}^2 & w_4 & w_3 f' & 0 & L_3 & -(L - L_4) \end{bmatrix}$$
$$\times \begin{bmatrix} dL_1 \\ dL_2 \\ dL_4 \\ dK_3 \\ dT_3 \\ dw_3 \\ dw_4 \end{bmatrix} = \begin{bmatrix} 0 \\ -w_3 ds_2 \\ 0 \\ 0 \\ 0 \\ 0 \\ 0 \end{bmatrix} \tag{11.19}$$

It could be calculated that the value of the coefficient matrix (11.19) is Δ_1.

Using the Cramer rule to solve Eq. (11.19) and Lemma 11.1, we can get Table 11.2 as follows:

To summarize, we obtain Proposition 11.2:

Proposition 11.2 In addition to having the same economic effect as Proposition 11.1, wage subsidies for the advanced agricultural sector will also increase the land use of the advanced agricultural sector and reduce that of the traditional agricultural sector.

There are some researches considering wage subsidies to rural sector in the existing theoretical literatures which consider labor transfer, most of them build a two-sector (manufacturing sector and rural sector) or three-sector (manufacturing sector, informal sector, and rural sector) model and don't set apart the rural sector. For example, in the two-sector researches, Corden and Findlay (1975) draw a conclusion that in the absence of capital mobility, a wage subsidy in agriculture leaves output of manufactures unchanged, while capital mobility will bring about some fall in output of manufactures. McCool (1982) concludes that a subsidy to agricultural wages does not affect wages in the manufacturing sector neither does it affect the gross return to capital or the capital intensity in either sector. In the three-sector models, the economic impacts of wage subsidy on the agriculture mostly relate to labor employment and social welfare. Gupta (1993) concludes that a wage subsidy to the rural sector increases the level of unemployment when the informal sector produces non-trade intermediate goods. Under the assumption that capital in the urban formal sector is internationally mobile and rural capital is specific, Din (1996) concludes that a rural wage subsidy raises the rural output and the return to capital specific to rural sector, depresses the outputs of both urban region, and leaves national welfare unchanged. Under the general informal sector condition, Yabuuchi and Beladi (2001) get that wage subsidies to the rural sector, improve national welfare, and decrease the level of unemployment. Though Proposition 11.2 in this chapter has some differences with the above researches, because this chapter divides the rural sector into two parts, so Proposition 11.2 in this chapter is more accurate and applicable than the existing researches.

Using the advanced agricultural sector as an example, the wage subsidies for the advanced agricultural sector would have no effect on employment and capital level in this sector in Li and Shen (2012). However, this chapter shows that wage subsidies could increase the labor and capital employment. The reason for the distinction is that wage subsidies in the three-sector model would not affect capital employment in the advanced agricultural sector, but will increase capital employment in this sector under the four-sector model that this chapter applies. Further, increase in capital employment would lead to increase in labor employment and thus would affect the entire economy.

Compared to interest rate subsidizing policies, wage subsidies for the advanced agricultural sector decrease the cost of labor employment and have a more direct impact of increasing labor employment in this sector. Under the condition that the production technology level does not change in the short run, the production scale

Table 11.3 The calculation result of Eq. (11.20) (please refer to Appendix B for the details of the calculation procedure)

	dL_1	dL_2	dL_3	dL_4	dK_1	dK_3	dT_3	dT_4	dr	dw_2	dw_3	dw_4	$d\tau$
ds_3	–	/	+	/	–	+	+	–	0	/	/	/	/

Note: The meaning of above signs is the same as in Table 11.1

of this sector must increase, as does land employment. However, the source of land is only the traditional agricultural sector, which is indicated by Proposition 11.2.

3.3 The Economic Impact of Land Subsidies for the Advanced Agricultural Sector

If the government subsidizes land for the advanced agricultural sector with the rate of s_3, then Eq. (11.15) becomes:

$$p_3 g F_T^3 = \tau(1 - s_3) \tag{11.15'}$$

The total differential of (11.5), (11.6), (11.7), (11.8), (11.9), (11.10), (11.11), (11.12), (11.13), (11.14), (11.15′), (11.16), and (11.17′) is:

$$\begin{bmatrix} F_{LL}^1 & 0 & 0 & -F_{LK}^1 & 0 & 0 & 0 \\ 0 & 0 & 0 & p_3\left(g'F_L^3 + gF_{LL}^3 f'\right) & p_3 g F_{LT}^3 & -1 & 0 \\ 0 & 0 & F_{LL}^4 & 0 & -F_{LT}^4 & 0 & -1 \\ p_1 F_{KL}^1 & 0 & 0 & -\left[p_1 F_{KK}^1 + p_3\left(g'' F^3 + g' F_L^3 f'\right)\right] & -p_3 g' F_T^3 & 0 & 0 \\ 0 & 0 & -F_{TL}^4 & p_3\left(g'F_T^3 + gF_{TL}^3 f'\right) & p_3 g F_{TT}^3 + F_{TT}^4 & 0 & 0 \\ 1 & 1 & 1 & f' & 0 & 0 & 0 \\ \overline{w_1} & w_2 + L_2 p_2 F_{LL}^2 & w_4 & w_3 f' & 0 & L_3 & -(L - L_4) \end{bmatrix} \times \begin{bmatrix} dL_1 \\ dL_2 \\ dL_4 \\ dK_3 \\ dT_3 \\ dw_3 \\ dw_4 \end{bmatrix} = \begin{bmatrix} 0 \\ 0 \\ 0 \\ 0 \\ -\tau ds_3 \\ 0 \\ 0 \end{bmatrix} \tag{11.20}$$

Apparently, the value of the coefficient matrix (11.20) is Δ_1.

Using the Cramer rule to solve Eq. (11.20) and according to the Lemmas 11.1 and 11.2, we get Table 11.3 as follows:

To summarize, we obtain Proposition 11.3:

Proposition 11.3 The economic effect of both land subsidies and wage subsidies in the advanced agricultural sectors is the same.

Land subsidies for the advanced agricultural sector will reduce the cost of land use in this sector and thus increase the land use. It should be noted that, compared to interest and wage subsidies, land subsidies for the advanced agricultural sector would have a more direct impact on increasing land use in this sector. Assuming that the production technology level does not change in the short run, the production scale of this sector must increase, as will the employment of labor and capital. The source of labor is the laborers who would have moved to the urban formal sector; the source of capital is from the urban formal sector. This is indicated by Proposition 11.3. Besides, except this chapter, the existing four-sector models (such as Gupta (1997a), and Beladi et al. (2010)) don't take into account the land factor, so our conclusion regarding land subsidies for the advanced agricultural sector is new.

3.4 *The Impact of Changes in Labor and Capital Endowment on the Economy*

When the labor endowment increases, the total differential of (11.5), (11.6), (11.7), (11.8), (11.9), (11.10), (11.11), (11.12), (11.13), (11.14), (11.15), (11.16), and (11.17′) is the following Eq. (11.21):

$$\begin{bmatrix} F^1_{LL} & 0 & 0 & -F^1_{LK} & 0 & 0 & 0 \\ 0 & 0 & 0 & p_3\left(g'F^3_L + gF^3_{LL}f'\right) & p_3gF^3_{LT} & -1 & 0 \\ 0 & 0 & F^4_{LL} & 0 & -F^4_{LT} & 0 & -1 \\ p_1F^1_{KL} & 0 & 0 & -\left[p_1F^1_{KK} + p_3\left(g''F^3 + g'F^3_Lf'\right)\right] & -p_3g'F^3_T & 0 & 0 \\ 0 & 0 & -F^4_{TL} & p_3\left(g'F^3_T + gF^3_{TL}f'\right) & p_3gF^3_{TT} + F^4_{TT} & 0 & 0 \\ 1 & 1 & 1 & f' & 0 & 0 & 0 \\ \overline{w_1} & w_2 + L_2p_2F^2_{LL} & w_4 & w_3f' & 0 & L_3 & -(L - L_4) \end{bmatrix} \times \begin{bmatrix} dL_1 \\ dL_2 \\ dL_4 \\ dK_3 \\ dT_3 \\ dw_3 \\ dw_4 \end{bmatrix} = \begin{bmatrix} 0 \\ 0 \\ 0 \\ 0 \\ 0 \\ dL \\ w_4dL \end{bmatrix} \tag{11.21}$$

Apparently, the value of the coefficient matrix (11.21) is Δ_1.

When the capital endowment increases, the total differential of (11.5), (11.6), (11.7), (11.8), (11.9), (11.10), (11.11), (11.12), (11.13), (11.14), (11.15), (11.16), and (11.17′) is (11.22):

$$
\begin{bmatrix}
F_{LL}^{1} & 0 & 0 & -F_{LK}^{1} & 0 & 0 & 0 & 0 \\
0 & 0 & 0 & 0 & p_3\left(g'F_L^3 + gF_{LL}^3 f'\right) & p_3 g F_{LT}^3 & -1 & 0 \\
0 & 0 & F_{LL}^4 & 0 & 0 & -F_{LT}^4 & 0 & -1 \\
p_1 F_{KL}^1 & 0 & 0 & p_1 F_{KK}^1 & -p_3\left(g'' F^3 + g' F_L^3 f'\right) & -p_3 g' F_T^3 & 0 & 0 \\
0 & 0 & -F_{TL}^4 & 0 & p_3\left(g'F_T^3 + gF_{TL}^3 f'\right) & p_3 g F_{TT}^3 + F_{TT}^4 & 0 & 0 \\
1 & 1 & 1 & 0 & f' & 0 & 0 & 0 \\
0 & 0 & 0 & 1 & 1 & 0 & 0 & 0 \\
\overline{w_1} & w_2 + L_2 p_2 F_{LL}^2 & w_4 & 0 & w_3 f' & 0 & L_3 & -(L - L_4)
\end{bmatrix}
\times \begin{bmatrix} dL_1 \\ dL_2 \\ dL_4 \\ dK_1 \\ dK_3 \\ dT_3 \\ dw_3 \\ dw_4 \end{bmatrix}
= \begin{bmatrix} 0 \\ 0 \\ 0 \\ 0 \\ 0 \\ 0 \\ dK \\ 0 \end{bmatrix}
\tag{11.22}
$$

We assume that the value of the coefficient matrix (11.22) is Δ_2, and then we can calculate that $\Delta_2 = -\Delta_1$.

Using the Cramer rule and according to Lemmas 11.1 and 11.2, we get the following Table 11.4:

To summarize, we obtain Propositions 11.4 and 11.5.

Proposition 11.4 The increase of labor endowment does not affect interest, but it has the following economic impacts:

1. Increase the labor and capital employment of the urban formal sector
2. Decrease the labor, capital, and land employment of the advanced agricultural sector
3. Increase the land employment of the traditional agricultural sector

Proposition 11.5 The increase of capital endowment does not affect interest, but it has the following economic impact:

1. The employment of labor, capital, and land in the advanced agricultural sector increases, and its wage increases.

Table 11.4 The result of the change of capital and labor endowment (please refer to Appendix C for the detailed calculation)

	dL_1	dL_2	dL_3	dL_4	dK_1	dK_3	dT_3	dT_4	dr	dw_2	dw_3	dw_4	$d\tau$
dL	+	/	–	/	+	–	–	+	0	/	/	/	/
dK	/	/	+	–	/	+	+	–	0	/	+	/	/

Note: The meaning of above signs is the same as in Table 11.1

2. The employment of labor and land of the traditional agricultural sector decreases.

The analysis of economic impacts of changes in factor endowment on the rural sector is a classic theme in the existing labor transferring researches. These researches always take the rural sector as a whole and focus on the impacts of factor endowment changes on labor employment and social welfare, among which Beladi and Naqvi (1988) is a typical one. Beladi and Naqvi (1988) take land factor into account in their model and conclude that increase in capital endowment will reduce urban unemployment rate and increase in labor endowment aggravates urban unemployment. On the other hand, Yabuuchi (1998) finds the relationship between capital endowment and labor employment through the analysis of unemployment rate; he concludes that with certain condition, increase in capital endowment leads to a fall in urban unemployment. Because this chapter segments the rural sector, so we could discuss the impacts of endowment changes on the economy more explicitly, in especial we could separately analyze the impacts on the two rural sectors. From Propositions 11.4 and 11.5, the impacts of endowment changes on the two rural sectors are different, so the different impacts can't be summarized through a one-rural-sector model; furthermore, this difference didn't get reflected in the previous researches.

The increase of labor endowment means the increase of labor supply; when we consider the four-sector model which contains advanced agricultural sector, Proposition 11.4 tells us the increase of labor supply will raise the labor employment of the urban formal sector. The decrease in the labor employment of the advanced sector is, on the other hand, due to the decrease of capital employment in the advanced sector, and hence the decrease of land employment, the reduced land employment in the advanced agricultural sector, then returns to the traditional agricultural sector. In the three-sector model of Li and Shen (2012), the increase in labor endowment is absorbed by unemployment in the urban sector. The increase of capital endowment mainly affects the formal sector and the advanced agricultural sector, both of which use capital. With the increased use of capital by the advanced agricultural sector, its employment increases. The source of labor is the traditional agricultural sector, which then results in decreased employment in this sector. On the other hand, the reason the advanced sector is able to attract labor is because of its rising wages, which are indicated by Proposition 11.5. But in the three-sector model, the increase of capital endowment has no effect on capital, labor employment, and wages in the advanced agricultural sector.

4 Conclusion

This chapter establishes a four-sector model and analyzes the economic effect of the policies to promote the development of the advanced agriculture. The main content of this chapter includes the development policies commonly involved in mainstream economic analyses and their effect on economic development. We determined from our analysis that interest, wage, and land rent subsidization policies have a similar effect on labor and capital employment. This provides a good policy environment for the development of the advanced agricultural sector and broadens the scope of policy choices. According to Propositions 11.1 and 11.2, compared to interest subsidies for the advanced agricultural sector, wage and land subsidies would have a stronger effect on the development of advanced agricultural sector and should be the first choice for policymakers. In addition, in this chapter, we also compared some of our conclusions with those of three-sector and four-sector models. Generally, when the unemployment problem is significant in the economy, the conclusions based on a three-sector model considering unemployment rate should be adopted, but when the urban informal sector is growing and taking a larger part of the economy, the conclusions of this chapter should be considered. However, we would also like to explain that, in our established model, there are still some undecided items which need to be determined under some specific conditions. Furthermore, wage and rent subsidization policies have a more direct impact on land employment than interest subsidization policies. With respect to economic development, we determined that increasing capital endowment in the economy increases wages in the advanced agricultural sector. These conclusions will provide guidance to policymakers in their all-important task of rural development.

Appendices

Appendix A

The dynamic adjustment procedure:

$$\dot{L}_1 = d_1\left(p_1 F_L^1 - \overline{w_1}\right) \tag{11.A1}$$

$$\dot{L}_2 = d_2\left(p_2 F_L^2 - w_2\right) \tag{11.A2}$$

$$\dot{L}_3 = d_3\left(p_3 g F_L^2 - w_3\right) \tag{11.A3}$$

$$\dot{L}_4 = d_4\left(F_L^4 - w_4\right) \tag{11.A4}$$

$$\dot{K}_1 = d_5\left(p_1 F_K^1 - r\right) \tag{11.A5}$$

$$\dot{K}_3 = d_6\left(p_3 g' F^3 - r\right) \tag{11.A6}$$

$$\dot{T}_3 = d_7\left(p_3 g F_T^3 - \tau\right) \tag{11.A7}$$

$$\dot{T}_4 = d_8\left(F_T^4 - \tau\right) \tag{11.A8}$$

$$\dot{w}_2 = d_9(L_1 + L_2 + L_3 + L_4 - L) \tag{11.A9}$$

$$\dot{w}_3 = d_{10}(L_3 - f(K_3)) \tag{11.A10}$$

$$\dot{w}_4 = d_{11}(L_1\overline{w_1} + L_2w_2 + L_3w_3 - (L - L_4)w_4) \tag{11.A11}$$

$$\dot{r} = d_{12}(K_1 + K_3 - K) \tag{11.A12}$$

$$\dot{\tau} = d_{13}(T_3 + T_4 - T) \tag{11.A13}$$

The total differential of (11.A1), (11.A2), (11.A3), (11.A4), (11.A5), (11.A6), (11.A7), (11.A8), (11.A9), (11.A10), (11.A11), (11.A12), and (11.A13) can be written as the following Jacobian matrix:

$$|J| = \begin{bmatrix} d_1p_1F_{LL}^1 & 0 & 0 & 0 & d_1p_1F_{LK}^1 & 0 & 0 & 0 & 0 & 0 & 0 & 0 & 0 \\ 0 & d_2p_2F_{LL}^2 & 0 & 0 & 0 & 0 & 0 & 0 & -d_2 & 0 & 0 & 0 & 0 \\ 0 & 0 & d_3p_3gF_{LL}^3 & 0 & 0 & d_3p_3g'F_L^3 & d_3p_3gF_{LT}^3 & 0 & 0 & -d_3 & 0 & 0 & 0 \\ 0 & 0 & 0 & d_4F_{LL}^4 & 0 & 0 & 0 & d_4F_{LT}^4 & 0 & 0 & -d_4 & 0 & 0 \\ d_5p_1F_{KL}^1 & 0 & 0 & 0 & d_5p_1F_{KK}^1 & 0 & 0 & 0 & 0 & 0 & 0 & -d_5 & 0 \\ 0 & 0 & d_6p_3g'F_L^3 & 0 & 0 & d_6p_3g''F^3 & d_6p_3g'F_T^3 & 0 & 0 & 0 & 0 & -d_6 & 0 \\ 0 & 0 & d_7p_3gF_{TL}^3 & 0 & 0 & d_7p_3g'F_T^3 & d_7p_3gF_{TT}^3 & 0 & 0 & 0 & 0 & 0 & -d_7 \\ 0 & 0 & 0 & d_8F_{TL}^4 & 0 & 0 & 0 & d_8F_{TT}^4 & 0 & 0 & 0 & 0 & -d_8 \\ d_9 & d_9 & d_9 & d_9 & 0 & 0 & 0 & 0 & 0 & 0 & 0 & 0 & 0 \\ 0 & 0 & d_{10} & 0 & 0 & -d_{10}f' & 0 & 0 & 0 & 0 & 0 & 0 & 0 \\ d_{11}\overline{w_1} & d_{11}w_2 & d_{11}w_3 & d_{11}w_4 & 0 & 0 & 0 & 0 & d_{11}L_2 & d_{11}L_3 & -d_{11}(L-L_4) & 0 & 0 \\ 0 & 0 & 0 & 0 & d_{12} & d_{12} & 0 & 0 & 0 & 0 & 0 & 0 & 0 \\ 0 & 0 & 0 & 0 & 0 & 0 & d_{13} & d_{13} & 0 & 0 & 0 & 0 & 0 \end{bmatrix}$$
$$= -d_1d_2d_3d_4d_5d_6d_7d_8d_9d_{10}d_{11}d_{12}d_{13}p_1\Delta_1$$

Under the condition of a stable system, there must be $|J| < 0$, and thus $\Delta_1 > 0$.

Appendix B

If the government subsidizes loan interest, wage and land rent for the advanced agricultural sector with the rates of s_1, s_2, and s_3, respectively, Eq. (11.14) becomes:

$$p_2g'(K_2)F^2 = r(1 - s_1) \tag{11.14$'$}$$

Equation (11.11) becomes:

$$p_3gF_L^3 = w_3(1 - s_2) \tag{11.11$'$}$$

Equation (11.15) becomes:

$$p_3gF_T^3 = \tau(1 - s_3) \tag{11.15$'$}$$

Then, the total differential of (11.5), (11.6), (11.7), (11.8), (11.9), (11.10), (11.11′), (11.12), (11.13), (11.14′), (11.15′), (11.16), and (11.17′) can be organized as follows:

$$\begin{bmatrix} F^1_{LL} & 0 & 0 & -F^1_{LK} & 0 & 0 & 0 \\ 0 & 0 & 0 & p_3\left(g'F^3_L + gF^3_{LL}f'\right) & p_3gF^3_{LT} & -1 & 0 \\ 0 & 0 & F^4_{LL} & 0 & -F^4_{LT} & 0 & -1 \\ p_1F^1_{KL} & 0 & 0 & -\left[p_1F^1_{KK} + p_3\left(g''F^3 + g'F^3_Lf'\right)\right] & -p_3g'F^3_T & 0 & 0 \\ 0 & 0 & -F^4_{TL} & p_3\left(g'F^3_T + gF^3_{TL}f'\right) & p_3gF^3_{TT} + F^4_{TT} & 0 & 0 \\ 1 & 1 & 1 & f' & 0 & 0 & 0 \\ \overline{w_1} & w_2 + L_2p_2F^2_{LL} & w_4 & w_3f' & 0 & L_3 & -(L - L_4) \end{bmatrix}$$
$$\times \begin{bmatrix} dL_1 \\ dL_2 \\ dL_4 \\ dK_3 \\ dT_3 \\ dw_3 \\ dw_4 \end{bmatrix} = \begin{bmatrix} 0 \\ -w_3ds_2 \\ 0 \\ rds_1 \\ -\tau ds_3 \\ 0 \\ 0 \end{bmatrix} \tag{11.B1}$$

By dynamic adjustment, we get that the value of the coefficient matrix (11.B1) $\Delta_1 > 0$.

Let $a = F^1_{LL}$, $b = p_1F^1_{KL}$, $c = \overline{w_1}$, $d = w_2 + L_2p_2F^2_{LL}$, $e = F^4_{LL}$, $f = -F^4_{TL} = -F^4_{LT}$, $g = w_4$, $h = -F^1_{LK}$, $j = p_3\left(g'F^3_L + gF^3_{LL}f'\right)$, $k = -\left[p_1F^1_{KK} + p_3\left(g''F^3 + g'F^3_Lf'\right)\right]$, $m = p_3\left(g'F^3_T + gF^3_{TL}f'\right)$, $n = f'$, $p = w_3f'$, $q = p_3gF^3_{LT}$, $s = -p_3g'F^3_T$, $t = p_3gF^3_{TT} + F^4_{TT}$, $u = L_3$, $v = -(L - L_4)$.

Using the Cramer rule to solve (11.B1), we get:

$$dL_1/ds_1 = -F^1_{KL}r\left\{\left(p_3gF^3_{TT} + F^4_{TT}\right)\left[w_2 + L_2p_2F^2_{LL} - w_4\right] + p_3gF^3_{TT}F^4_{LL}(L - L_4) - F^4_{TL}p_3gL_3F^3_{LT}\right\}/\Delta_1 < 0$$

$$dL_2/ds_1(<,=,>)0$$

$$dL_4/ds_1(<,=,>)0$$

$$dK_3/ds_1 = -ar\left(dt - gt + fqu + f^2v - etv\right)/\Delta_1 > 0$$

$$dK_1/ds_1 = -dK_3/ds_1 < 0$$

$$dL_3/ds_1 = f'dK_3/ds_1 > 0$$

$$dT_3/ds_1(<,=,>)0$$

$$dw_3/ds_1(<,=,>)0$$

$$dw_4/ds_1(<,=,>)0$$

$$dr/ds_1 = p_1F^1_{KL}dL_1/ds_1 + p_1F^1_{KK}dK_1/ds_1 = 0$$

$$d\tau/ds_1 = F^4_{TL}dL_4/ds_1 + F^4_{TT}dT_4/ds_1(<,=,>)0$$

$$dL_1/ds_2 = w_3fhsu/\Delta_1 < 0$$

$$dL_2/ds_2 = w_3u(akt - bht - ams - fhs + afns)/\Delta_1(<,=,>)0$$
$$dL_4/ds_2 = w_3u(bht - akt + ams)/\Delta_1(<,=,>)0$$
$$dK_3/ds_2 = -w_3afsu/\Delta_1 > 0$$
$$dK_1/ds_2 = -dK_3/ds_2 < 0$$
$$dL_3/ds_2 = f'dK_3/ds_2 > 0$$
$$dT_3/ds_2 = w_3fu(ak - bh)/\Delta_1 > 0$$
$$dw_3/ds_2(<,=,>)0$$
$$dw_4/ds_2 = -w_3u\left(bf^2h - beht - af^2k + aekt - aems\right)/\Delta_1(<,=,>)0$$
$$dr/ds_2 = p_1F^1_{KL}dL_1/ds_2 + p_1F^1_{KK}dK_1/ds_2 = 0$$
$$d\tau/ds_2 = F^4_{TL}dL_4/ds_2 + F^4_{TT}dT_4/ds_2(<,=,>)0$$
$$dL_1/ds_3 = -\tau hs(g - d + ev)/\Delta_1 < 0$$
$$dL_2/ds_3(<,=,>)0$$
$$dL_4/ds_3(<,=,>)0$$
$$dK_3/ds_3 = as\tau(g - d + ev)/\Delta_1 > 0$$
$$dK_1/ds_3 = -dK_3/ds_3 < 0$$
$$dL_3/ds_3 = f'dK_3/ds_3 > 0$$
$$dT_3/ds_3 = \tau(bh - ak)(g - d + ev)/\Delta_1 > 0$$
$$dw_3/ds_3 = \tau(bhq - akq + ajs)(g - d + ev)/\Delta_1(<,=,>)0$$
$$dw_4/ds_3(<,=,>)0$$
$$dr/ds_3 = p_1F^1_{KL}dL_1/ds_3 + p_1F^1_{KK}dK_1/ds_3 = 0$$
$$d\tau/ds_3 = F^4_{TL}dL_4/ds_3 + F^4_{TT}dT_4/ds_3(<,=,>)0$$

Appendix C

When the labor endowment increases, the total differential of (11.5), (11.6), (11.7), (11.8), (11.9), (11.10), (11.11), (11.12), (11.13), (11.14), (11.15), (11.16), and (11.17′) can be written as the following (11.21):

$$\begin{bmatrix} F_{LL}^1 & 0 & 0 & -F_{LK}^1 & 0 & 0 & 0 \\ 0 & 0 & 0 & p_3\left(g'F_L^3 + gF_{LL}^3 f'\right) & p_3 g F_{LT}^3 & -1 & 0 \\ 0 & 0 & F_{LL}^4 & 0 & -F_{LT}^4 & 0 & -1 \\ p_1 F_{KL}^1 & 0 & 0 & -\left[p_1 F_{KK}^1 + p_3\left(g'' F^3 + g' F_L^3 f'\right)\right] & -p_3 g' F_T^3 & 0 & 0 \\ 0 & 0 & -F_{TL}^4 & p_3\left(g'F_T^3 + gF_{TL}^3 f'\right) & p_3 g F_{TT}^3 + F_{TT}^4 & 0 & 0 \\ 1 & 1 & 1 & f' & 0 & 0 & 0 \\ \overline{w_1} & w_2 + L_2 p_2 F_{LL}^2 & w_4 & w_3 f' & 0 & L_3 & -(L - L_4) \end{bmatrix} \times \begin{bmatrix} dL_1 \\ dL_2 \\ dL_4 \\ dK_3 \\ dT_3 \\ dw_3 \\ dw_4 \end{bmatrix} = \begin{bmatrix} 0 \\ 0 \\ 0 \\ 0 \\ 0 \\ dL \\ w_4 dL \end{bmatrix} \tag{11.C1}$$

Apparently, the value of the coefficient matrix (11.C1) is Δ_1.

When the capital endowment increases, the total differential of (11.5), (11.6), (11.7), (11.8), (11.9), (11.10), (11.11), (11.12), (11.13), (11.14), (11.15), (11.16), and (11.17′) is (11.22) as follows:

$$\begin{bmatrix} F_{LL}^1 & 0 & 0 & -F_{LK}^1 & 0 & 0 & 0 & 0 \\ 0 & 0 & 0 & 0 & p_3\left(g'F_L^3 + gF_{LL}^3 f'\right) & p_3 g F_{LT}^3 & -1 & 0 \\ 0 & 0 & F_{LL}^4 & 0 & 0 & -F_{LT}^4 & 0 & -1 \\ p_1 F_{KL}^1 & 0 & 0 & p_1 F_{KK}^1 & -p_3\left(g'' F^3 + g' F_L^3 f'\right) & -p_3 g' F_T^3 & 0 & 0 \\ 0 & 0 & -F_{TL}^4 & 0 & p_3\left(g'F_T^3 + gF_{TL}^3 f'\right) & p_3 g F_{TT}^3 + F_{TT}^4 & 0 & 0 \\ 1 & 1 & 1 & 0 & f' & 0 & 0 & 0 \\ 0 & 0 & 0 & 1 & 1 & 0 & 0 & 0 \\ \overline{w_1} & w_2 + L_2 p_2 F_{LL}^2 & w_4 & 0 & w_3 f' & 0 & L_3 & -(L - L_4) \end{bmatrix} \times \begin{bmatrix} dL_1 \\ dL_2 \\ dL_4 \\ dK_1 \\ dK_3 \\ dT_3 \\ dw_3 \\ dw_4 \end{bmatrix} = \begin{bmatrix} 0 \\ 0 \\ 0 \\ 0 \\ 0 \\ 0 \\ dK \\ 0 \end{bmatrix} \tag{11.C2}$$

Assume that the value of the matrix (11.C2) is Δ_2, then $\Delta_2 = -\Delta_1$. Using the Cramer rule to solve (11.C1) and (11.C2), we get:

$$dL_1/dL = fhs(d - g)/\Delta_1 > 0$$

$$dL_2/dL(<, =, >)0$$

$$dL_4/dL = -(d - g)(akt - bht - ams)/\Delta_1(<, =, >)0$$

$$dK_3/dL = -afs(d - g)/\Delta_1 < 0$$

$$dK_1/dL = -dK_3/dL > 0$$
$$dL_3/dL = f' dK_3/dL < 0$$
$$dT_3/dL = -f(bh - ak)(d - g)/\Delta_1 < 0$$
$$dw_3/dL = -f(bhq - akq + ajs)(d - g)/\Delta_1(<, =, >)0$$
$$dw_4/dL = -f(d - g) \left(bf^2h - beht - af^2k + aekt - aems\right)/\Delta_1(<, =, >)0$$
$$dr/dL = p_1 F^1_{KL} dL_1/dL + p_1 F^1_{KK} dK_1/dL = 0$$
$$d\tau/dL = F^4_{TL} dL_4/dL + F^4_{TT} dT_4/dL(<, =, >)0$$
$$dL_1/dK(<, =, >)0$$
$$dL_2/dK(<, =, >)0$$
$$dL_4/dK = -ht(d - c)(z - s)/\Delta_2 < 0$$
$$dK_1/dK(<, =, >)0$$
$$dK_3/dK = (cfhs - dfhs)/\Delta_2 > 0$$
$$dL_3/dK = f' dK_3/dK > 0$$
$$dT_3/dK = (dfhz - cfhz)/\Delta_2 > 0$$
$$dw_3/dK = cfh(js - zq)/\Delta_2 > 0$$
$$dw_4/dK(<, =, >)0$$
$$dr/dK = p_1 F^1_{KL} dL_1/dK + p_1 F^1_{KK} dK_1/dK = 0$$
$$d\tau/dK = F^4_{TL} dL_4/dK + F^4_{TT} dT_4/dK(<, =, >)0$$

In the above, the letters a, b, c, d, e, f, g, h, j, k, m, n, p, q, s, t, u, and v have the same meaning as in Appendix B. Besides, $y = p_1 F^1_{KK}$, $z = -p_3\left(g'' F^3 + g' F^3_L f'\right)$.

References

Beladi, H., Chakrabarti, A., & Marjit, S. (2010). Skilled-unskilled wage inequality and urban unemployment. *Economic Inquiry*, 48(4), 997–1007.

Beladi, H., Chakrabarti, A., & Marjit, S. (2010). Skilled-unskilled wage inequality and urban unemployment. *Economic Inquiry, 48*(4), 997–1007.

Brecher, R. A., & Alejandro, C. F. (1977). Tariffs, foreign capital and immiserating growth. *Journal of International Economics, 7*(4), 317–322.

Chandra, V., & Khan, M. (1993). Foreign investment in the presence of an informal sector. *Economica, 60*(237), 79–103.

Chao, C.-C., & Yu, E. S. H. (1992). Capital markets, urban unemployment and land. *Journal of Development Economics, 38*, 407–413.

Chaudhuri, S. (2006). Labor market reform, welfare and unemployment in a small open economy. *Keio Economics Studies, 43*(2), 1–17.

Chaudhuri, S. (2007). Foreign capital, welfare and urban unemployment in the presence of agricultural dualism. *Japan and the World Economy, 19*, 149–165.
Corden, W. M., & Findlay, R. (1975). Urban unemployment, intersectional capital mobility and development policy. *Economica, 42*(142), 59–78.
Din, M. (1996). International capital mobility and development policy in a dual economy. *Review of International Economics, 6*, 185–201.
Gupta, M. (1993). Rural-urban migration, informal sector and development policies: A theoretical analysis. *Journal of Development Economics, 41*, 137–151.
Gupta, M. (1997a). Informal sector and informal capital market in a small open less-developed economy. *Journal of Development Economics, 52*(2), 409–428.
Gupta, M. (1997b). Foreign capital and the informal sector: Comments on Chandra and Khan. *Economica, 64*(254), 353–363.
Grinols, E. L. (1991). Unemployment and foreign capital: The relative opportunity costs of domestic labor and welfare. *Economica, 58*(229), 107–121.
Harris, J., & Todaro, M. (1970). Migration, unemployment and development: A two-sector analysis. *American Economic Review, 60*, 126–142.
Khan, M. A., & Naqvi, S. N. H. (1983). Capital markets and urban unemployment. *Journal of International Economics, 15*, 367–385.
Li, X. C., & Shen, Q. (2012). A study on the urban private capital in the modern agriculture sector and the transfer of labor. *Journal of Economic Policy Reform, 15*(2), 135–152.
McCool, T. (1982). Wage subsidies and distortionary taxes in a mobile capital Harris-Todaro model. *Economica, 49*(193), 69–79.
Yabuuchi, S. (1998). Urban unemployment, factor accumulation, and welfare. *Review of Development Economics, 2*(1), 31–40.
Yabuuchi, S., & Belaid, H. (2001). Urban unemployment, informal sector and development policies. *Journal of Economics, 74*(3), 301–314.
Zheng, J. C., Liu, H. Z., Zhou, J. T., Zhen, R. H., & Li, N. (2009). Study on the goals and models of advanced agricultural development in Jiangsu Province. *Jiangsu Agricultural Academic Journal, 25*(1), 1–5.

Chapter 12
Unemployment, Wage Inequality, and International Factor Movement in the Presence of Agricultural Dualism

Xiaochun Li and Yuanting Xu

Abstract This chapter investigates how the international factor movements affect the unemployment and skilled–unskilled wage inequality with the existence of a modern agricultural sector. Our research has the new feature that we not only consider that the rural labor migrates to the urban sector but also to the modern agricultural sector. The main conclusions are that the unskilled labor outflow certainly decreases the wage inequality and unemployment rate and the influences that skilled labor movement and capital inflow have on wage inequality and unemployment rate are dependent on the factor intensity between the urban and modern agricultural sectors.

Keywords Wage inequality • Unemployment • International factor movement • Agricultural dualism

1 Introduction

It is common for most developing countries to develop domestic economies with the aid of foreign capital and technology. As such, it is particularly important to investigate how the international economy affects domestic employment and wage inequality for developing countries. Academics have already completed some research on this topic: Feenstra and Hanson (1996), Marjit et al. (2004), Marjit and Kar (2005), Chaudhuri and Yabuuchi (2007), Yabuuchi and Chaudhuri (2007), etc. The researchers above analyzed the influence of trade liberalization and international factor movement on the wage inequality in developing countries. Yabuuchi (2007), Beladi et al. (2008, 2010), and Chaudhuri and Banerjee (2010) not only considered

X. Li (✉)
Business School, Nanjing University, Nanjing, China
e-mail: xiaochun@nju.edu.cn

Y. Xu
School of Economics, Nanjing University, 22 Hankou Road, Nanjing, Jiangsu 210093, China

X. Li (ed.), *Labor Transfer in Emerging Economies*, New Frontiers in Regional Science: Asian Perspectives 12, DOI 10.1007/978-981-10-3569-2_12

the influence on wage inequality, but they also investigated the impact of trade liberalization and international factor movement on unemployment of unskilled labor in developing countries in addition to the impact on wage inequality.

Among them, Beladi et al. (2008) assumed that in the agricultural sector, capital corresponding to unit skilled labor is higher than that in the urban sector. Under this premise, this research had several conclusions: the impacts that skilled labor outflow had on wage inequality and unemployment are dependent on the intensity difference of skilled labor and capital between urban and agricultural sectors, the impacts that foreign capital inflow had on wage inequality and unemployment are also dependent on it, and unskilled labor outflow would increase the wage inequality and unemployment rate under certain conditions. Such a premise may not be applicable for other developing countries. For example, in rural areas of China, generally, family is the unit of production and management, which rarely uses capital. Traditional means of agricultural production also do not require higher technology. Therefore, their conclusions cannot be applied directly to developing countries like China.

In addition, modern agriculture has improved rapidly in some developing countries such as China and India. In fact, there is no consistent definition of "modern agriculture" in academia. Li and Shen (2012) held that modern agriculture is defined as newly developing agriculture that emphasizes market demand and adopts modern facilities and technologies to achieve higher yields than traditional agriculture. Because of the rise of modern agriculture, labor migration has been endowed with new meaning. This is not only because the modern agricultural sector uses skilled labor but also because rural unskilled labor would migrate only to the urban sector before the development of the modern agricultural sector. However, another option for labor transfer emerged after the modern agricultural sector appeared. It is worth noting how such a transfer affects employment and wage inequality. Actually, Chaudhuri (2008), in a working paper, considered wage inequality in developing countries in the presence of agricultural dualism. However, it weakened the meaning of modern agriculture by not including skilled labor and capital in the modern agricultural sector.

In order to investigate the influences that international factor movement has on employment and wage inequality with the existence of modern agriculture, this chapter constructs a three-sector model. This chapter includes the understanding that unskilled labor in traditional rural areas migrates to both urban and modern agricultural sectors, and we also include skilled labor and capital as production factors in the modern agricultural sector.

2 The Model

We consider a small open developing economy with three sectors that are the urban formal sector, modern agricultural sector, and traditional agricultural sector. The economy uses four production factors, which are skilled labor LS, unskilled labor LU, capital K, and land T. Urban sector X1 uses skilled labor, unskilled labor, and capital to produce the import-competing goods. Modern agricultural sector X2 uses skilled labor, unskilled labor, capital, and land to produce the exportable goods. Traditional agricultural sector X3 uses unskilled labor and land to produce the exportable goods. Hence, the production functions of the urban, modern agricultural, and traditional agricultural sectors are given by

$$X_1 = F^1(L_{S1}, L_{U1}, K_1) \tag{12.1}$$

$$X_2 = F^2(L_{S2}, L_{U2}, K_2, T_2) \tag{12.2}$$

$$X_3 = F^3(L_{U3}, T_3) \tag{12.3}$$

$F^j(j = 1, 2, 3)$ are production functions increasing corresponding to each factor and satisfying linear homogenous and strictly quasi-concave properties.

Under the condition that the markets are perfectly competitive, we could obtain that

$$a_{S1}w_S + a_{U1}\bar{w}_U + a_{K1}r = p_1 \tag{12.4}$$

$$a_{S2}w_S + a_{U2}\bar{w}_U + a_{K2}r + a_{T2}\tau = p_2 \tag{12.5}$$

$$a_{U3}w + a_{T3}\tau = p_3 \tag{12.6}$$

where a_{ij} represents that the factor i used in producing a unit product in the jth sector, w_S is the wage rate of skilled labor in urban and modern agricultural sectors, $\bar{w}_U$ is the downward rigid wage rate of unskilled labor in the urban and modern agricultural sectors, w is the wage rate of unskilled labor used in the traditional agricultural sector, r is the interest rate of capital in urban and modern agricultural sectors, s is the rent of land used in two agricultural sectors, and p_j $(j = 1,2,3,)$ represents the product prices of urban sector, modern agricultural sector, and traditional agricultural sector, respectively. The product price of the modern agricultural sector is different from that of traditional agricultural sector owing to capital and technology used to produce high value-added agricultural products in the modern agricultural sector. Therefore, the modern agricultural sector has a higher efficiency in land utilization than the traditional sector, and it reduces costs through economies of scale. Generally, the product price of the modern agricultural sector is higher than that of traditional agricultural sector. In this chapter, we assume that all the products are tradable, and hence the product prices are given internationally.

Generally, developing countries lack skilled labor. Therefore, we assume that skilled labor is fully employed, there is no unemployment, and labor moves freely between the urban and modern agricultural sectors. This chapter assumes that the wage rates of unskilled labor in the urban and modern agricultural sectors are given exogenously, which means downward rigid. One needs to note that some existing research, such as Gupta (1997a, b), sets the wage rate for the modern agricultural sector to be flexible following the former set of the wage rate for the agricultural sector. In many developing countries, such as China, modern agriculture first appeared in city surrounds, which are convenient and closer to roads and railways. These areas are easily affected by cities and also their policies. Therefore, the wages of unskilled labor in those areas must be the same as in the urban sector. If not, the unskilled labor will leave this sector and directly immigrate to the urban areas to find jobs [for a detailed explanation, see Du and Jin (2012)]. Hence, we set the wage rate of the unskilled labor in the modern agricultural sector to be downward rigid as in the urban sector. However, in the traditional agricultural sector, the wage rate of unskilled labor is flexible. We use LUU to denote the number of unemployed unskilled labor in the urban and modern agricultural sectors and use k to denote the unemployment rate of unskilled labor in these two sectors; hence $\lambda = L_{UU}/(L_{U1} + L_{U2}) = L_{UU}/(a_{U1}X_1 + a_{U2}X_2)$. Therefore, in the unskilled labor market equilibrium, the wage rate in the traditional agricultural sector equals the expected wage income in the urban and modern agricultural sectors, which is equal to the downward rigid wage rate $\bar{w}_U$multiplied by the probability of finding a job in these two sectors $(L_{U1} + L_{U2})/(L_{U1} + L_{U2} + L_{UU})$. Thus, the unskilled labor allocation mechanism is shown as

$$w = \frac{L_{U1} + L_{U2}}{L_{U1} + L_{U2} + L_{UU}} \bar{w}_U \tag{12.7a}$$

$$(1 + \lambda)w = \bar{w}_U \tag{12.7b}$$

The market-clearing conditions of the four factors, unskilled labor, skilled labor, capital, and land, could be shown as follows:

$$a_{U1}X_1 + a_{U2}X_2 + a_{U3}X_3 + \lambda a_{U1}X_1 + \lambda a_{U2}X_2 = L_U \tag{12.8}$$

$$a_{S1}X_1 + a_{S2}X_2 = L_S \tag{12.9}$$

$$a_{K1}X_1 + a_{K2}X_2 = K \tag{12.10}$$

$$a_{T2}X_2 + a_{T3}X_3 = T \tag{12.11}$$

where L_U, L_S, K, and T represent the endowments of unskilled labor, skilled labor, capital, and land, respectively.

The basic theoretical model has been built, which consists of the eight equations (12.4), (12.5), and (12.6), (12.7b) and (12.8), (12.9), (12.10), and (12.11). Eight endogenous variables are determined, and they are w_S, w, r, s, k, X_1, X_2, and X_3.

Unskilled labor is divided into three sectors, noting that the wage rate of the unemployed labor is zero. Therefore, the average wage rate of unskilled labor yields

$$w_A = \lambda_{U1}\bar{w}_U + \lambda_{U2}\bar{w}_U + \lambda_{U3}w \tag{12.12a}$$

where k_{ij} is the allocative share of factor i in the jth sector (e.g., $\lambda_{S1} = a_{S1}X_1/L_S$). According to Eqs. (12.7b), (12.8), and (12.12a), Eq. (12.12a) could be rewritten as

$$w_A = w \tag{12.12b}$$

That is, the average wage rate of unskilled labor is equal to that in the traditional agricultural sector. Therefore, when $\widehat{w}_S - \widehat{w} > (<)0$, the inequality between skilled labor and unskilled labor increases (decreases).

Factor intensities between these sectors play an important role in the following discussion. Therefore, in this chapter, we make the following assumptions:

Assumption 12.1

$$K_1/L_{S1} < K_2/L_{S2} \Leftrightarrow \wedge_{KS} = \lambda_{K1}\lambda_{S2} - \lambda_{S1}\lambda_{K2} < 0 \Leftrightarrow \Theta_{KS} = \theta_{K1}\theta_{S2} - \theta_{S1}\theta_{K2} < 0$$

where θ_{ij} is the distributive share of factor i in the jth sector (e.g., $\theta_{S1} = w_S a_{S2}/p_1$), Λ_{KS} is the comparison of the amount of capital corresponding to unit skilled labor between the urban and modern agricultural sectors, and Θ_{KS} is the comparison of skilled labor cost and capital cost in production price between the urban and modern agricultural sectors.

Assumption 12.1 means that the amount of capital corresponding to unit skilled labor in the modern agricultural sector is higher than that in the urban sector, either in a physical sense or in a value sense. This is similar to the assumption in Beladi et al. (2008) that the amount of capital corresponding to unit skilled labor in the agricultural sector is higher than that in the urban sector. The difference is that the comparison in this chapter is between the urban and modern agricultural sectors. This assumption is common in the early developing stage of the modern agriculture. Although urban and modern agricultural sectors both use skilled labor and capital, the modern agricultural sector employs less skilled labor comparatively in the early developing stage. Therefore, in this stage, the amount of capital corresponding to unit skilled labor is more than that in the urban sector.

Assumption 12.2

$$T_2/L_{U2} > T_3/L_{U3} \Leftrightarrow \wedge_{TU} = \lambda_{T2}\lambda_{U3} - \lambda_{U2}\lambda_{T3} > 0$$

where Λ_{TU} is the comparison of the amount of land corresponding to unit unskilled labor between modern and traditional agricultural sectors.

Assumption 12.2 means that the amount of land corresponding to unit unskilled labor in the modern agricultural sector is higher than that in traditional agricultural sector, which is the same as the assumption in Chaudhuri (2008). This is because the amount of unskilled labor in the traditional agricultural sector is higher. In addition, the technology that the modern agricultural sector applied is more advanced; hence, the unskilled labor that unit land needed to produce is less.

The two assumptions above have similar or common points with the related assumptions in the existing research, which considers the wage inequality of skilled and unskilled labor. However, the two assumptions are set for the economy concluding modern agricultural sector, which is different from the assumptions in the existing research. Under these assumptions, we investigate how the international movements of three factors affect the wage inequality and unemployment rate in the developing countries.

3 Unemployment, Wage Inequality, and International Factor Movement

3.1 International Unskilled Labor Movement

We consider the impacts that the international unskilled labor movement has on the wage inequality and unemployment in the developing countries, considering both the unskilled labor outflow and the unskilled labor inflow. Although the former situation is common in developing countries, the latter one is also reasonable and exists in the real economy.

Differentiating Eqs. (12.4), (12.5), and (12.6), (12.7b), and (12.8), (12.9), (12.10), and (12.11) and solving the simultaneous equations, we could obtain the following:

$$\widehat{w}_S/\widehat{L}_U = \Lambda_{KS}\lambda_{T3}\theta_{T2}\theta_{U3}w\lambda/\Delta > 0 \tag{12.13}$$

$$\widehat{w}/\widehat{L}_U = \Lambda_{KS}\lambda_{T3}\Theta_{KS}\theta_{T3}w\lambda/\Delta < 0 \tag{12.14}$$

$$(\widehat{w}_S - \widehat{w})/\widehat{L}_U = \Lambda_{KS}\lambda_{T3}(\theta_{K1}\theta_{T2}\theta_{U3} - \Theta_{KS}\theta_{T3})w\lambda/\Delta > 0 \tag{12.15}$$

$$\widehat{\lambda}/\widehat{L}_U = -\frac{1+\lambda}{\lambda}\widehat{w}/\widehat{L}_U = \Lambda_{KS}\lambda_{T3}\Theta_{KS}\theta_{T3}w(1+\lambda)/\Delta > 0 \tag{12.16}$$

where Δ is the determinant of the coefficient matrix of the simultaneous equations. Using the dynamic adjustment process for the supply side in the present model, we obtain that $\Delta < 0$under the assumption that the equilibrium in this chapter is stable.

The four equations above are correct under Assumption 12.1. We therefore obtain the following proposition:

Proposition 12.1 Under Assumption 12.1, the unskilled labor inflow increases the skilled–unskilled wage inequality and unemployment rate of unskilled labor; conversely, the unskilled labor outflow decreases the wage inequality and unemployment rate.

With the unchanged product prices in all sectors, we have chosen to analyze the outflow of unskilled labor from developing countries. Developing countries have a large population of unskilled labor, much of which is unemployed. The outflow of unskilled labor decreases the labor supply, causing the wage rate of unskilled labor to increase and the unemployment rate to decrease. In the traditional agricultural sector, the increasing wage rate of unskilled labor decreases the rent of land with an unchanged product price in this sector. Land moves perfectly between the two agricultural sectors; therefore, the cost of renting land in the modern agricultural sector declines. The product price and the wage rate of unskilled labor are exogenously given. Hence, the decreasing cost of renting land increases the cost of employing skilled labor and capital. It is important to understand that the wage rate of skilled labor and interest rate of capital vary inversely in the urban and modern agricultural sectors and that the product price and the wage rate of unskilled labor are exogenously given in the urban sector. Therefore, the cost of employing skilled labor and capital (in the unit product price) remains unchanged. According to Assumption 12.1, the wage rate of skilled labor must decrease, and the interest rate of capital must increase in order to satisfy the cost of the two factors in the modern agricultural sector increases and that in urban sector remains unchanged. Hence, the wage rate of unskilled labor increases, the wage rate of skilled labor decreases, and the skilled–unskilled wage inequality decreases.

Conversely, we can analyze the situation in which unskilled labor flows into developing countries. Under the model and the assumptions in this chapter, the outflow of unskilled labor not only decreases the unemployment rate of unskilled labor, but also narrows the wage inequality. The results are different from the results in Yabuuchi (2007) and Beladi et al. (2008). In their research, the outflow of unskilled labor increases the wage inequality and unemployment rate under certain conditions.

3.2 International Skilled Labor Movement

We consider the international skilled labor movement. Solving the earlier simultaneous equations, we can obtain:

$$\text{if } \Lambda_{KU}\begin{cases} > (\Lambda_{TU}\lambda_{K1} + \lambda_{U1}\lambda_{K2}\lambda_{T3})/\lambda_{T3}\lambda \\ = (\Lambda_{TU}\lambda_{K1} + \lambda_{U1}\lambda_{K2}\lambda_{T3})/\lambda_{T3}\lambda\text{; we can obtain:} \\ < (\Lambda_{TU}\lambda_{K1} + \lambda_{U1}\lambda_{K2}\lambda_{T3})/\lambda_{T3}\lambda \end{cases}$$

$$\frac{\widehat{w}_S}{\widehat{L}_S} = \frac{(\Lambda_{TU}\lambda_{K1} - \Lambda_{KU}\lambda_{T3}\lambda + \lambda_{U1}\lambda_{K2}\lambda_{T3})\theta_{K1}\theta_{T2}\theta_{U3}w\lambda}{\Delta}\begin{cases} > 0 \\ = 0 \\ < 0 \end{cases} \tag{12.17}$$

$$\frac{\widehat{w}}{\widehat{L}_S} = \frac{(\Lambda_{TU}\lambda_{K1} - \Lambda_{KU}\lambda_{T3}\lambda + \lambda_{U1}\lambda_{K2}\lambda_{T3})\Theta_{KS}\theta_{T3}w\lambda}{\Delta}\begin{cases} < 0 \\ = 0 \\ > 0 \end{cases} \tag{12.18}$$

$$\frac{\widehat{w}_S - \widehat{w}}{\widehat{L}_S} = \frac{(\Lambda_{TU}\lambda_{K1} - \Lambda_{KU}\lambda_{T3}\lambda + \lambda_{U1}\lambda_{K2}\lambda_{T3})(\theta_{K1}\theta_{T2}\theta_{U3} - \Theta_{KS}\theta_{T3})w\lambda}{\Delta}\begin{cases} > 0 \\ = 0 \\ < 0 \end{cases} \tag{12.19}$$

$$\frac{\widehat{\lambda}}{\widehat{L}_S} = \frac{-(\Lambda_{TU}\lambda_{K1} - \Lambda_{KU}\lambda_{T3}\lambda + \lambda_{U1}\lambda_{K2}\lambda_{T3})\Theta_{KS}\theta_{T3}w(1+\lambda)}{\Delta}\begin{cases} > 0 \\ = 0 \\ < 0 \end{cases} \tag{12.20}$$

where $\Lambda_{KU} = \lambda_{K1}\lambda_{U2} - \lambda_{U1}\lambda_{K2}$ is the comparison of the amount of capital corresponding to unit unskilled labor between the urban and modern agricultural sectors.

The four equations above are correct under Assumptions 12.1 and 12.2. We can obtain the following proposition:

Proposition 12.2 Under Assumptions 12.1 and 12.2, when $\Lambda_{KU} < \frac{\Lambda_{TU}\lambda_{K1}+\lambda_{U1}\lambda_{K2}\lambda_{T3}}{\lambda_{T3}\lambda}$, the skilled labor inflow decreases the skilled–unskilled wage inequality and unemployment rate of unskilled labor; conversely, the skilled labor outflow increases the wage inequality and unemployment rate. When $\Lambda_{KU} > \frac{\Lambda_{TU}\lambda_{K1}+\lambda_{U1}\lambda_{K2}\lambda_{T3}}{\lambda_{T3}\lambda}$, the skilled labor inflow increases the wage inequality and unemployment rate; conversely, the skilled labor outflow decreases the wage inequality and unemployment rate.

Skilled labor in developing countries will sometimes leave because of lower wages. In reality, there are also some situations in which skilled labor moves into developing countries. With the fluctuation of the word economic situation, some developed countries have had a high unemployment rate, resulting in unemployed and retired skilled labor moving into the developing countries to find job opportunities. Therefore, in this chapter we not only consider skilled labor outflow but also skilled labor inflow.

With the unchanged product price in all sectors, we have chosen to analyze the inflow of skilled labor into developing countries. We consider the different situations that compare the amount of capital corresponding to unit unskilled labor between the urban and modern agricultural sectors. If $\Lambda_{KU} < \frac{\Lambda_{TU}\lambda_{K1}+\lambda_{U1}\lambda_{K2}\lambda_{T3}}{\lambda_{T3}\lambda}$, the skilled labor inflow increases the skilled labor supply, causing the wage rate of skilled labor to decrease. The product price and the wage rate of unskilled labor in the urban sector are exogenously given. Hence, the cost of employing skilled labor and capital (in the unit product price) of this sector remains unchanged and the interest rate of capital rises. Skilled labor and capital move freely between urban and modern agricultural sectors; therefore, according to Assumption 12.1, the cost of employing skilled labor and capital (in the unit product price) of this sector increases. With the downward rigid wage rate of unskilled labor in the modern agricultural sector, the rent of land in this sector declines. Land moves freely between the two agricultural sectors; therefore, the decreasing rent of land increases the wage rate in the traditional agricultural sector. The endowment of the unskilled sector remains unchanged in the economy. The increasing average wage rate of unskilled labor demonstrates that the total demand for unskilled labor increases and the unemployment rate decreases. Hence, under this situation, the skilled labor inflow decreases the skilled–unskilled wage inequality and the unemployment rate of unskilled labor. Conversely, if $\Lambda_{KU} > \frac{\Lambda_{TU}\lambda_{K1}+\lambda_{U1}\lambda_{K2}\lambda_{T3}}{\lambda_{T3}\lambda}$, this means that the difference of the amount of capital corresponding to unit skilled labor between the urban and modern agricultural sectors is large enough. With Assumption 12.1, we can conclude that the amount of skilled labor corresponding to unit unskilled labor in the urban sector far outweighs that in the modern agricultural sector. Compared with the modern agricultural sector, the urban sector production relies more on skilled labor. When skilled labor flows into the developing countries, the urban sector attracts the skilled labor by increasing its wage rate. Therefore, the domestic wage rate of skilled labor increases. Using the same method, we can conclude that the wage rate of unskilled labor decreases, which means that the domestic wage inequality and unemployment rate increases.

We can also analyze the situation that the skilled labor outflows from developing countries. Under the model and assumptions in this chapter, the influence that the inflow or outflow of skilled labor has on the wage inequality and unemployment rate depends on the intensities of unskilled labor and capital between the urban and modern agricultural sectors. This conclusion is different from the conclusions in Yabuuchi (2007) and Beladi et al. (2008). In their research, the impacts that skilled labor has on the wage inequality and unemployment rate depend on the intensities of skilled labor and capital between urban and agricultural sectors. Hence, the developing countries should pay attention to the intensities of unskilled labor and capital between the urban and modern agricultural sectors when confronting the policies for attracting skilled labor. Otherwise, these polices would increase the wage inequality and the unemployment rate.

3.3 International Capital Inflow

Generally, the developing countries lack capital. Hence, the governments adopt the capital-attracting policies to facilitate economic growth. Therefore, we mainly consider the international capital inflow. Solving the simultaneous equations:

$$\text{if } \Lambda_{SU}\begin{cases} > (\Lambda_{TU}\lambda_{S1}+\lambda_{U1}\lambda_{S2}\lambda_{T3})/\lambda_{T3}\lambda \\ = (\Lambda_{TU}\lambda_{S1}+\lambda_{U1}\lambda_{S2}\lambda_{T3})/\lambda_{T3}\lambda \\ < (\Lambda_{TU}\lambda_{S1}+\lambda_{U1}\lambda_{S2}\lambda_{T3})/\lambda_{T3}\lambda \end{cases}, \text{ we can obtain:}$$

$$\frac{\widehat{w}_S}{\widehat{L}_S} = \frac{(-\Lambda_{TU}\lambda_{S1} + \Lambda_{SU}\lambda_{T3}\lambda - \lambda_{U1}\lambda_{S2}\lambda_{T3})\theta_{K1}\theta_{T2}\theta_{U3}w\lambda}{\Delta}\begin{cases} <0 \\ =0 \\ >0 \end{cases} \tag{12.21}$$

$$\frac{\widehat{w}}{\widehat{L}_S} = \frac{(-\Lambda_{TU}\lambda_{S1} + \Lambda_{SU}\lambda_{T3}\lambda - \lambda_{U1}\lambda_{S2}\lambda_{T3})\Theta_{KS}\theta_{T3}w\lambda}{\Delta}\begin{cases} >0 \\ =0 \\ <0 \end{cases} \tag{12.22}$$

$$\frac{\widehat{w}_S - \widehat{w}}{\widehat{K}} = \frac{(-\Lambda_{TU}\lambda_{S1} + \Lambda_{SU}\lambda_{T3}\lambda - \lambda_{U1}\lambda_{S2}\lambda_{T3})(\theta_{K1}\theta_{T2}\theta_{U3} - \Theta_{KS}\theta_{TS})w\lambda}{\Delta}\begin{cases} <0 \\ =0 \\ >0 \end{cases} \tag{12.23}$$

$$\frac{\widehat{\lambda}}{\widehat{L}_S} = \frac{-(-\Lambda_{TU}\lambda_{S1} + \Lambda_{SU}\lambda_{T3}\lambda - \lambda_{U1}\lambda_{S2}\lambda_{T3})\Theta_{KS}\theta_{T3}w(1+\lambda)}{\Delta}\begin{cases} <0 \\ =0 \\ >0 \end{cases} \tag{12.24}$$

where $\Lambda_{SU} = \lambda_{S1}\lambda_{U2} - \lambda_{U1}\lambda_{S2}$ is the comparison of the amount of skilled labor corresponding to unit unskilled labor between the urban and modern agricultural sectors.

The four equations above are correct under Assumptions 12.1 and 12.2. We therefore obtain the following proposition:

Proposition 12.3 Under Assumptions 12.1 and 12.2, when

$$\Lambda_{SU} < \frac{\Lambda_{TU}\lambda_{S1} + \lambda_{U1}\lambda_{S2}\lambda_{T3}}{\lambda_{T3}\lambda},$$

the international capital inflow increases the skilled–unskilled wage inequality and unemployment rate of unskilled labor. Conversely, when $\Lambda_{SU} > \frac{\Lambda_{TU}\lambda_{S1}+\lambda_{U1}\lambda_{S2}\lambda_{T3}}{\lambda_{T3}\lambda}$, it decreases the wage inequality and unemployment rate.

With the unchanged product price in all sectors, we have chosen to analyze the inflow of capital into developing countries. We consider the different situations that compare the amount of skilled labor corresponding to unit unskilled labor between the urban and modern agricultural sectors. If $\Lambda_{SU} < \frac{\Lambda_{TU}\lambda_{S1}+\lambda_{U1}\lambda_{S2}\lambda_{T3}}{\lambda_{T3}\lambda}$, the capital inflow decreases the domestic interest rate of capital. The product price and the wage rate of unskilled labor in the urban sector are exogenously given. Hence, the domestic wage rate of skilled labor increases. Conversely, if $\Lambda_{SU} > \frac{\Lambda_{TU}\lambda_{S1}+\lambda_{U1}\lambda_{S2}\lambda_{T3}}{\lambda_{T3}\lambda}$, this means that the difference in the amount of skilled labor corresponding to unit unskilled labor between the urban and modern agricultural sector is large enough. With Assumption 12.1, although the amount of capital corresponding to unit skilled labor in the urban sector is less than that in the modern agricultural sector, the difference between them is relatively small. Hence, we can conclude that the amount of capital corresponding to unit unskilled labor in the urban sector far outweighs that in the modern agricultural sector. Compared with the modern agricultural sector, urban sector production relies more on capital. When capital flows into the developing countries, the urban sector attracts the capital by increasing its interest rate. Therefore, the domestic interest rate of capital increases. With the unchanged product price and wage rate of unskilled labor in the urban sector, the wage rate of skilled labor declines. Using the same method in Proposition 12.2, we can draw the conclusion.

To developing countries, it is common for the governments to adopt the capital-attracting policies for economic development. Under the model and assumptions in this chapter, the influences that the capital inflow has on the wage inequality and unemployment rate depend on the intensities of skilled labor and unskilled labor between the urban and modern agricultural sectors. This conclusion is different from the conclusions in Yabuuchi (2007) and Beladi et al. (2008). In their research, the impacts that capital inflow has on the wage inequality and unemployment rate depend on the intensities of skilled labor and capital between the urban and agricultural sectors. Therefore, developing countries should pay attention to the intensities of skilled labor and unskilled labor between the urban and modern agricultural sectors when confronting capital-attracting policies. Otherwise, these polices could increase the wage inequality and the unemployment rate.

4 Conclusions

Academia and government have always been concerned about the wage inequality and unemployment in developing countries. The governments of developing countries are actively formulating policies to deal with the wage inequality and unemployment. This chapter establishes a three-sector labor migration model involving the urban sector, modern agricultural sector, and traditional agricultural sector. Under the premises of the paper, the main conclusions can be summarized as follows. The unskilled labor outflow certainly decreases the wage inequality and unemployment rate. However, the influences that the skilled labor movement and capital inflow have on wage inequality and unemployment rate are dependent on the factor intensity between the urban and modern agricultural sectors. Therefore, the governments of developing counties should take the factor intensity between domestic sectors into consideration when confronting policies to attract the talent and capital inflow. In order to formulate policies, those variables are reasonable and in favor of decreasing wage inequality and unemployment rate.

There are two main contributions offered in this chapter. The first involves including the modern agricultural sector in research and sets its unskilled labor wage as downward rigid, which corresponds to economic reality in developing countries. The second involves clarifying the influence of factors that affect wage inequality and unemployment rate with regard to the skilled labor movement and capital inflow. These factors are not included in the conclusions reached in existing researches. These new ideas will contribute greatly to policy formulation in developing countries.

Particularly, the subjects studied in this paper such as employment, income inequality, international factor flow, and modern agriculture have almost covered all major problems in Asian developing economies. The conclusion of this chapter will have certain model significance for the economy of the Asian countries.

References

Beladi, H., Chaudhuri, S., & Yabuuchi, S. (2008). Can international factor mobility reduce wage inequality in a dual economy. *Review of International Economics, 16*, 893–903.

Beladi, H., Chakrabarti, A., & Marjit, S. (2010). Skilled–unskilled wage inequality and urban unemployment. *Economic Inquiry, 48*, 997–1007.

Chaudhuri, S. (2008). Fair wage hypothesis, foreign capital inflow and skilled–unskilled wage inequality in the presence of agricultural dualism. Available online at: http://papers.ssrn.com/sol3/papers.cfm?abstract_id=1226048

Chaudhuri, S., & Banerjee, D. (2010). Foreign capital inflow, skilled-unskilled wage inequality and unemployment of unskilled labor in a fair wage model. *Economic Modelling, 27*, 477–486.

Chaudhuri, S., & Yabuuchi, S. (2007). Economic liberalization and wage inequality in the presence of labor market imperfection. *International Review of Economics and Finance, 16*, 592–603.

Du, X., & Jin, A. (2012). The analysis of peasant household characteristics and conditions of production and management in Zhejiang Modern Agricultural Parks-based on the survey of Modern Bamboo Park in Anji, Suichang and Qingyuan county. *Chinese Agricultural Science Bulletin, 28*, 74–79.

Feenstra, R. C., & Hanson, G. H. (1996). Foreign investment, outsourcing and relative wages. In R. C. Feenstra, G. M. Grossman, & D. A. Irwin (Eds.), *The political economy of trade policy: Essays in honor of Jagdish N. Bhagwati*. Cambridge, MA: MIT Press.

Gupta, M. R. (1997a). Informal sector and informal capital market in a small open less-developed economy. *Journal of Development Economics, 52*, 409–428.

Gupta, M. R. (1997b). Foreign capital and the informal sector: Comments on Chandra and Khan. *Economica, 64*, 353–363.

Li, X., & Shen, Q. (2012). A study on the urban private capital in the modern agriculture sector and the transfer of labor. *Journal of Economic Policy Reform, 15*, 135–152.

Marjit, S., & Kar, S. (2005). Emigration and wage inequality. *Economic Letters, 88*, 141–145.

Marjit, S., Beladi, H., & Chakrabarti, A. (2004). Trade and wage inequality in developing countries. *Economic Inquiry, 42*, 295–303.

Yabuuchi, S. (2007). Unemployment and international factor movement in the presence of skilled and unskilled labor. *Review of Development Economics, 11*, 437–449.

Yabuuchi, S., & Chaudhuri, S. (2007). International migration of labor and skilled- unskilled wage inequality in a developing economy. *Economic Modelling, 24*, 128–137.

Chapter 13
Environment and Economy in the Modern Agricultural Development

Xiaochun Li and Yunyun Wu

Abstract This chapter establishes a three-sector general equilibrium model to investigate the environmental and economic effects of policies intended to promote modern agriculture. In the model, two situations are considered: in the first situation, the perfect mobility of capital between the capital-consuming sectors is assumed, and in the second situation, there is perfect mobility of land between the land-using sectors, keeping perfect mobility of capital assumption unchanged. The main conclusion is that the environmental effect of interest subsidization for modern agricultural sector is superior to other subsiding policies of factor prices.

Keywords Environment • Labor migration • Modern agriculture

1 Introduction

The term "modern agriculture" generally refers to the newly emergent agricultural sector, which produces its output using labor and capital as input and achieves higher yields than traditional agriculture. In recent years, many emerging economies such as India, China, and Brazil have taken modern agriculture as an impetus and vigorously promoted it. China exemplifies this practice: scholars have calculated the agricultural modernization development level from 1980 to 2008 and found that the development level of the national agricultural modernization is on an upward trend and the composite index of the development level has increased by 102% since 1980 (Xin and Jiang 2010). However, along with the flourishing of modern agriculture, environmental pollution has become increasingly evident in developing countries. Continuing with China as the example, the amount of carbon dioxide emission per capita has increased by 8% for 40 years, and the average value from 1998 to 2010 reaches 4.078 metric tons, almost twice that of the period from 1978 to 1997. Figure 13.1 shows the

X. Li (✉)
Business School, Nanjing University, Nanjing, China
e-mail: xiaochun@nju.edu.cn

Y. Wu
School of Economics, Nanjing University, 22 Hankou Road, Nanjing, Jiangsu 210093, China

X. Li (ed.), *Labor Transfer in Emerging Economies*, New Frontiers in Regional Science: Asian Perspectives 12, DOI 10.1007/978-981-10-3569-2_13

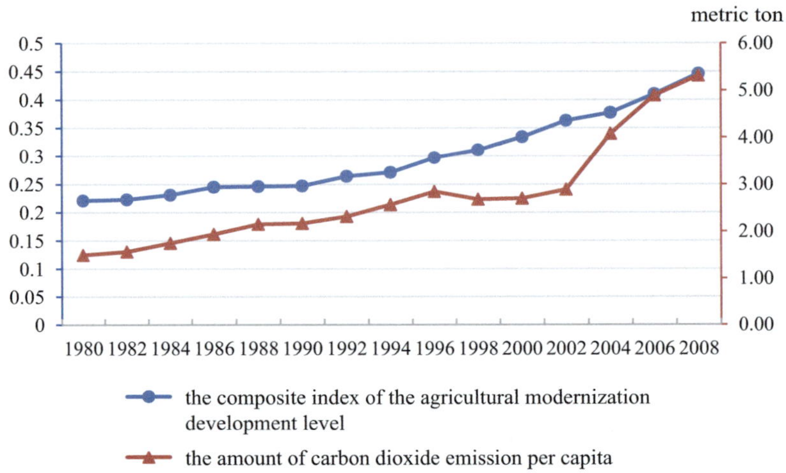

Fig. 13.1 The tendencies in the development of modern agricultural and environmental pollution. (Data sources: the data of the composite index of the agricultural modernization development level comes from Xin and Jiang 2010 and that of the carbon dioxide emission per capita comes from World Bank 2014)

composite index of the agricultural modernization development level and the amount of carbon dioxide emission per capita from 1980 to 2008 in China. Based on Fig. 13.1, we can see that the tendencies in the development of modern agriculture and environmental pollution are mutually correlative during the same period.

Thus, we must ask whether there is a particular mechanism that involves the two aforementioned issues. To date, no research has endeavored to combine the factors of modern agriculture and environmental pollution into a unifying framework. While some studies have considered modern agriculture and environmental pollution, they have treated them individually in the context of labor migration.

Various articles have divided the rural sector into the modern and traditional agricultural sectors in order to analyze economic development and labor migration. Examples include Gupta (1997a, b), Chaudhuri (2006, 2007), Li and Shen (2012), and Li et al. (2013). Particularly, Gupta (1997a) separated the modern agricultural sector from the traditional agricultural sector and employed a four-sector model to analyze the impact of changes in commodity price within a small, open, developing economy. Moreover, Gupta (1997b) considered a small open economy consisting of four sectors. He elaborated upon the invalidity of the proposition of Brecher and Alejandro when incorporating the costs of migration and skill acquisition. Furthermore, Chaudhuri (2006, 2007) divided the rural sector into a modern agricultural sector and a traditional agricultural sector. The former work explored the appropriateness and importance of labor market reform in developing countries that employ the three-sector general equilibrium model. The latter addressed the issue of why developing countries demand foreign capital despite the detrimental effects predicted by conventional literature regarding a three-sector model. Li and Shen (2012) and Li et al. (2013) studied the economic effects of government development policies with the introduction of urban private capital to the modern agricultural sector. Different from Gupta (1997a, b) and Chaudhuri (2006, 2007), they asserted that wages in the modern agricultural sector are higher than in the traditional agricultural sector, which is closer to the reality of the development of the modern agricultural sector in developing countries.

As for environmental pollution and labor migration, if the urban manufacturing sector absorbs rural emigrant labors, it will alter the scale and activity of manufacturing production. However, the expansion of the manufacturing sector will generate more pollution, which is known as the scalar effect of environmental pollution (Grossman and Krueger 1995). The literature regarding environmental pollution via labor migration includes Beladi and Rapp (1993), Beladi and Frasca (1999), and others. Beladi and Rapp (1993) examined the backward incidence of pollution abatement policies on some key variables of interest in a closed economy consisting of two sectors: an urban polluting sector and a rural nonpolluting sector. Beladi and Frasca (1999) took Beladi and Rapp (1993) one step further by using a three-sector model that incorporated an urban, nonpolluting sector.

The environmental factor remains largely ignored in the study of modern agriculture. Correspondingly, in the analysis of the environmental pollution induced through labor migration, the study of modern agriculture is ignored. However, in developing economies the relationship between modern agriculture and environmental pollution is clearly discernible. Because modern agriculture requires an adequate ecological environment, labor and capitalization, it competes with the urban sector for production factors on the basis of fixed endowment, whereby the higher development of modern agriculture increases the demand for such factors, thus creating an upward spiral. Therefore, the development of modern agriculture reduces the amount of production factors acquired by the urban sector, which is accompanied by changes in urban production scale and environmental quality. However, the issue becomes more complicated in the actual economic life, so it should be analyzed more specifically but also with greater consideration for the real world. Accordingly, as a means to clarify the environmental and economic impacts of modern agricultural development, this chapter establishes a three-sector general equilibrium model and conducts a comparative static study to investigate the environmental and economic effects of policies for the promotion of modern agricultural development. There are two situations under consideration: in the first situation, the perfect mobility of capital between the capital-consuming sectors is assumed, and in the second situation, there is perfect mobility of land between the land-using sectors, while the perfect mobility of capital assumption is unchanged. We find that the environmental effects of policies designed to promote modern agricultural development in the two situations differ significantly. In the first situation, wage subsidization for the modern agricultural sector has no environmental consequence, but interest subsidization improves environmental quality and raises the output of the modern agricultural sector. However, in the second situation, the subsidization of wages and rent for the modern agricultural sector lead to environmental deterioration, whereas interest subsidization has a positive environmental effect under certain conditions.

The paper is organized as follows. We examine the environmental and economic effects of policies for the promotion of modern agricultural development in the first situation in Sect. 2 and investigate that in the second situation in Sect. 3. Finally, concluding remarks can be found in Sect. 4.

2 Capital Enters the Modern Agricultural Sector

2.1 Model

This chapter considers a small open dual economy with three sectors. The urban sector uses two factors of production: labor and capital. The rural sector is further subdivided into two subsectors: a modern agricultural sector which uses capital and labor and a traditional agricultural sector which only uses labor. Among them, the modern agricultural sector is a newly emergent one. Labor is mobile from the traditional agricultural sector to the urban sector and the modern agricultural sector, whereas there is perfect mobility of capital between the urban and modern agricultural sectors. We further assume that, according to Copeland and Taylor (1999), the production procedures of the two agricultural sectors depend on environmental factor, whereby improvements within the environment create correspondingly higher levels of output. However, urban production generates environmental pollution, which imposes damage to the environment through agents such as air and water. All the markets are perfectly competitive, and the factor endowments are exogenously given. The production function of each of the said sectors is

$$X_1 = F^1(L_1, K_1), \tag{13.1}$$

$$X_2 = E^{\varepsilon_2} F^2(L_2, K_2), \tag{13.2}$$

$$X_3 = E^{\varepsilon_3} F^3(L_3), \tag{13.3}$$

where X_i, (i =1, 2, 3) indicates the output of the urban sector, modern agricultural sector, and traditional agricultural sector, respectively; L_i (i =1, 2, 3) indicates their respective quantity of labor; K_1 and K_2 are the capital utilized by the urban sector and modern agricultural sector, respectively; and K_2 is the loan from the urban sector.[1] Denote that E is the quality of environment after pollution. E^{ε_2} and E^{ε_3}, with the property of $0 < \varepsilon_2, \varepsilon_3 < 1$, represent the effects of environment on the modern agricultural productivity and traditional productivity, respectively. Thus,

[1]The long-existing institutional obstacles in developing countries have resulted in the stagnation of capital flows between the urban and rural sectors (Li and Shen 2012). However, certain developing countries have promoted the "modern agriculture" business, leading urban capital to flow to rural sector.

$$E = \bar{E} - \lambda X_1, \tag{13.4}$$

where $\bar{E}$ is the environmental endowment when there is no pollution in the economy, which is regarded as given; λ expresses the units of pollution generated by one unit of production of urban sector.

To maximize the profit of each sector, we have the following equations:

$$P_1 F_L^1(L_1, K_1) = \bar{w}_1, \tag{13.5}$$

$$P_2 E^{\varepsilon_2} F_L^2(L_2, K_2) = w_2, \tag{13.6}$$

$$E^{\varepsilon_3} F_L^3(L_3) = w_3, \tag{13.7}$$

$$P_1 F_K^1(L_1, K_1) = r, \tag{13.8}$$

$$P_2 E^{\varepsilon_2} F_K^2(L_2, K_2) = r. \tag{13.9}$$

Here, the subscript in F^i denotes the partial derivative (e.g., $F_L^1 = \partial F^1/\partial L_1$). P_1 and P_2 indicate the product prices of the urban sector and the modern agricultural sector in terms of the traditional agricultural sector, respectively. r is the interest rate. w_1, w_2, and w_3 indicate the wage rate in the urban sector, the modern agricultural sector, and the traditional agricultural sector, respectively. The urban wage rate shows downward rigidity because of labor unions and ubiquitous local protectionism, so $w_1 = \bar{w}_1$ is an exogenous variable; the wage rate in the traditional agricultural sector is flexible.

Furthermore, we assume that labor in the traditional agricultural sector cannot be fully transferred to the modern agricultural sector, and the absorption of labor by the modern agricultural sector is constrained by capital in this sector. Thus, the relationship between its employed labor and capital is as follows:

$$L_2 = A_1 {K_2}^{\alpha}, \tag{13.10}$$

where A_1 indicates the variety coefficient of the modern agricultural production, which is regarded as given. $0 < \alpha < 1$ is set as the basis for the development of the modern agriculture, and this chapter researches this situation in particular. Therefore, the wage rate in the modern agricultural sector exceeds that in the traditional sector, and it is determined by the following (Similar settings please refer to Gupta 1994):

$$w_2 = w_2(w_3, K_2).$$

When K_2=0, we assume w_2=w_3, which means without capital investment, the modern agricultural sector deteriorates to the traditional agricultural sector; when K_2>0, we assume w_2>w_3, because the capital used improves labor efficiency, causing a higher marginal productivity of labor.

Let $\bar{L}$ be the endowment of labor in the entire economy and L_u be the urban unemployment, there is

$$L_1 + L_2 + L_3 + L_u = \bar{L}. \quad (13.11)$$

Let $\mu = L_u / L_1$ be the unemployment rate of the urban sector; thus, Eq. (13.11) becomes

$$(1 + \mu)L_1 + L_2 + L_3 = \bar{L}. \quad (13.11')$$

Let $\bar{K}$ be the endowment of capital in the entire economy. Capital in the economy is fully employed by the urban and modern agriculture sectors:

$$K_1 + K_2 = \bar{K}. \quad (13.12)$$

With regard to the labor allocation mechanism, we assume that workers in traditional agricultural sector will compare the actual wage in their sector with the expected wage of the urban sector and the modern sector and will move to the other two sectors if the expected wage is higher. At the equilibrium point, we have

$$w_3 = \frac{L_1}{(1 + \mu)L_1 + L_2}\bar{w}_1 + \frac{L_2}{(1 + \mu)L_1 + L_2}w_2. \quad (13.13)$$

According to Eq. (13.13), we could describe the labor transfer mechanism in the economy as follows by reorganizing this equation:

$$\bar{w}_1 L_1 + w_2 L_2 = w_3[(1 + \mu)L_1 + L_2] = w_3(\bar{L} - L_3). \quad (13.13')$$

The basic model has been established. In Eqs. (13.1) to (13.10), (13.11′), (13.12), and (13.13′), there are 13 endogenous variables, namely, X_1, X_2, X_3, E, L_1, L_2, L_3, K_1, K_2, μ, w_2, w_3, and r, and 6 exogenous variables, $\bar{E}$, $\bar{L}$, $\bar{K}$, $\bar{w}_1$, P_1, and P_2.

2.2 *Analysis*

We begin the analysis by considering the environment. Totally differentiating Eq. (13.4), we obtain

$$dE = -\lambda dX_1 = -\lambda F_L^1 dL_1 - \lambda F_K^1 dK_1. \quad (13.14)$$

The environmental quality is affected by the two factor inputs in the urban sector. In addition, development policies for one sector always focus on price subsidization for production factor. Accordingly, we will separately analyze wage subsidization and interest subsidization for the modern agricultural sector to expose the environmental effects as well as economic effects.

Table 13.1 The effects of wage subsidization for the modern agricultural sector

	dL_1	dL_2	dL_3	dK_1	dK_2	$d\mu$	dE
ds_1	0	0	–	0	0	+	0
	dw_2	dw_3	dr	dX_1	dX_2	dX_3	
ds_1	+	0	0	0	0	–	

Note: "+" and "−" mean that the changes of s_1 make the endogenous variables change in the same and opposed directions, respectively; "0" means that the changes of s_1 have no impacts on endogenous variables

2.2.1 The Effects of Wage Subsidization for the Modern Agricultural Sector

If the government implements policy to subsidize wages in the modern agricultural sector and the rate of subsidy is s_1, then Eq. (13.6) becomes

$$P_2 E^{\varepsilon_2} F_L^2(L_2, K_2) = w_2(1 - s_1). \tag{13.6*}$$

Substitute Eqs. (13.4), (13.5), (13.10), and (13.12) into Eq. (13.6*) and make s_1 =0 at the initiation of the subsidy policy. Then, total differentiation of Eq. (13.6*) yields

$$\Phi \frac{dK_1}{ds_1} + \frac{1}{w_2}\frac{dw_2}{ds_1} = 1, \tag{13.15}$$

where $\Phi = \varepsilon_2 \lambda X_1/EK_1 + (1-\alpha)K_2 F_{LK}^2/F_L^2 K_2 > 0$. Wage subsidization for the modern agricultural sector not only directly affects the wage rate in this sector but also affects the capital utilized by the urban sector through capital mobility. Therefore, we should turn to the capital market.

Using Eqs. (13.5), (13.8), (13.10), and (13.12) and then total differentiation of Eq. (13.9) yields

$$\Psi dK_1 = 0, \tag{13.16}$$

where $\Psi = \varepsilon_2 \lambda X_1/EK_1 + (1-\alpha)F_{KK}^2/F_K^2$, and the sign of Ψ is ambiguous (the first term of Ψ is positive, while the second term of Ψ is negative since $0 < \alpha < 1$). Note that $\theta_{KK} = F_{KK}^2 K_2/F_K^2$ measures the partial curvature of the production function, and $|\theta_{KK}| > aK_2X_1/K_1E$ is assumed where $a = \varepsilon_2\lambda/(1-\alpha) > 0$. This condition asserts that the capital elasticity of its marginal product (or interest) in the modern agricultural sector is large enough. Therefore, $\Psi < 0$ and, hence, Eq. (13.16) implies $dK_1 = 0$, also Eq. (13.15) becomes $dw_2/ds_1 = w_2 > 0$.

Substituting these results into the model, we obtain the effects of wage subsidization for the modern agricultural sector on other endogenous variables and get Table 13.1 (please refer to Appendix A for the details of the calculation).

Table 13.2 The effects of interest subsidization for the modern agricultural sector

	dL_1	dL_2	dL_3	dK_1	dK_2	$d\mu$	dE
ds_2	−	+	[−]	−	+	[+]	+
	dw_2	dw_3	dr	dX_1	dX_2	dX_3	
ds_2	+	+	0	−	+	[−]	

Note: "+" and "−" mean that the changes of s_2 make the endogenous variables change in the same and opposed directions, respectively; "0" means that the changes of s_2 have no impacts on endogenous variables; "[+]" and "[−]" mean that the changes of s_2 make the endogenous variables change in the same and opposed directions under specific conditions (as shown in Appendix B)

To summarize, we obtain Proposition 13.1.

Proposition 13.1 *Wage subsidization for the modern agricultural sector has no environmental consequence, but reduces the quantity of labor in traditional agricultural sector and raises urban unemployment, moreover, raises the wage rate in modern agricultural sector, and lowers the output of traditional agricultural sector.*

Wage subsidization for the modern agricultural sector reduces its labor using cost, so the modern agricultural sector raises wage rate so as to absorb more labor. However, it has no effect on the labor of modern agricultural sector according to Table 13.1. This is because the wage subsidization does not affect capital market, and the absorption of labor by the modern agricultural sector is constrained by capital in this sector. Given the interest rate r and urban wage $\bar{w}_1$, the output in the urban sector is constant, thereby keeping the environmental quality unchanged. In addition, some of the laborers in the traditional agricultural sector are attracted by the higher expected wage of the other two sectors, but they come to the urban sector and become the urban unemployed because of the unchanging L_1 and L_2.[2]

2.2.2 The Effects of Interest Subsidization for the Modern Agricultural Sector

If the interest of modern agricultural sector is subsidized and the subsidy rate is s_2, then Eq. (13.9) becomes

$$P_2 E^{\varepsilon_2} F_K^2(L_2, K_2) = r(1 - s_2). \tag{13.9*}$$

Let $s_2 = 0$ at the initiation of the subsidy policy and use Eqs. (13.4), (13.5), (13.8), (13.10), and (13.12), then total differentiation of Eq. (13.9*) yields

[2]It is implicitly assumed that unemployed labor is supported by employed labor, such as other members of the family, or alternatively that the job is allocated daily (or monthly and so on) to all applicants by lottery.

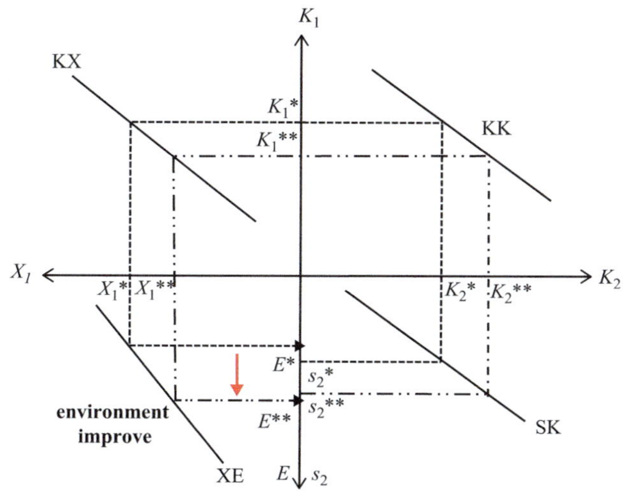

Fig. 13.2 Partial environmental effects of interest subsidization for the modern agricultural sector

$$\frac{dK_1}{ds_2} = \frac{1}{\Psi} < 0, \tag{13.17}$$

where $\Psi < 0$. From Eq. (13.17), it is clear that interest subsidization for the modern agricultural sector raises its capital demand, thereby reducing the capital utilized by the urban sector.

Substituting Eq. (13.17) into the model, we obtain the effects of interest subsidization for the modern agricultural sector on other endogenous variables and get Table 13.2 (please refer to Appendix B for the details of the calculation).

To sum up, we arrive at Proposition 13.2.

Proposition 13.2 *Interest subsidization for the modern agricultural sector contributes to environmental improvement and exerts the following economic impacts:*

1. *It raises the wage rates in the modern and traditional agricultural sectors.*
2. *It lowers the capital of the urban sector but raises that of the modern agricultural sector.*
3. *The quantity of labor in the urban sector reduces and when* $\varepsilon_2 w_2 L_2 > \varepsilon_3 w_3 (\bar{L} - L_3)$ *and* $K_1 L_2 / L_1 K_2 > \bar{w}_1 / \alpha w_2$ *that in the traditional agricultural sector reduces, while that in the modern agricultural sector raises; when* $\varepsilon_2 w_2 L_2 > \varepsilon_3 w_3 (\bar{L} - L_3)$, *the urban unemployment rate raises.*
4. *The output of urban sector falls and that of traditional agricultural sector falls if* $\varepsilon_2 w_2 L_2 > \varepsilon_3 w_3 \bar{L}$ *but that of modern agricultural sector rises.*

The environmental effects of interest subsidization for modern agricultural sector are superior to those obtained from wage subsidization. Interest subsidization lowers the cost of capital using the modern agricultural sector, whereby more capital leaves the urban to the modern agricultural sector, leading to an increase of labor demand in the modern agricultural sector but a decrease of labor demand in the urban sector. The former puts an upward pressure on the wage rate in the modern agricultural, while the latter reduces the output of urban sector and then improves the quality of environment. The partial environmental impact of Proposition 13.2 could be illustrated by Fig. 13.2. We use four curves to describe the mechanism. First, using Eq. (13.9*), we can derive a positive relationship between K_2 and s_2, and this is shown by the SK curve in the K_2 -s_2 plane. Moreover, from Eq. (13.12) we obtain the negatively sloped KK line in the K_2 -K_1 plane. Furthermore, Eq. (13.1) is represented by the KX curve in the X_1-K_1 plane. Finally, the inverse relationship between X_1 and E given by Eq. (13.4) can be shown by the XE curve in the X_1-E plane. Therefore, when the government raises the rate of interest subsidization for the modern agricultural sector from s_2* to s_2**, the capital utilized by the modern agricultural sector increases from K_2* to K_2**, and the capital utilized by the urban sector decreases from K_1* to K_1** accordingly, whereby the output in the urban sector falls from X_1* to X_1**, and the environmental quality improves from E* to E**. In addition, the improvement of environment and the increase of factor inputs facilitate the development of modern agriculture.

Li and Shen (2012) adopted a three-sector general equilibrium model and analyzed the economic effects of policies for the modern agricultural development when urban private capital has entered into the modern agricultural sector. They found that interest subsidization for the modern agricultural sector actually reduces the quantity of labor in the traditional agricultural sector. But taking environment into account, the same occurs only under specific conditions. The reasons for the distinction are as follows. The modern agricultural sector is a better destination with higher wage, and labor is more likely to flow into the modern agricultural sector than the traditional sector. However, interest subsidization for the modern agricultural sector has a positive effect on the environment, thereby promoting the traditional agricultural sector and increasing its factor employments. Therefore, the quantity of labor in the traditional agricultural sector depends on the labor absorptive capacity of modern agricultural sector and the environmental benefits.

3 Analysis in the Presence of Land Factor

3.1 Model

The importance of the land factor becomes more obvious when the modern agricultural sector has accumulated considerable capital. It is necessary to extend the model to include the land factor which is used in these two agricultural sectors. Thus, we could distinguish the agricultural sectors from urban sector. Further, there is perfect mobility of land between the traditional agricultural sector and the modern agricultural sector. In the same setup, the production function of each sector is replaced by the following equations:

$$X_1 = F^1(L_1, K_1), \tag{13.1'}$$

$$X_2 = E^{\varepsilon_2} F^2(L_2, K_2, T_2), \tag{13.2'}$$

$$X_3 = E^{\varepsilon_3} F^3(L_3, T_3). \tag{13.3'}$$

T_2 and T_3 indicate the land inputs in the modern agricultural sector and the traditional agricultural sector, respectively.

Adding the land factor, Eqs. (13.6), (13.7), and (13.9) become

$$P_2 E^{\varepsilon_2} F_L^2(L_2, K_2, T_2) = w_2, \tag{13.6'}$$

$$E^{\varepsilon_3} F_L^3(L_3, T_3) = w_3, \tag{13.7'}$$

$$P_2 E^{\varepsilon_2} F_K^2(L_2, K_2, T_2) = r. \tag{13.9'}$$

Further, we assume that labor migration from the traditional agricultural sector to the modern sector is not "limitless," and the absorption of labor by the modern agricultural sector is constrained by capital and land in this sector. Thus, Eq. (13.10) takes the following form:

$$L_2 = A_2 {K_2}^{\beta} T_2^{\gamma}, \tag{13.10'}$$

where $0 < \beta < 1$ and $0 < \gamma < 1$, A_2 indicates the variety coefficient of the modern agricultural production. Similar setup to the previous section, the wage rate in the modern agricultural sector is determined by $w_2 = w_2\ (w_3, K_2, T_2)$ with the properties $w_2 = w_3$ for $K_2 = 0$, which means without capital investment, the modern agricultural sector deteriorates to the traditional agricultural sector; $w_2 > w_3$ for $K_2 > 0$; $w_2 < \bar{w}_1$ for $T_2 > 0$.

If τ is the land rent, we could obtain the following two equations based on profit maximization:

$$P_2 E^{\varepsilon_2} F_T^2(L_2, K_2, T_2) = \tau, \tag{13.18}$$

$$E^{\varepsilon_3} F_T^3(L_3, T_3) = \tau. \tag{13.19}$$

Let $\bar{T}$ be the endowment of land in the entire economy, which is exogenous. Land in the economy is fully used by the two agricultural sectors:

$$T_2 + T_3 = \bar{T}. \tag{13.20}$$

In Eqs. (13.1′), (13.2′), (13.3′), (13.4), (13.5), (13.6′), (13.7′), (13.8), (13.9′), (13.10′), (13.11′), (13.12), (13.13′), and (13.18), (13.19), and (13.20), there are

Table 13.3 The effects of wage subsidization for the modern agricultural sector

	dL_1	dL_2	dL_3	dK_1	dK_2	dT_2	dT_3	$d\mu$
ds_1	+	\	\	+	–	+	–	\
	dE	dw_2	dw_3	dr	$d\tau$	dX_1	dX_2	dX_3
ds_1	–	\	\	0	–	+	\	\

Note: "+" and "–" mean that the changes of s_1 will make the endogenous variables change in the same and opposed directions, respectively; "0" means that the changes of s_1 have no impacts on endogenous variables; "\" means the changes of s_1 have ambiguous impacts on endogenous variables

altogether 16 endogenous variables, namely, $X_1, X_2, X_3, E, L_1, L_2, L_3, K_1, K_2, T_2, T_3$, μ, w_2, w_3, τ, and r, and 7 exogenous variables, $\bar{E}$, $\bar{L}$, $\bar{K}$, $\bar{T}$, $\bar{w}_1$,P_1, and P_2.

3.2 *Analysis*

3.2.1 The Effects of Wage Subsidization for the Modern Agricultural Sector

If the government subsidizes the wages of the modern agricultural sector with the rate of s_1, then Eq. (13.6′) becomes

$$P_2 E^{\varepsilon_2} F_L^2(L_2, K_2, T_2) = w_2(1 - s_1). \tag{13.6′*}$$

Differentiating Eqs. (13.4), (13.5), (13.6′*), (13.7′), (13.8), (13.9′), (13.10′), (13.12), (13.13′), and (13.18), (13.19), and (13.20) and writing in a matrix notation, we can obtain the following equation:

$$\begin{bmatrix} A & M & (w_2)^{-1} & 0 & 0 \\ B & N & 0 & 0 & 0 \\ C & P & 0 & 0 & S \\ D & Q & 0 & (w_3)^{-1} & T \\ G & R & L_2 & -(\bar{L} - L_3) & w_3 \end{bmatrix} \begin{bmatrix} dK_1 \\ dT_2 \\ dw_2 \\ dw_3 \\ dL_3 \end{bmatrix} = \begin{bmatrix} 1 \\ 0 \\ 0 \\ 0 \\ 0 \end{bmatrix} ds_1. \tag{13.21}$$

Define the determinant of the coefficient matrix in Eq. (13.21) as Δ and we obtain $\Delta > 0$ by stability (please refer to Appendix C for the details of the calculation). Solving Eq. (13.21) by using Cramer's rule, we can get Table 13.3 as follows (please refer to the Appendix D for details of the calculation procedure):

Summarizing the results in Table 13.3, we arrive at the following proposition.

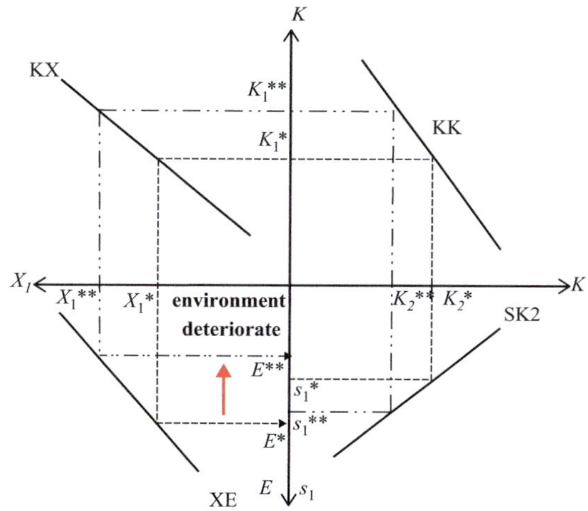

Fig. 13.3 The environmental effects of wage subsidization for the modern agricultural sector incorporating land factor

Proposition 13.3 *In the presence of land factor, wage subsidization for the modern agricultural sector deteriorates the quality of environment and exert the following economic impacts: raising the quantity of labor, capital and output in the urban sector, decreasing the capital but increasing the land input in the modern agricultural sector, reducing the land input in the traditional agricultural sector, and lowering the land rent.*

The results show sharp contrast to those obtained in Proposition 13.1. Wage subsidization for the modern agricultural sector lowers the cost of labor use, causing a tendency toward raising the quantity of labor. However, according to Table 13.3, wage subsidization for the modern agricultural sector causes its land input to raise and its capital to fall due to the substitute relations among labor, capital, and land factors. Thus, the change in the quantity of labor in the modern agricultural is uncertain. Furthermore, capital flows back to urban sector from the modern agricultural sector, expanding the urban sector and, hence, leading to a deterioration of environment. This mechanism could be illustrated by Fig. 13.3. In the same setup, we use the KK, KX, and XE curves to describe the mechanism. Moreover, using Eq. (13.6′*), we can derive an inverse relationship between K_2 and s_1 that has been explained above, and this is shown by the SK2 curve in the K_2 - s_1 plane. Therefore, when government raises the rate of wage subsidization for modern agricultural sector from s_1* to s_1**, the capital utilized by the modern agricultural sector decreases from K_2* to K_2**, and capital utilized by the urban sector increases from K_1* to K_1** accordingly, rising the output of urban sector from X_1* to X_1**. As a result, the environmental quality deteriorates from E* to E**.

3.2.2 The Effects of Interest Subsidization and Rent Subsidization for the Modern Agricultural Sector

If interest in the modern agricultural sector is subsidized with the rate of s_2, then Eq. (13.9′) becomes

$$P_2 E^{\varepsilon_2} F_K^2(L_2, K_2, T_2) = r(1 - s_2). \tag{13.9′*}$$

And if the government subsidizes land rent in the modern agricultural sector with the rate s_3, then Eq. (13.18) becomes

$$P_2 E^{\varepsilon_2} F_T^2(L_2, K_2, T_2) = \tau(1 - s_3). \tag{13.18*}$$

Differentiating Eqs. (13.4), (13.5), (13.6′), (13.7′), (13.8), (13.9′*), (13.10′), (13.12), (13.13′), (13.18*), (13.19), and (13.20) and writing in matrix notation, we can obtain the following equation:

$$\begin{bmatrix} A & M & (w_2)^{-1} & 0 & 0 \\ B & N & 0 & 0 & 0 \\ C & P & 0 & 0 & S \\ D & Q & 0 & (w_3)^{-1} & T \\ G & R & L_2 & -(\bar{L} - L_3) & w_3 \end{bmatrix} \begin{bmatrix} dK_1 \\ dT_2 \\ dw_2 \\ dw_3 \\ dL_3 \end{bmatrix} = \begin{bmatrix} 0 \\ 1 \\ 0 \\ 0 \\ 0 \end{bmatrix} ds_2 + \begin{bmatrix} 0 \\ 0 \\ 1 \\ 0 \\ 0 \end{bmatrix} ds_3. \tag{13.22}$$

In order to calculate the effect of interest subsidization, we make the following assumption:

Assumption M<0 *and* $P[1 + T(\bar{L} - L_3)] < S[Q(\bar{L} - L_3) + R/w_3]$.

Under this assumption, according to Cramer's rule with respect to ds_2 in Eq. (13.22), we can obtain $dK_1/ds_2 = MSL_2/w_2 + \{P[1 + T(\bar{L} - L_3)] - S[Q(\bar{L} - L_3) + R/w_3]\}/w_2 < 0$. According to Eqs. (13.4), (13.5), and $dK_1 / ds_2 < 0$, we can get that $dE/ds_2 > 0$, which means that interest subsidization for the modern agricultural sector will deteriorate environmental quality.

With respect to ds_3 in Eq. (13.22), we can obtain that incorporating land factor, rent subsidization for the modern agricultural sector has the same effect as wage subsidization (please refer to Appendix E for the details of the calculation). The partial effects of rent subsidization could be illustrated as follows. Rent subsidization for the modern agricultural sector reduces the cost of land use and increases land input. However, since the substitute relations between capital and land factors, an increase of land input in the modern agricultural sector causes a decrease of its capital, whereby capital flows back to urban sector from the modern agricultural sector. Consequently, the urban sector expands its production scale and raises the output, resulting in the environmental deterioration. As for other economic effects, we can find answers from substitute relation among factors.

To summarize, we obtain Proposition 13.4.

Proposition 13.4 *In the presence of land factor, the interest subsidization for modern agricultural sector raises the capital utilized by the modern agricultural sector and favors the environment if* $M<0$ *and* $P[1+T(\bar{L}-L_3)] < S[Q(\bar{L}-L_3)+R/w_3]$, *whereas rent subsidization for modern agricultural sector has the same environmental and economic effects as wage subsidization in Proposition* 13.3.

4 Conclusion

The capital factor is the primary problem in the development of the modern agricultural sector, which can be separated from the traditional agricultural sector only when there is capital investment. After solving the capital problem, the importance of the land factor becomes more obvious. Accordingly, this article employs a comparative static method to investigate the environmental and economic effects of the policies intended to promote modern agriculture in the following two situations: in the first situation, the perfect mobility of capital between the capital-consuming sectors is assumed, and in the second situation, there is perfect mobility of land between the land-using sectors, keeping perfect mobility of capital assumption unchanged. The former highlights the role of capital in modern agricultural development, while the latter focuses on the relative substitution between the capital factor and the land factor when the modern agricultural sector has accumulated considerable capital. (Mainly, it reflects the function of the land factor.) We thereby obtain four propositions and, in the process, conclude that the environmental effect of interest subsidization for modern agricultural sector is superior to other subsiding policies of factor prices. As for wage subsidization in the modern agricultural sector, the environmental effects in the first situation are better than those in the second situation. Consequently, in a developing country with serious environmental problems, one policy implication could be proposed whereby interest subsidization for the modern agricultural sector should be the first choice in policy development. As for the related economic impacts, please refer to the specific propositions.

Appendices

Appendix A

Substituting $dK_1/ds_1=0$, $dw_2/ds_1=w_2>0$ into Eqs. (13.1), (13.2), (13.3), (13.4), (13.5), (13.6), (13.7), (13.8), (13.9), (13.10), (13.11), (13.12), and (13.13), we get $\frac{dL_1}{ds_1}=\frac{dE}{ds_1}=\frac{dK_2}{ds_1}=\frac{dL_2}{ds_1}=\frac{dr}{ds_1}=\frac{dX_2}{ds_1}=\frac{dX_1}{ds_1}=\frac{dw_3}{ds_1}=0$, $\frac{d\mu}{ds_1}>0$, $\frac{dL_3}{ds_1}<0$, $\frac{dX_3}{ds_1}<0$.

Appendix B

Substituting $dK_1/ds_2=1/\Psi<0$ into Eqs. (13.1), (13.2), (13.3), (13.4), (13.5), (13.6), (13.7), (13.8), (13.9), (13.10), (13.11), (13.12), and (13.13), we get $\frac{dL_1}{ds_2}<0, \frac{dE}{ds_2}>0, \frac{dK_2}{ds_2}>0, \frac{dL_2}{ds_2}>0, \frac{dr}{ds_2}=0, \frac{dX_1}{ds_2}<0, \frac{dX_2}{ds_2}>0, \frac{dw_2}{ds_2}>0, \frac{dw_3}{ds_2}>0$. When $\varepsilon_2 w_2 L_2 > \varepsilon_3 w_3(\bar{L}-L_3)$, $d\mu\ /\ ds_2>0$; when $\varepsilon_2 w_2 L_2 > \varepsilon_3 w_3(\bar{L}-L_3)$ and $k_1/k_2 > \bar{w}_1/(\alpha w_2)$, $dL_3/ds_2<0$; when $\varepsilon_2 w_2 L_2 > \varepsilon_3 w_3 \bar{L}$, $dX_3/ds_1<0$.

Appendix C

Differentiating Eqs. (13.4), (13.5), (13.6′*), (13.7′), (13.8), (13.9′), (13.10′), (13.12), (13.13′), (13.18), (13.19), and (13.20) and writing in a matrix notation, we can obtain the following equation:

$$\begin{bmatrix} A & M & (w_2)^{-1} & 0 & 0 \\ B & N & 0 & 0 & 0 \\ C & P & 0 & 0 & S \\ D & Q & 0 & (w_3)^{-1} & T \\ G & R & L_2 & -(\bar{L}-L_3) & w_3 \end{bmatrix} \begin{bmatrix} dK_1 \\ dT_2 \\ dw_2 \\ dw_3 \\ dL_3 \end{bmatrix} = \begin{bmatrix} 1 \\ 0 \\ 0 \\ 0 \\ 0 \end{bmatrix} ds_1, \qquad (13.21)$$

where

$$A = \frac{\varepsilon_2 \lambda X_1}{EK_1} + \frac{\beta L_2 F_{LL}^2 + K_2 F_{LK}^2}{F_L^2 K_2},\ B = \frac{\varepsilon_2 \lambda X_1}{EK_1} + \frac{\beta L_2 F_{KL}^2 + K_2 F_{KK}^2}{F_K^2 K_2}, C = \frac{(\varepsilon_2-\varepsilon_3)\lambda X_1}{EK_1}$$
$$+\frac{\beta L_2 F_{TL}^2 + K_2 F_{TK}^2}{F_T^2 K_2},\ D = \frac{\varepsilon_3 \lambda X_1}{EK_1} > 0,\ G = \frac{\bar{w}_1 L_1}{K_1}$$
$$-\frac{w_2 \beta L_2}{K_2}, M = -\frac{\gamma L_2 F_{LL}^2 + T_2 F_{LT}^2}{F_L^2 T_2},\ N = -\frac{\gamma L_2 F_{KL}^2 + T_2 F_{KT}^2}{F_K^2 T_2} < 0,$$
$$P = -\left(\frac{\gamma L_2 F_{TL}^2 + T_2 F_{TT}^2}{F_T^2 T_2} + \frac{F_{TT}^3}{F_T^3}\right) > 0, Q = \frac{F_{LT}^3}{F_L^3} > 0,$$
$$R = \frac{w_2 \beta L_2}{T_2} > 0,\ S = \frac{F_{TL}^3}{F_T^3} > 0,\ T = -\frac{F_{LL}^3}{F_L^3} > 0.$$

The determinant of square matrix in Eq. (13.21) is $\Delta = -\{S[w_2 L_2(AN-BM) + (BR-GN) + (\bar{L}-L_3)w_3(BQ-DN)]\}/w_2 w_3. +[1+(\bar{L}-L_3)T](BP-CN)/w_2$. Since the sign of Δ cannot be directly determined, we will use dynamic adjustment to decide its sign.

Let

$$\dot{L}_1 = d_1\left(P_1 F_L^1(L_1, K_1) - \bar{w}_1\right), \tag{13.C1}$$

$$\dot{L}_2 = d_2\left(P_2 E^{\varepsilon_2} F_L^2(L_2, K_2, T_2) - w_2\right), \tag{13.C2}$$

$$\dot{L}_3 = d_3\left(E^{\varepsilon_3} F_L^3(L_3, T_3) - w_3\right), \tag{13.C3}$$

$$\dot{K}_1 = d_4\left(P_1 F_K^1(L_1, K_1) - r\right), \tag{13.C4}$$

$$\dot{K}_2 = d_5\left(P_2 E^{\varepsilon_2} F_K^2(L_2, K_2, T_2) - r\right), \tag{13.C5}$$

$$\dot{T}_2 = d_6\left(P_2 E^{\varepsilon_2} F_T^2(L_2, K_2, T_2) - \tau\right), \tag{13.C6}$$

$$\dot{T}_3 = d_7\left(E^{\varepsilon_3} F_T^3(L_3, T_3) - \tau\right), \tag{13.C7}$$

$$\dot{w}_2 = d_8\left(L_2 - A_2 {K_2}^{\beta} T_2^{\gamma}\right), \tag{13.C8}$$

$$\dot{w}_3 = d_9(\bar{w}_1 L_1 + w_2 L_2 - w_3(\bar{L} - L_3)), \tag{13.C9}$$

$$\dot{r} = d_{10}(K_1 + K_2 - \bar{K}), \tag{13.C10}$$

$$\dot{\tau} = d_{11}(T_2 + T_3 - \bar{T}), \tag{13.C11}$$

$$\dot{E} = d_{12}\left(E - \bar{E} + \lambda F^1\right), \tag{13.C12}$$

where "." represents differentiation with respect to time and d_j (j=1,2...,12) is the positive coefficient measuring the speed of adjustment and d_j >0.

The determinant of the Jacobian matrix of Eqs. (13.C1), (13.C2), (13.C3), (13.C4), (13.C5), (13.C6), (13.C7), (13.C8), (13.C9), (13.C10), (13.C11), and (13.C12) is

$$|J| = \begin{vmatrix}
d_1P_1F_{LL}^1 & 0 & 0 & d_1P_1F_{LK}^1 & 0 & 0 & 0 & 0 & 0 & 0 & 0 & 0 \\
0 & d_2P_2E^{\varepsilon_2}F_{LL}^2 & 0 & 0 & d_2P_2E^{\varepsilon_2}F_{LK}^2 & d_2P_2E^{\varepsilon_2}F_{LT}^2 & 0 & -d_2 & 0 & 0 & 0 & d_2P_2\varepsilon_2E^{\varepsilon_2-1}F_L^2 \\
0 & 0 & d_3E^{\varepsilon_3}F_{LL}^3 & 0 & 0 & 0 & d_3E^{\varepsilon_3}F_{LT}^3 & 0 & -d_3 & 0 & 0 & d_3\varepsilon_3E^{\varepsilon_3-1}F_L^3 \\
d_4P_1F_{KL}^1 & 0 & 0 & d_4P_1F_{KK}^1 & 0 & 0 & 0 & 0 & 0 & -d_4 & 0 & 0 \\
0 & d_5P_2E^{\varepsilon_2}F_{KL}^2 & 0 & 0 & d_5P_2E^{\varepsilon_2}F_{KK}^2 & d_5P_2E^{\varepsilon_2}F_{KT}^2 & 0 & 0 & 0 & -d_5 & 0 & d_5P_2\varepsilon_2E^{\varepsilon_2-1}F_K^2 \\
0 & d_6P_2E^{\varepsilon_2}F_{TL}^2 & 0 & 0 & d_6P_2E^{\varepsilon_2}F_{TK}^2 & d_6P_2E^{\varepsilon_2}F_{TT}^2 & 0 & 0 & 0 & 0 & -d_6 & d_6P_2\varepsilon_2E^{\varepsilon_2-1}F_T^2 \\
0 & 0 & d_7E^{\varepsilon_3}F_{TL}^3 & 0 & 0 & 0 & d_7E^{\varepsilon_3}F_{TT}^3 & 0 & 0 & 0 & -d_7 & d_7\varepsilon_3E^{\varepsilon_3-1}F_T^3 \\
0 & d_8 & 0 & 0 & -d_8\beta\frac{L_2}{K_2} & -d_8\gamma\frac{L_2}{T_2} & 0 & 0 & 0 & 0 & 0 & 0 \\
d_9\bar{w}_1 & d_9w_2 & d_9w_3 & 0 & 0 & 0 & 0 & d_9L_2 & -d_9(\bar{L}-L_3) & 0 & 0 & 0 \\
0 & 0 & 0 & d_{10} & d_{10} & 0 & 0 & 0 & 0 & 0 & 0 & 0 \\
0 & 0 & 0 & 0 & 0 & d_{11} & d_{11} & 0 & 0 & 0 & 0 & 0 \\
d_{12}\lambda F_L^1 & 0 & 0 & d_{12}\lambda F_K^1 & 0 & 0 & 0 & 0 & 0 & 0 & 0 & d_{12}
\end{vmatrix}.$$

It can also be written as follows: $|J| = -P_1F_{LL}^1 r\tau w_2 w_3 d_1 d_2 \ldots d_{12}\Delta$. Under the condition of a stable system, there must be $|J| > 0$, and thus Δ >0.

Appendix D

Using Cramer's rule to solve Eq. (13.21), we get $dK_1/ds_1 = -L_2SN/\Delta w_3 > 0$, $dT_2/ds_1 = L_2BS/\Delta w_3$. Note that $\Gamma_{KK} = F_{KK}^2 K_2/F_K^2$, which denotes the capital elasticity of its marginal product (or interest rate) in the modern agricultural sector; $\Gamma_{KL} = F_{KL}^2 L_2/F_K^2$, which denotes the labor elasticity of the marginal product of capital (or interest rate) in the modern agricultural sector. We assume that $|\beta\Gamma_{KL}+\Gamma_{KK}|< e$, where $\beta\Gamma_{KL}+\Gamma_{KK}$ is the resultant capital elasticity of interest rate in the modern agricultural sector,$e=\varepsilon_2\lambda K_2X_1/EK_1$. Because we separate land factor from capital, it makes the interest rate less sensitive to capital factor' s change. Hence, $B>0$ and $dT_2/ds_1>0$.

Substituting the above results into Eqs. (13.1′), (13.2′), (13.4), (13.8), (13.10′), (13.12), (13.18), and (13.20), we can obtain the following:

$$\frac{dK_2}{ds_1}<0,\quad \frac{dT_3}{ds_1}<0,\quad \frac{dr}{ds_1}=0,\quad \frac{dE}{ds_1}<0,\quad \frac{dX_1}{ds_1}>0,$$

$$\frac{dL_2}{ds_1}=-\frac{L_2SL_2}{\Delta w_3}\left[\frac{\gamma K_2F_{KK}^2-\beta T_2F_{KT}^2}{F_K^2K_2T_2}+\frac{\gamma\varepsilon_2\lambda X_1}{T_2EK_1}\right],$$

$$\frac{dX_2}{ds_1}=\frac{L_2S}{\Delta w_3}\left[\frac{\varepsilon_2\lambda X_1X_2N}{EK_1}+rN-w_2L_2\left(\frac{\gamma K_2F_{KK}^2-\beta T_2F_{KT}^2}{F_K^2K_2T_2}+\frac{\gamma\varepsilon_2\lambda X_1}{T_2EK_1}\right)\right].$$

Appendix E

Using Cramer's rule to solve Eq. (13.22), we get
$\frac{dK_1}{ds_3}=\frac{-N[(\bar{L}-L_3)T+1]}{\Delta w_2}>0,\ \frac{dT_2}{ds_3}=\frac{B[(\bar{L}-L_3)T+1]}{\Delta w_2}>0.$

Substituting the results of Eq. (13.22) into Eqs. (13.1′), (13.2′), (13.4), (13.8), (13.10′), (13.12), (13.18), and (13.20), we obtain the following:

$$\frac{dK_2}{ds_3}<0,\frac{dT_3}{ds_3}<0,\quad \frac{dr}{ds_3}=0,\quad \frac{dE}{ds_3}<0,\quad \frac{dX_1}{ds_3}>0,\quad \frac{d\tau}{ds_3}<0,$$

$$\frac{dL_2}{ds_3}=\left(\frac{\beta N}{K_2}+\frac{\gamma B}{T_2}\right)\frac{L_2[(\bar{L}-L_3)T+1]}{\Delta w_2},$$

$$\frac{dX_2}{ds_3}=\left[\frac{\varepsilon_2\lambda X_1X_2N}{EK_1}+rN+w_2L_2\left(\frac{\beta N}{K_2}+\frac{\gamma B}{T_2}\right)\right]\frac{[(\bar{L}-L_3)T+1]}{\Delta w_2}$$

References

Beladi, H., & Frasca, R. (1999). Pollution control under an urban binding minimum wage. *The Annals of Regional Science, 33*, 523–533.

Beladi, H., & Rapp, J. (1993). Urban unemployment and the backward incidence of pollution control. *The Annals of Regional Science, 27*, 153–163.

Chaudhuri, S. (2006). Labour market reform, welfare and unemployment in a small open economy. *Keio Economics Studies, 43*, 1–17.

Chaudhuri, S. (2007). Foreign capital, welfare and urban unemployment in the presence of agricultural dualism. *Japan and the World Economy, 19*, 149–165.
Copeland, B., & Taylor, M. (1999). Trade, spatial separation, and the environment. *Journal of International Economics, 47*, 137–168.
Grossman, G., & Krueger, B. (1995). Economic growth and the environment. *Quarterly Journal of Economics, 110*, 353–377.
Gupta, M. (1994). Foreign capital, income inequality and welfare in a Harris-Todaro model. *Journal of Development Economics, 45*, 407–414.
Gupta, M. (1997a). Informal sector and informal capital market in a small open lessdeveloped economy. *Journal of Development Economics, 52*, 409–428.
Gupta, M. (1997b). Foreign capital and the informal sector: Comments on Chandra and Khan. *Economica, 64*, 353–363.
Li, X., & Shen, Q. (2012). A study on urban private capital and the transfer of labor in the modern agriculture sector. *Journal of Economic Policy Reform, 15*, 135–152.
Li, X., Shen, Q., Gu, C., & Ni, M. (2013). Analyzing the effect of advanced agriculture development policy. *Journal of Economic Policy Reform, 16*, 349–367.
World Bank. (2014). World development indicators: Energy dependency, efficiency and carbon dioxide emissions. http://data.worldbank.org.cn/indicator/EN.ATM.CO2E.PC/countries/A5-CN?display=graph
Xin, L., & Jiang, H. (2010). Setting up evaluation index system and calculation development level of China agricultural modernization. *Research of Agricultural Modernization, 31*, 646–650.

MIX
Papier aus verantwortungsvollen Quellen
Paper from responsible sources
FSC® C105338

If you have any concerns about our products,
you can contact us on
ProductSafety@springernature.com

In case Publisher is established outside the EU,
the EU authorized representative is:
Springer Nature Customer Service Center GmbH
Europaplatz 3, 69115 Heidelberg, Germany

Printed by Libri Plureos GmbH
in Hamburg, Germany